T0323669

Management Tools

No organisation is immune from the influence of management tools. Such tools as norms, indicators, ranking, evaluation grids and management control systems have moved outside the managerial and consultancy realm within which they were first developed to reach public administrations and policy-makers, as well as a range of other governmental and non-governmental organisations. Taking management tools out of the practical and utilitarian contexts to which they are often consigned and approaching them from a social analytical perspective, this book gives primacy to these everyday objects that constitute the background of organisational life and remain too often unquestioned. Bringing together developing streams of research from anthropology, political science, social psychology, sociology, accounting, organisation theory and management, Ève Chiapello and Patrick Gilbert offer an unprecedented theoretical synthesis that will help managers, scholars and policy-makers to unpack the functional and dysfunctional roles and effects of management tools within and across organisations.

ÈVE CHIAPELLO is Professor at École des hautes études en sciences sociales (EHESS), Paris, where she holds a chair in the 'Sociology of the transformation of capitalism'. She was previously Professor at the HEC School of Management, Paris. Her previously published works comprise numerous articles and books including: *Artistes versus Managers* (1998), and *Le nouvel esprit du capitalisme* (1999, with Luc Boltanski, translated into nine languages, including English in 2005).

PATRICK GILBERT holds a Ph.D. in Management and graduated in Organizational Psychology. He is Emeritus Professor at the Sorbonne Business Scool (IAE Paris) and Research Director at the *Mutations Anticipations Innovations* Chair. He is also a member of the board of several scientific societies, such as the Association francophone de Gestion des Ressources Humaines (AGRH) and Association Internationale de Psychologie du Travail de Langue Française (AIPTLF).

Management Tools

A Social Sciences Perspective

ÈVE CHIAPELLO
École des Hautes Etudes en Sciences Sociales, Paris

PATRICK GILBERT
IAE Paris – Sorbonne Business School

In collaboration with
MARION BRIVOT, CARINE CHEMIN-BOUZIR AND
BÉNÉDICTE GRALL

CAMBRIDGE
UNIVERSITY PRESS

CAMBRIDGE
UNIVERSITY PRESS

University Printing House, Cambridge CB2 8BS, United Kingdom

One Liberty Plaza, 20th Floor, New York, NY 10006, USA

477 Williamstown Road, Port Melbourne, VIC 3207, Australia

314–321, 3rd Floor, Plot 3, Splendor Forum, Jasola District Centre,
New Delhi – 110025, India

79 Anson Road, #06–04/06, Singapore 079906

Cambridge University Press is part of the University of Cambridge.

It furthers the University's mission by disseminating knowledge in the pursuit of
education, learning, and research at the highest international levels of excellence.

www.cambridge.org
Information on this title: www.cambridge.org/9781108428958
DOI: 10.1017/9781108553858

© Ève Chiapello and Patrick Gilbert 2019

This edition is an adapted translation of *Sociologie des outils de gestion: Introduction à
l'analyse sociale de l'instrumentation de gestion*, published by La Découverte in 2014
(9782707151452).

First published 2019

Printed and bound in Great Britain by Clays Ltd, Elcograf S.p.A.

A catalogue record for this publication is available from the British Library.

Library of Congress Cataloging-in-Publication Data
Names: Chiapello, Ève, author. | Gilbert, Patrick, author.
Title: Management tools : a social sciences perspective / Ève Chiapello, École des
Hautes Etudes en Sciences Sociales, Paris, Patrick Gilbert, IAE Paris ; in collaboration
with [three others].
Other titles: Sociologie des outils de gestion. English
Description: Cambridge, United Kingdom ; New York, NY : Cambridge University Press,
[2019] | "This edition is an adapted translation of Sociologie des outils de gestion:
introduction a l'analyse sociale de l'instrumentation de gestion, published by
La Decouverte in 2014."
Identifiers: LCCN 2019007595 | ISBN 9781108428958 (hardback : alk. paper) |
ISBN 9781108451727 (pbk. : alk. paper)
Subjects: LCSH: Management–Social aspects. | Organizational sociology.
Classification: LCC HD30.19 C4513 2019 | DDC 302.3/5–dc23
LC record available at https://lccn.loc.gov/2019007595

ISBN 978-1-108-42895-8 Hardback

Contents

Figures

Tables

Acknowledgements

This book owes its origins to a French-language book published in 2013 (Chiapello and Gilbert, 2013). It contains the first two parts (containing five chapters) and conclusion of the French book, slightly amended for the English-language version.[1] Chapter 6, which is new for this edition, presents ideas previously discussed in Chiapello and Gilbert (2016).

The whole is the result of a research and teaching project nourished by the authors' previous work, in the sociology of accounting for one (Berland and Chiapello, 2009; Bourguignon and Chiapello, 2005; Chiapello, 2005, 2007; Chiapello and Desrosières, 2006),[2] and for the other, in human resources management (Gilbert, 1998a, 1998b) and information systems (Gilbert and Gonzalez, 2000; Gilbert and Leclair, 2004). This work was enriched along the way by countless conversations and discussions.

The event that set us on this journey was the 'Social and behavioural approaches to management tools'[3] seminar we set up in 2005 in connection with the Master in Research on Organisations[4] run jointly by HEC School of Management[5] and IAE

---

[1] It does not, however, contain the third part, comprising four case studies written by Corine Eyraud, Bénédicte Grall, Carine Chemin-Bouzir and Céline Baud.

[2] We should also mention the organisation of the 'First sociology and quantification days' (in collaboration with Alain Desrosières, Carlos Ramirez and Fabrice Bardet) in May 2002, the coordination (with Carlos Ramirez) of a special 'sociology of accounting' issue of *Comptabilité-Contrôle-Audit* in June 2004 (Chiapello and Ramirez, 2004), and the co-editing (with Richard Baker) of an issue of *Accounting, Auditing & Accountability Journal* focusing on the influence of French Theory on accounting research in 2011 (Chiapello and Baker, 2011).

[3] Original French title: *Approches sociales et comportementales des outils de gestion*.

[4] *DEA Organisation appliquée*.

[5] Ève Chiapello was a Professor at HEC School of Management, Paris until March 2013. Since then she has been a Research Director at EHESS, Paris (*École des Hautes Etudes en Sciences Sociales*; School for the Advanced Studies in Social Sciences).

de Paris.[6] The discussions contained in Chapter 6 also benefited from Ève Chiapello's 2014–15 EHESS seminar, and bibliographic research conducted by Mehdi Arfaoui (Ph.D. student, EHESS).

Our reflections were stimulated by the work done with junior researchers, particularly Carine Chemin-Bouzir, who prepared her Ph.D. at IAE de Paris, and Marion Brivot, who has a doctorate from HEC. The research work undertaken by Céline Baud, Bénédicte Grall, Luis Cuenca and Nathalie Stempak for their HEC doctoral thesis was also a constant source of considerations about the way management tools are used, and analysis of more general transformations in business organisations and the economic system. Bénédicte Grall also helped us to identify important publications related to certain schools of thought. For five years (2007–12), the Renault-Polytechnique-HEC Chair in Multicultural Management (in collaboration with Eric Godelier of the École Polytechnique) provided another arena for experimentation with our view of the way organisations operate in an international context (Chiapello and Godelier, 2015a, 2015b). Every year, four to six teams of students carried out research comparing management practices in France with Japan, India and Korea.

Further advances came about through our participation in Ph.D. examination panels (especially in sociology, for the theses presented by Pauline Barraud de Lagerie (IEP Paris) and Benjamin Lemoine (École des Mines), and management, for Valérie Michaud (UQAM)), and Research Supervisor qualifications[7] (especially in management for Annick Bourguignon and Ewan Oiry, and sociology for Valérie Boussard and Corine Eyraud).

There were also many useful encounters and discussions with colleagues: naturally, with colleagues linked to HEC (Hélène Löning, Claire Dambrin) and IAE de Paris (José Allouche, Géraldine Schmidt, Hélène Rainelli) in the course of research or doctoral seminars, but

---

[6] *IAE de Paris* is the School of Management of University of Paris 1-La Sorbonne (*Institut d'Administration des Entreprises*).

[7] *Habilitation à diriger des recherches.*

also with colleagues from other institutions, including Alain Desrosières (INSEE), Valérie Boussard (Université de Paris-Nanterre), Fabian Muniesa (Mines ParisTech), Corine Eyraud (Université de Provence), Dominique Bouteiller (HEC Montreal), François-Xavier de Vaujany and Bernard Colasse (Université de Paris-Dauphine), Yves Cohen (EHESS), Maya Leroy (Agro Paristech), François Pichault (Université de Liège) and Frédérique Pigeyre (Université de Paris-Est). Productive interactions with other colleagues – who are too numerous to name individually – occurred at symposia and conferences (*Association Française de Sociologie, Association francophone de Gestion des Ressources Humaines, Association Internationale de Psychologie du Travail de Langue Française*), visits to other universities, and debates inside research teams.

This intellectual journey was punctuated by milestones in the form of intermediate publications. Philippe Steiner and François Vatin provided the initial opportunity to provide a first introduction to the sociology of management tools when they invited us to contribute to their book *Traité de sociologie économique* (Chiapello and Gilbert, 2009). An article discussing the clinical critique of management tools, published in *Le travail humain* (Chiapello and Gilbert, 2012), was a chance to test our prototype method for exposing the research theses contributing to social analysis of management tools, and launch the debate.

To bring this work to fruition, we benefited from input from other researchers sharing our interest in studying management tools, who very willingly agreed to write for the book. Bénédicte Grall (lecturer at the Conservatoire National des Arts et Métiers), Marion Brivot (associate professor at Université Laval au Québec) and Carine Chemin-Bouzir (associate professor at Neoma Business School) were all involved in the literature review;[8] the book would have been the

---

[8] Thesis 4 was written by Carine Chemin-Bouzir, thesis 6 was written by Marion Brivot and thesis 7 by Bénédicte Grall. Their signature is found in a footnote at the start of each thesis.

poorer without their contribution. They also agreed to update their parts of the book in preparation for publication of the English-language version.

Finally, we would like to express our very sincere thanks to Jean-Pascal Gond (professor at Cass Business School). We are indebted to him as the first person to express enthusiasm for our plan to adapt the original French book for an English-language readership. He was also instrumental in establishing our initial contacts with Cambridge University Press. The book has been translated thanks to financial support from IAE de Paris and the Anneliese Maier Research Award grant received by Ève Chiapello from the Foundation Alexander Von Humbolt. Yuewu Duan (Ph.D., IAE de Paris), Medhi Arfaoui (Ph.D., EHESS) and Philipp Golka (Post-Doc, University of Hamburg) also took part in reviews of the English version. We extend our warmest gratitude to all these people. However, as the time-honoured expression goes, responsibility for the overall construction of the book and the arguments developed in it remains entirely our own.

This book is especially dedicated to Alain Desrosières, who passed away on 15 February 2013. Our many discussions with him and our reading of his work were a crucial part of the genesis of this book, and he is sadly missed.

How to Use This Book

This book is for anyone who wants a relatively comprehensive exploration of much of the social thinking on management tools. It has been written for people who are interested in the way management tools are influencing individual and group behaviours in organisations.

It can be used in a number of ways, depending on the reader's specialisation, experience and interests. It can be read from beginning to end because it follows an organised sequence. But each chapter, and each of the ten theses in the second part, can also be read separately, as appropriate to the area of literature the reader wants to address. It can be used both as a textbook for a course, and as a reference book that is consulted to inform thinking or analysis.

The book originated in our teaching and research supervision activities, and was initially conceived as a reference manual for doctoral or post-doctoral research, since no book existed that gave an overview of the wide range of management tool-related research going on in a number of management disciplines, and more broadly in the social sciences. The second part provides a digest of the major theoretical streams that are casting light on the question. It contains summary tables describing the object of study, the theses and their contributions. Each thesis is backed up with an extensive bibliography for further reading. We consider these theses complementary, to be called on as and when relevant to the management situations and economic climates encountered. The appendices offer suggestions for successful social science research that takes management tools seriously, and a guide for combining approaches as appropriate to the research questions addressed.

The book can thus be used to construct a Ph.D. or Research Master level course in Management, Sociology or Political Sciences designed to train students in these approaches. After an introductory session based on Chapters 1 and 2, a certain number of theses from the second part can be selected for closer examination in dedicated sessions. As well as the part of the book presenting the chosen thesis, it is advisable to have the students read some of the key works cited. Chapter 6 and the conclusion are useful for a final summing-up session. For assessment, we recommend asking the students to carry out a study of a management tool.

A similar approach can also be used to construct classes for top-level business schools where 'management tools' are not supposed to be taken for granted, and teaching is informed by cutting-edge research. In such establishments the book can be used as a supplementary resource for MBA, MSc, and Executive MBA teaching. MBA and EMBA module students are always keen to learn about management tools, and this book is an excellent instrument for bringing fundamental social science debates on the potential and limitations of such tools into the classroom. For instance, the book can be given to practitioners/MBA students as a comprehensive guide for analysing a specific tool in their workplace, with the potential to serve as a textbook for an entire module. Business school students who already have some professional experience are often very interested in re-examining familiar management tools under different analysis grids. For this type of student, we recommend focusing work on the ideas from the second part, which they must learn to handle. It is also important to have them work in small groups on real-life case studies chosen by the students themselves, which will require them to collect additional documents, visit businesses and conduct interviews. Our teaching experience suggests that students always love management tools and want to learn about them.

A course of this kind can provide an enjoyable complement to an Organisational Behaviour or Organisation Theory course. Chapter 2 of this book, which reviews organisation theories from the perspective of management tools, provides a good way in to the subject. The book also could be adapted to develop an ad hoc module on tools for specific disciplines, for example HRM tools (e.g., HR planning, job evaluation),

Strategy tools (e.g., Five Forces, PESTEL, BCG Matrix), Sustainability-CSR tools (e.g., GRI, reporting tools, business case and supply-chain analysis tools, norms and standards for implementing sustainability, CSR ratings), accounting and control tools (e.g., performance indicators, accounting standards) or marketing tools (e.g., customer-management tools, segmentation), using the different perspectives to unpack a pre-selected set of tools from the disciplines. In this case, the teacher must take care to select appropriate additional reading.

Finally, outside the academic world, practising professionals who specialise in a functional field (management control, HR management, information systems, operations management, or other fields), working in business or as consultants, can make use of the analysis grids provided for their diagnoses. The third part provides a grid for the systematic study of the effects of any management tool. The methodological complements of the conclusion and the appendices also supply useful resources for conducting an in-depth study.

Introduction

Organisations as Worlds of Management Tools

Let's imagine an ordinary employee, Smith, a member of the marketing team of a fictional company whose name, Tools Ltd, echoes the theme of this book. On a Monday morning after a pleasant weekend Smith goes into the entrance hall of a multi-company building in a business district on the outskirts of a large city. It is 09.10 when he presents his smart card at the doorway. In doing this he encounters a technical arrangement that does not give him any more pause for thought than the turnstile on the underground, his usual mode of transport. The door opens obligingly for him, but of course if it hadn't done so Smith would have had an anxious moment. Then again, the security guard would have come and put things right. It would have been just one of those little vexations of modern life.

Smith now approaches the array of lifts that will take him up to his company's offices, on the twentieth floor. In Tools Ltd reception, he smiles at the receptionist, and, looking up, glances absent-mindedly at the Charter of Company Values displayed behind the reception desk. It comprises the commitments to which each 'Toolsian' should subscribe. These amount to ten points ('Like the Ten Commandments', Smith says sardonically to himself): ethics, clarity, professionalism, timekeeping, transparency, a devoted project team, responsiveness, safety, follow-up, traceability. At the Chairman's invitation, each of the workers in the company has signed the charter 'to demonstrate his or her commitment'. How far does it commit them? It is difficult to say exactly. We would have to examine carefully how the document is used, the view management and employees take of it, and any potential sanctions for failing to respect its values. At all events, 'The Charter' at Tools Ltd is not insignificant. Less material than the automatic door, it has no less regulatory function, and numerous deciding factors relate to it. It aims to embed in employees a vision of reality that is profitable for the company's management and to stimulate conduct that corresponds to that vision. From this perspective it appears to be a genuine 'management tool'. However, it could be seen very differently: far from being an effective instrument, it could be doing little more than flagging up a vague ambition in a public place. This is because the quality of a management tool depends on its context.

As he goes on, Smith submits to being checked by a different smart card from the one that gave him access to the lifts. This one has greater significance. With the exception of the management team, everyone at Tools Ltd scans this particular smart card; there is guaranteed working time, plus flexible time, and by the end of the week all employees must have completed their contracted hours. It is possible to be credited with hours and pool them to take half-days off. Now and again Smith tries to take a Friday afternoon off in order to extend his weekend, which he has just done. This 'smart-carding' also constitutes a management tool. It defines work periods and checks and interprets time with reference to regulations associated with labour law and internal constraints (operating rules). It covers a broad spectrum. It has an influence not only on Smith's professional life, but also on the organisation of his private life – those Friday afternoons he is fond of – and his relations with those around him. And with many Smiths benefiting from similar arrangements, every Friday afternoon it adds to the volume of traffic on the roads and to the demand on public transport.

Our hero makes his way into the open space, thinking nostalgically of the time when individual managers had their own office. He remembers the arguments the management team made at the time to justify the new-style workspaces, which, they said, 'allow for more conviviality and collaboration between teams, and improved circulation of information, and in this way foster transparency'. He greets his colleagues Sophie and Chris, already at their desks. They get up and invite him to go with them to the coffee machine area. They tell him that there will be a delay in developing the new customer relationship management (CRM) application. Smith is not an IT expert but he understands clearly that this could be a potential source of problems for him: he is responsible for the quality of the information about customers' characteristics supplied to the sales force. There are all kinds of customers: good ones, who generate a substantial amount of business, help think up new products and are loyal to the company; and bad ones who pay late or not at all, complain all the time, demand information before buying from the competition and end up costing more than they bring in. Smith's role is to make the most of this information and disseminate it. To do this he relies on customer categorisation. CRM and the analysis of customers are tools used to inform the company's commercial policy.

Back at his desk Smith settles down in front of his computer, presses the start button and a few seconds later enters a password (his daughter's date of birth). Following an unvarying procedure he then consults the shared diary and discovers with alarm that he has a staff meeting from 10 a.m. to 12 noon – and he had planned to spend the morning thoroughly reorganising his files! His expression darkens: 'They might have warned me!' He goes to his message-board, which requires a new password (the last six digits of his mobile phone number). He finds a message from his boss, marked top priority, detailing the aim of the meeting ('Setting up a continuous improvement approach in the marketing department') and inviting everyone to consider what contribution they could make. An attachment specifies the nature of the approach and presents a schedule. Smith notes that the message was sent to everybody on Saturday morning. 'That's just not on!' he growls.

Smith gets to the meeting room a few minutes before 10 a.m. Prominent on the back wall are 'The Principles of a Good Meeting' (Responsiveness, Synergy and Innovation, Interaction, Group decision-making based on consensus and commitment). Tools Ltd is very keen on valorising effective conduct. Each principle is illustrated with amusing cartoon-type images. At the other end of the meeting table an unfamiliar figure is busying himself with his tablet and the video-projector. A small group of colleagues begins to arrive, including Sophie, who sits next to him.

The head of department enters around 10 a.m., greets those present with a slight nod and grumbles about latecomers. Then he opens the meeting and hands over to the unfamiliar figure, who turns out to be a consultant. He details the 1–2–3 method on which the continuous improvement approach will be based. He explains that this pragmatic method, perfected in the 1980s in the USA, is acclaimed by today's top companies, to which it has brought considerable increases in productivity. A short training period will ensure success. 'Any questions?' 'Yes, what are the cost implications of the proposed training, which has not been allowed for in section budgets?' 'How do we keep track of the return on investment?' 'Will it be necessary to use scorecards [an array of indicators associated with objectives]?' The consultant gives perfunctory replies ('ROI calculations are integrated into the 1–2–3 method'), as does the head of department ('As for the implications, we'll see'; 'Scorecards, excellent idea – make a proposal'). Hands go up, with more questions, but it is already 12.05 and the time for discussion is over. The head of department closes the meeting: 'I must stress the seriousness of this approach, which will be shown in the performance appraisal system.' Sophie turns to Smith, 'Well, what do you make of that?' 'Typical Monday morning', mutters our hero, who is given to sarcasm.

At this point we begin to get an idea about what sorts of things are called 'management tools' (charter of values, staff card, continuous improvement approach, principles of a good meeting, 1–2–3 method, cost implications, return on investments, scorecards, performance appraisal system, and so on). We notice the kinship they share with other technical facilities (controlled access, computers, message-boards, video-projectors), forms of time organisation (flexible timetable), space (open space), and company context (Tools Ltd, aptly named, loves all kinds of rationalisation). We also see the diversity of human agents caught up in their use to various degrees and concerned with their effects both inside and outside the organisation. And we begin to see how we might fill a book dedicated to management tools and their deployment.

It is probably clear from this introduction that management tools interest us in relation to individuals, groups and human society in general. We approach the subject from a social analysis perspective.

This approach takes management tools out of the practical and utilitarian context to which they are often consigned and maintains that management techniques warrant close examination. Both management and management tools are important to understand for social scientists: we cannot disregard their significance to organisations and the economy. Moreover, we cannot understand organisational behaviour if we fail to pay attention to management tools and techniques. The stakes are also theoretical: taking an interest in management tools beyond the narrow field of their use enables us to see things that are not otherwise apparent.

The social analysis of management tools and techniques considers those as social facts. Social sciences – sociology in particular – allow us to avoid a strictly rational consideration of management actions and to re-embed them within social relationships and structures: social representations, value systems, rules of the game, and power relations can illuminate and even explain management actions. But the conceptual foundation of social analysis of management techniques is anthropological, in the sense that it puts to work all of the human and social sciences. The history and philosophy of techniques provide the core understanding of the relationship between people and techniques. Psychology and ergonomics offer analytical frameworks for systems of instrumented activities. Institutional economics prioritises the influence of rules in individual agents' decision-making. Lastly, management science itself has amassed a series of research results that call the classic vision into question.

Academic work in the disciplines we have mentioned is substantial but highly disparate: we miss a structured synthesis enabling students and researchers to go deeper in the field. Our aim is to fill that gap. This book has been conceived as a methodological and reflective work that will give the reader an extensive, detailed and systematic review of the literature in the field, while taking care to locate each element in the context of a broad interrogation.

We hope that our approach will facilitate the development of a body of research in various social science disciplines (management science, sociology, political science, social psychology) that will embark on an analysis of social and organisational phenomena through an attention to the tools of organisational activities. Our book focuses on the 'management tools' used to coordinate the activities of organisations (mainly companies) and to check their results. We believe that it can also provide inspiration and a methodology for the study of what we call 'political instruments' – that is, tools that aim to manipulate actors and situations outside the organisation, not for profit but to enhance the well-being of individuals (in terms of education, health, safety, social participation) and the natural world (protecting biodiversity, managing natural resources), or to regulate and arbitrate between conflicting interests in diverse fields.[1]

There are three parts to this book.

The first is devoted to broad issues and to establishing a conceptual basis for considering the instrumentation of management. First (Chapter 1), we introduce the big questions that we address throughout the book: What is the discussion of management techniques based on? What is a management tool? How do management tools relate to management techniques? We then (Chapter 2) examine traditional approaches drawn from organisation theory, viewing them both as departure points and as frontiers to be challenged.

---

[1] The state can use both 'management tools' (for managing its finances or personnel) and 'policy instruments' (for example, aid procedures for certain populations, mechanisms for authorising certain activities, quality norms or obligatory safety practices). The 'new public management' tends to blur the frontiers between the instrumentation of public policies and the management of the services that put them into effect, for example through the development of evaluation practices as it is often a short step between the evaluation of public policies to the performance of those enacting the policy.

The second part of the book addresses the analysis of management tools through ten theses emerging from a full review of the literature. These theses are grouped into three categories of approach. The first (Chapter 3, critical approaches) examines management tools as instrumentalising and fostering the phenomena of domination and exploitation. The second (Chapter 4, institutionalist approaches) examines the role played by institutions in the development of management tools. The third (Chapter 5, interactional approaches) looks at the interaction between management tools and actors. These approaches are studied systematically using the same analytical framework that aims to reveal their particular contributions.

The third part (Chapter 6, the agency of management tools) provides a synthetic framework that draws on the theses discussed above to answer two theoretical questions, which are also practical ones: How do tools act and influence situations? What are their real functions beyond those officially stated?

We conclude by elaborating a synthesis of our social analysis perspective and demonstrating the contribution this approach can make to some classic questions in social sciences.

By the end of this book the reader will judge whether we have fulfilled our aim. We hope that at the very least he or she will have acquired an overview of all the recent theoretical advances on the subject of the instrumentation of management and will be equipped with an array of approaches associated with theoretical frameworks. While these approaches differ, they all challenge traditional approaches and open up new research perspectives, constituting highly effective instruments for analysing numerous phenomena.

PART I **Theoretical Foundations for Thinking about Management Instrumentation**

The purpose of Part I is to lay the groundwork for the analysis of management instruments by positioning the study of management tools in the broader perspective of the study of techniques and the analysis of classical management tools. In so doing, this Part clarifies the historical and anthropological foundations for the study of management tools and provides the liminal definitions of the notions used in the remainder of the book (e.g., objects, techniques, tools). Part I is composed of two chapters.

Chapter 1 introduces the debate on views of management tools, as they relate to the technical field, and as they relate to the social field. We identify three habitual attitudes to the technical field: denial of the technical, technophilia, and technophobia. These ideal-type stances translate the behaviours most often adopted in response to management tools, which are considered as autonomous objects cut off from social reality. They are closed-ended and cannot grasp the full complexity and relevance of these tools. Drawing on the anthropology of techniques, and thereby stressing the specific nature of management techniques applied to human interactions, we intend to break away from the indifference/attraction/repulsion triptych. This reflection leads to a proposed description of management tools and their various aspects.

Chapter 2 continues this reflection with a presentation of the traditional approaches to management tools in organisation theory. These approaches oscillate between rationality and normativity (Barley and Kunda, 1992). For rational theories, the stance is generally technophile. Normative theories, which were constructed as an alternative to rational theories, adopt a stance that is sometimes technophobic, and sometimes in denial of techniques, pointing up the role of informal factors in the organisation. Based on this reading of the foundations of thought in management sciences, we describe how the theory has evolved as increasing attention has been paid to management tools. In its time, the socio-technical approach instigated at the Tavistock Institute in the 1950s, which opposed the prevailing technological determinism of the period, marked a significant shift in the way techniques are considered in organisational change. Behavioural organisation theory then contributed further pioneering work, taking an interest in the formal rules that are the very essence of management tools. This paved the way for an expanding body of research at the intersection between management tools and social behaviours which has been ongoing since the 1980s as reflections have broadened out. In France, the initiative was taken by the top engineering schools' management research laboratories. Elsewhere, most particularly in the United Kingdom and primarily in accounting, sociology-inspired research began to develop. By the turn of the twenty-first century, social science research had multiplied, and the following parts of this book are mainly devoted to this more recent work.

Part I thus circumscribes our approach and highlights the specific contribution of the work, which is presented from Part II onwards. Chapter 1 closely defines our proposed social science-inspired perspective on management tools, which makes them into remarkable analysers of the contemporary world. Chapter 2 reviews the way they have traditionally been approached by social sciences and organisation theory, underlining the gaps and blind spots in these approaches, and the path beyond that is proposed in the rest of the book.

I Theoretical Foundations

From the Study of Technique to the Analysis of Management Tools

The need to take into account technique in analyses of social phenomena now seems obvious, given the place that it occupies in our industrialised societies, which George Friedmann, one of the founders of the sociology of work, said arises within a 'technical civilisation' (Friedmann, 1964). And technique does not exist on its own without the technical objects that the tools constitute. However, for a long time, objects considered as something belonging to the natural order, appeared as intruders in the human sciences (Blandin, 2002, p. 7).

Denaturalisation of objects began in the course of the 1960s, in France, with the semiotics of objects by Roland Barthes (Barthes, 1972) and his successors, particularly Baudrillard (1996) and in the 1980s in Great Britain with the emergence of material culture studies (Buchli, 2002; Lemonnier, 1986), and their interest in the relationships between objects, culture and power. A radical change took place at the beginning of the 1990s with researchers focusing on studying the role of objects in social arrangements (Conein et al., 1993) or even in endowing objects with real social agency (Callon, 1984; Latour, 2000). We identify ourselves as part of that movement.

What is the specific role of a tool among objects? François Dagognet (1989, 1996) supplies the groundwork for a clarification. As a philosopher of technique he first proposes to distinguish objects from things. He explains that if a thing (a lump of wood, a stone or a leaf, for example) relates to nature, then the object relates directly to the subject, by way of the human intervention that created it and the technique that allowed it to be produced. Dagognet then points out that the tool fits into a particular category of objects: it is an 'object of the object' (1996, pp. 20–2), which is used to intervene with other objects.

Management, as an administrative technique, relies on many tools. However, these tools are rarely considered for their own sake. There is a kind of absence here. To start thinking about this, this chapter first clarifies the diversity and limits of spontaneous approaches to technique, which vary between indifference and more stringent criticism, by way of proselytism. This analysis opens the way to an introduction of the contribution of anthropology of techniques, in a broad sense including the ethnology, history and sociology of techniques for the study of management tools. At first sight such references may strike the specialist in management as bold or somewhat exotic, but in the field of management those concerned with the study of techniques still find very few fellow voices. Studies conducted using the anthropology of techniques are highly instructive, even if they do not address directly management techniques. Anthropologists conceive technique as a social phenomenon from the outset. According to Marcel Mauss, André Leroi-Gourhan and André-Georges Haudricourt, technique is a socialised action, and management fits perfectly into that category. We will then be able to define management as a specific 'intangible technique' and propose a definition of 'management tool' congruent with the proposed approach.

SPONTANEOUS DISCOURSE ABOUT TECHNIQUE

To deem that technique and social matters are interdependent does not imply either indifference to the first or exaggeration of its effects. Technical objects deserve to be understood as specific phenomena, and warrant a specific analysis. However, some denial of technique (a sort of 'techno-indifference') has always existed, and, when technique is acknowledged discussion often remains organised along a technophile/technophobe opposition.

Denial of Technique, or the Insignificance of the Object

Denial of technique, or at least the tendency to keep it in the shadows, and to minimise its role and effects, is often found in the classic oppositions of science and technique or art and technique, in which technique, as opposed to culture, is pushed into the background.

Since the Enlightenment, technique has commonly been viewed as subordinate to science. The notion flowing from this was that if we wanted access to science we had to distance ourselves from technique. But techniques have their own rationale and do not boil down to scientific applications. What is more, technique can evolve independently of science, as is demonstrated in the empirical know-how of craftsmen. There is certainly knowledge in the technical field, but it is not always knowledge drawn from science. Besides, if it is possible to proceed from science to technique, it is quite possible to go the other way. Science arises from technique every time practice pushes theory forward: an instance is the steam engine, which was born of mechanical skill, and which also contributed to the development of the then non-existent field of thermodynamics (Daumas, 1963).

Added to a prevailing representation in which technique is subordinated to science is the concealment of technique from what is ordinarily understood by 'culture' and particularly from art. Many philosophers more or less banish technique from aesthetic discourse. Kant, for instance, states that art is a 'natural production of genius' and for Hegel it is a 'sensuous manifestation of the spirit'. If in former times the practice of art and technique were closely connected, nowadays the artist's activity is quite simply valorised above that of the artisan – or *a fortiori* the worker. While artists need technique, it is in transcending it that they secure recognition. A work of art is declared to be the fruit of artistic genius and not of material technique. More radically, in the prevailing representation of culture, art is the opposite of technique because it is directed first at aesthetic pleasure, while technique, whose criterion is effectiveness, only aspires to the useful. It is, however, difficult to conceive of an art that ignores technique: in that they are artificial, works of art are themselves akin to technical objects.

In science as in art it is the 'object' that has to be kept at a distance, in a form of rejection. An ardent defender of the object, Dagognet sees several explanations for this:

- Characterised first by its utility, the object is seen as the opposite of a thought: 'Thinkers are not much moved by the useful' (Dagognet, 1989, p. 45).
- Belonging to 'doing', the object could degrade 'being' (Dagognet, 1989, p. 47).
- Its status as external to the subject is perceived as a threat: 'What is worse than reification?' (Dagognet, 1996, p. 13).

If, in social sciences, especially those concerned with organisations, technique has been disregarded, ignored and belittled, it is also doubtless the case that it has revealed itself as invasive, particularly under the influence of engineers. Also, the assertion that 'techniques do not run organisations' (Reynaud, 1988) has been a baton passed between several generations of organisational sociologists.

The reluctance to integrate technique into culture, the insistence on erecting impenetrable borders between science and technique, or art and technique, the insistence that they should conform to a feeling of inferiority or superiority, closes the door on a more subtle understanding of human activities. Counter to this attitude, Dagognet (1989, p. 41), inspired by Marcel Mauss, maintains that the object is a 'total social fact' that we must learn to read and decrypt to discover the 'culture lodged within it'. However, when technique is not actually concealed from view, discussion about it is too frequently reduced to the argument between those who link the fate of society to the evolution of techniques (technophiles) and those who oppose them (technophobes).

Technophile Euphoria

If technique seen from the outside is often considered a cold, calculating affair, from within it is a passion that its defenders want to communicate to others. In that matter, the pleasure scientists and engineers find in proclaiming their aims to the world seems similar to the desire of the executives to market new technical objects.

With each wave of inventions technophile euphoria spreads out. It finds its bearings today particularly in the discourse of new technologies, following the communication utopia celebrated at the end of the 1960s by Marshall McLuhan with his 'global village' (McLuhan and Fiore, 1967). In ordinary usage 'technology' has become a grandiloquent superlative of 'technique' for which it is substituted at every opportunity. This term has come to designate modern, complex techniques, like information processing and communication. While 'technique' evokes the restricted and familiar know-how of the traditional industrial world, 'technology' is instinctively associated with modern values. So new technologies are characterised as 'cutting-edge' or 'advanced'.

Every novelty feeds the technophile deluge. Pioneers of artificial intelligence such as Hofstadter (1979) and Minsky (1985), whose works have been publicised widely in the media, have given prominence to the possibilities of simulating the human brain by using computers. These authors have more or less directly fostered the vision of a spiritual fusion between man and machine. Singularianism now predicts the ability of technologies like nanotechnology and biotechnology to massively increase human intelligence over the next decade and fundamentally reshape the economy and society (Kurzweil, 2005). One could also mention the utopia celebrating collective intelligence (Lévy, 1994) in the context of cyberspace, or cloud computing and the Web 2.0 as bearers of new promises.

The prestige of modern technology moves on in step with the development of the market and the reduction in purchasing and operating costs, as has been the case in developments from the telephone to the internet, which were initially the preserve of the elite.

Technophobic Reaction, or Technique as a Snare

In front of technophiles and their promises of progress stands the technophobic reaction. Long before the development of an intellectual criticism of techniques, the question had been addressed by Luddites and was the centre of some labour disputes in the context of industrialisation at the beginning of the nineteenth century. The actions of those 'machine breakers' could be seen as reactionary by those for whom the triumph of mechanisation was inevitable. But, as Thompson (1963, p. 543) put it: 'the character of Luddism was not that of a blind protest, or of a food riot (as took place in many other districts). Nor will it do to describe Luddism as a form of "primitive" trade unionism. [...] the men who organized, sheltered, or condoned Luddism were far from primitive. They were shrewd and humorous; next to the London artisans, some of them were amongst the most articulate of the "industrious classes".'

Even today Luddites are considered with condescension, as well as all those seen as their descendants: 'neo-luddite' is often used to insult indistinctly radical ecologists or those resisting the digital modernity. However, some do not hesitate to endorse this identity, as for example Chellis Glendinning, a psychologist, who published a neo-luddite manifesto in an alternative press magazine. She writes: 'The technologies created and disseminated by modern Western societies are out of control and desecrating the fragile fabric of life on Earth' (Glendinning, 1990, p. 51). A few years later, the essayist Kirkpatrick Sale (1996) came to prominence by smashing computers on the day of a public presentation of his book on Luddites.

On a less spectacular level, when social science specialists got over their indifference towards techniques, they often manifested some defiance in the face of those praising technique. In his presentation of the philosophy of technique Jean-Yves Goffi justly remarks that 'the number of authors who have endorsed the list of contemporary technophobia is almost infinite' (Goffi, 1988, p. 11).

Jacques Ellul typifies such an approach. As a philosopher of technical society and modernity he engages in a critical analysis of the ideology of technique, emphasising both its inexorable nature and the damage done by technical euphoria. In *The Technological Society* (1964) Ellul maintains that technique is now swallowing up civilisation. We no longer own technique but are part of it. He takes this notion further later, asserting that technique has ceased to be just an accumulation of techniques and has become a 'technological system' (Ellul, 1980). This system, developed as an intermediary between nature and man, has evolved to the extent that humans have lost all contact with their natural environment and are able to relate only to the intermediary. And this leads us to envisage an autonomous system of techniques that imposes its own rules on all humanity: 'Beyond a certain degree of technization, we pass from a society determined by natural factors to a society determined by technological factors' (Ellul, 1980, pp. 65–6). To say that technique is autonomous means 'that technology ultimately depends only on itself, it maps its own route, it is prime and not a secondary factor, it must be regarded as an "organism" tending toward closure and self-determination: it is an end in itself' (Ellul, 1980, p. 125).[1]

Later Ellul (1990) radicalises his argument. He inveighs against the fact that techniques are credited with many achievements, while their costs and dangers are kept hidden. Technique is henceforward presented as being both the only solution to our individual and collective problems and as the only possibility for progress – a bluff that is lodged in a discourse that greatly exaggerates technical possibilities and simultaneously draws a veil over its negative aspects.

False Debates and Real Impasses

Denial of technique, technophilia, technophobia – the autonomy of technique is the implicit assumption common to these apparently contradictory philosophical positions.

The partisans of denial systematically refuse to accord importance to technique. Scornfully, they keep it at arm's length, as if social matters could be considered independently of technique. As for technophobes and technophiles, while the values on which their judgements are based differ, they share the same basic conception that technique is omnipotent. Their apparent opposition conceals a deterministic vision fed by a technocentric model. Technophiles believe

---

[1] It should be noted that the 'technical principle' Ellul examines, defined as a research for effectiveness valorising specialised knowledge, is central to management.

that technical action can satisfy human needs and give humans control over their actions. Technophobes believe that technique sets itself against man, as Ellul (1990, pp. 147–8) says: technique 'is not interested in what serves humanity. Its only interest is in itself [...] It cannot occupy itself with the human except to subordinate it and to subject it to the demands of its own functioning.'

Even so, from the point of view of social analysis, we should note that distinct from technophile proselytism, which tends to conceal the damaging effects of technique in the name of progress and its requirements, the criticism of technique has the advantage of questioning the phenomenon of technique and 'denaturalising' it.

Getting away from the unproductive technophilia/technophobia opposition involves expanding the notion of technique in order to stop thinking of it in terms of attraction and repulsion, and rather in terms of method and attitude. In order to look at it differently we are going to turn to the particularly fruitful observations of the anthropology of techniques, which demonstrate from the outset that the technical is social and the social is technical.

THE CONTRIBUTIONS OF ANTHROPOLOGY

Considering Technique: The Technological Project

Marcel Mauss's (1872–1950) interest in the study of techniques ran very deep and his contribution to the debate is remarkable.[2] First, he proposed a method and a programme for the study of techniques, a 'technology' that constitutes second-degree thinking about techniques. There are two parts to this technology (Mauss, 1948, pp. 149–50):

In the first place, we have descriptive technology. This relates to:

1. Sources that are classified historically and geographically, such as tools, instruments, machines; the last two being analysed and assembled.

---

[2] See Vatin (2004) on this point.

2. Sources that are studied from physiological and psychological points of view; including the ways in which they use photographs, analyses, etc.
3. Sources that are organised according to the system of industry of each society studied, such as food, hunting, fishing, cooking, preserving, or clothing, or transport, and including general and specific usages, etc.

Onto this preliminary study of the material of techniques, must be superimposed the study of the function of these techniques, their interrelations, their proportions, their position in social life.

Any object must be studied (a) in itself; (b) in relation to its users; and (c) in relation to the whole of the system under scrutiny. [...] Then study similarly the mode of use and the production of each tool. (Mauss, 2007, pp. 27–8)

Following on from Mauss, one of his students, André-Georges Haudricourt (1911–96), an eclectic scholar, simultaneously botanist, linguist and ethnologist, showed his interest in the observation of techniques by drawing up a description of technological processes in relation to the analysis of the evolutionary processes of productive forces. From 'La technologie, science humaine' (1964) ('Technology: A human science'), we retain two key ideas that inspired the writing of this book.

The first thing is to note that the same object may be approached from different angles, each with its own values. When studying an object each point of view uncovers specific facts and deploys specific methods. Haudricourt (1964, p. 28, our translation) writes:

What characterises a science is the point of view, not the object. Take a table, for example. It can be studied from the physical point of view: one can study its weight, density, its resistance to pressure; or from the point of view of chemistry, its chance of catching fire, or being dissolved by acid; or biology, the age and species of the wood it is made of; and lastly, from the point of view of the human sciences, the origin and function of the table in human life.

Second, there is the idea of contextualising the technical object. This means abandoning the simplification of isolating the object under consideration from the environment in which it plays an assigned role and from the time in which it is developed. Haudricourt says that in order to understand the technical object 'one must surround it with all the human actions that produce it and make it work' (Haudricourt, 1955, p. 77, our translation).

This notion is also central in the work of Bertrand Gille (1920–80). Starting out from the proposition that there is no such thing as a technique in isolation and that we should refer to 'confluent techniques', this historian proposes the idea of the technical system, which he defines in the introductory chapter of his reference work *Histoire des techniques* (Gille, 1986) (*The History of Techniques*) as 'a coherent ensemble of mutually compatible structures'. For Gille, each age may be characterised by a synergy between various fundamental techniques that determine other human systems, such as economics or politics. He states that understanding technique has the advantage of engaging in a discussion with researchers in the social sciences (economics, sociology, linguistics, law, etc.), 'specialists in other systems'.

A tool is not an isolated thing: it exists in relation to others, an individual in a species. The palaeoanthropologist André Leroi-Gourhan (1911–86) analyses the techniques that underlie all others and establishes a typology of the tools that correspond to them in a remarkable two-volume work of classification, *Évolution et techniques. L'homme et la matière* (1943) (*Evolution and Techniques: The Man and the Matter*) and *Milieu et techniques* (1945) (*Environment and Techniques*). Leroi-Gourhan is the originator of the concept of the 'operational sequence', which has become the chief model in the study of material in the anthropology of techniques. This concept describes the sequence of operations that brings a primary material from its natural state to a fabricated state. Relying on Leroi-Gourhan (1993), we can argue that these products, as elements of social organisation, pre-exist the intelligence of whoever uses them, in the sense that individuals find them before them as the fruits of long collective experience and an accumulation of knowledge.

Following in the footsteps of Leroi-Gourhan, Pierre Lemonnier (1976), Robert Cresswell (1983) and Hélène Balfet (1991) take the concept of the 'operational sequence' further. In an article in *Dictionnaire de l'ethnologie et de l'anthropologie*, Lemonnier (1991, p. 697) (*Dictionary of Ethnology and Anthropology*), proposes a definition of technique as 'an ensemble setting four elements in play: a material that it works on; objects ("tools", "tools of the trade", "artefacts"); actions or sources of energy [...] which set these objects moving; specific representations that underlie the technical actions' (our translation). Lemonnier explains that (a) the 'material' acted upon may be the body, (b) the 'tool' may also be the body, and (c) the knowledge may be unconscious. A fifth element can also be added: 'the actors who perform the action'. He emphasises that techniques do something beyond acting on material, and wonders about what happens through objects that contribute to make a society. This entry point enables scientists to say things about societies that could not be said otherwise (Lemonnier, 2012).

Concerning the Study of Technique and Its Tools

As we have seen, a tool is part of a technical system. If this is circumscribed, how do we study a tool? Once again Mauss (2007, p. 24) supplies the framework of a method in a few words:

> The most insignificant tool should be named and located; by whom it is used, where was it found, how is it used and for what purpose, does it have a general purpose or a special one (e.g. the use of a knife)? It should be photographed as it is used, together with the object on which it is used, or with its end product; the photographs will show the various stages of production. The industrial system to which the object belongs should be identified; the study of a single tool normally implies the study of the craft as a whole.

The study of a tool includes the study of its history because, as Simondon (1980, p. 12) says, 'An individual technical object is not such and such a thing, something given hic et nunc, but something that has a genesis [. . .] the genesis of the technical object is part of its being.' So it is by way of analysis of the conditions prevailing at its origins, study of its 'social production' according to Perrin (1988), that we can identify the specificity of a tool. The evolution of techniques, far from being pre-programmed and imposing its own conditions on society, is shaped by numerous socio-economic, cultural and political factors that direct its development. Thus, since the beginning of the industrial revolution, innovation in machinery and means of production has been shaped by a concept of the organisation and division of labour specific to a dominant economic system, that of capitalist industrialised countries.

The work of Breton (1987) on the history of computers fits this perspective. Breton opposes an approach in terms of generations of technical objects: machines with electronic tubes (the first generation), computers with transistors (second generation), integrated circuits (third generation), microprocessors (fourth generation). He shows that the history of computing has several aspects, technical certainly, but also economic and social. For example, the computer was born of a convergence of scientific and military interests (Breton, 1987, p. 105); and furthermore, the genesis of the microcomputer owes as much to the social project of North American radicals reclaiming the democratisation of access to information as to the microprocessor (Breton, 1987, p. 211).

Some Lessons for the Study of Management Tools

From our readings of different authors, anthropologists, sociologists, historians and philosophers of techniques, we have drawn up five principles for analysis that guide our approach to management tools.

1. *Reduce the separation.* There is nothing to be gained and much to be lost by opposing the subject to the object, the technical

to the social. It would be better, as Dagognet suggests (1989, p. 164) to 'reduce the separation' for, as he points out, 'the designation as an object, refers indeed in itself to the subject' (1989, p. 20, our translation). Brandishing one against the other in the way that technophiles and technophobes do limits our understanding of both. Technique and social live in the same world and are entwined; they constitute analytical categories and not realities of the natural order. The lowliest of management tools (a management chart, a time sheet) is socially saturated and the social life of organisations is full of tools.

2. *Multiply points of view.* The management tool is not easily understood from just one angle. Being content with a single approach would mean reducing our scope of vision and not taking account of its complexity. So, following Haudricourt's advice we will try to multiply our points of view. We will adopt a plural approach to management tools, taking different theories into account without trying to combine them or to force them to converge.

3. *Identify the system.* Management tools take their place within a technical system made up of a group of interactive elements (conception of performance, state of the art, company strategy, etc.), which allows them to be maintained and developed. There is always a context. Studying an object for itself limits the analysis and quickly exhausts the proposition. It would be better to identify the system in which the management tool takes its place as Gille, Leroi-Gourhan and Lemonnier invite us to do.

4. *Study the instrumental genesis.* Guided by Simondon and Perrin, we will bear in mind that the actuality of a management tool and its being rooted in a management context should not conceal its history, the cultural, economic and social environment of its design or the intentions of its inventors. In order to understand this, it is best to analyse the conditions under which it is produced, that is, its 'instrumental genesis'.

5. *Proceed in a systematic manner.* The detailed analysis of a management tool supposes that there is a systematic approach that

goes beyond the immediate surface. Thus, following on from Mauss, we should try to describe what the tool is being applied to, identify the places where it is used and the profession that makes use of it. We should characterise its uses and note its effects. We should also attempt to describe the 'operational sequence' (Leroi-Gourhan) in which it has its place; that is to say the ordered sequence of actions it applies to objects, from their raw state to their finished product state.

We hope that, armed with these principles, we will be able to study all kinds of management tools, even though the frameworks may vary because of their particular nature and the fields in which they are applied.

MANAGEMENT AS AN INTANGIBLE TECHNIQUE

Management: A Technique Unlike Others

While management is recognised as one technique among others, it is nevertheless a technique unlike any other. The difficulty in characterising management is principally due to the diverse ways in which it manifests itself. The technique of management covers many varied fields (accounting, marketing, financial analysis, management control, etc.). Over and above this diversity, what is its place in the vast universe of techniques? What is its purpose?

For Leroi-Gourhan (1943, p. 18, our translation), 'material is what conditions all techniques'. What, then, is the material to which management techniques are applied? We think spontaneously of information, which is collected, analysed, transformed, formatted and disseminated. But management techniques apply more deeply to the human interactions they seek to coordinate. They prescribe formats for action and build a unit of action in a labour community. Beyond their primary rooting in organisations, they produce more broadly on a daily basis the economic system and the market arrangements (Dubuisson-Quellier, 1999; Cochoy, 1999).

Considering management as a technique and analysing it as such is the same as extending the meaning of technique from the material to the intangible, an extension that was made very early in ethnological studies.

The Specificity of Intangible Techniques

Marcel Mauss is recognised as having broadened the concept of technique. In his famous paper on 'Les techniques du corps' ('Techniques of the body'), presented to the French Society of Psychology on 17 May 1934, he stated: 'I call technique an action which is effective and traditional (and you will see that in this it is no different from the magical, religious or symbolic action). It has to be *effective* and *traditional* [underlined by Mauss]. There is no technique and no transmission in the absence of tradition. This above all is what distinguishes man from the animals: the transmission of his techniques and very probably their oral transmission' (Mauss, 1973, p. 75). By *techniques of the body* Mauss means 'the ways in which from society to society men know how to use their bodies' (Mauss, 1973, p. 70). He illustrates this idea by starting with everyday actions: walking, running and swimming. In these examples he shows that actions observed in a society that we might have believed were spontaneous and natural are in fact acquired social forms and differ from those found in other societies.

The classic conception of technique as belonging only to action on nature or on things is nevertheless maintained because it corresponds fairly well to the consensual idea of progress in an industrial society.

Nevertheless, intangible techniques have existed since the dawn of humanity. We might even maintain that they are older than material techniques since technique has its roots in magic. But, considered as sources of investment and vectors of progress, they have developed and are more sophisticated today: communication techniques, psychotherapies, techniques for territorial development, for planning, management techniques. These are not only modern techniques. Accounting and law,[3] for example, are very ancient examples of techniques.

They differ from techniques that have to do with the material world because nothing like social physics or social universal principles exists. Material objects exist outside us and are ruled by forces whose intensity and direction have nothing to do with human will. But it is different when it comes to objects to which intangible techniques are applied. Their effects are uncertain and differ according to the situations in which they are implemented. Management falls within these intangible techniques,[4] which has consequences for the functioning and effect of its tools.

WHAT IS A MANAGEMENT TOOL?

Like any technique, management is a practice with an array of tools. Managers make use of a number of tools that structure and define their activity: no management controller goes without a balanced scorecard; no human resources manager goes without job descriptions and professional interview forms; no marketing specialist goes without the tools of communication and promotion. But what is a 'management tool'?

A Common-Sense Notion

The expression 'management tool' is obviously not a scientific concept. Or at least it is no longer such. According to Hatchuel (2000), the notion of 'management tool' is indeed natural for the conception of management as a form of engineering, an idea dominant in the 1960s. But, even as used by classic authors of *scientific management*, has it ever been anything other than a common-sense notion? Later on, other authors proposed their own terminology to conceptualise it ('management apparatus', 'management instrument', 'management device').

---

[3] See Supiot (2002), an interesting reflection on the relationship between technique and law in the world of work.

[4] This in no way excludes their material inscription through objects, equipment, computers, etc.

As far as we are concerned, no single denomination is widely applicable. Each term, each definition, is linked to a research path. So, as we shall see in the second part of this book, each of the reviewed theses has developed its own vocabulary. The denominations put forward by each school of thought take on meaning within a particular theoretical framework and designate an object that can vary in size; for example, device is 'bigger' than tool. As Haudricourt (1964) said, the same object can be observed from different points of view and each of these can throw light on a part of the object.

Doubtless, the use of the word 'tool' is questionable, especially since it immediately evokes the idea of a world of objects and basic gestures where the complexity of social life is only present on the margins. But in its favour 'tool' has the simplicity of a collective representation available to all theoretical conceptualisations. Over and above the differences in points of view, it designates a class of objects that everybody agrees to recognise as being central to management practices. In order to focus our presentation and for the sake of temporary consensus, we propose to recognise as management tools a specific group of organisational objects that have characteristic traits and can be described in three ways (functional, structural and processual).

Describing a Management Tool

At this stage, we intend to offer an initial description. In order to describe a management tool we have to examine all its dimensions, both the most obvious, which flag up their material existence, as well as those that are hidden (implicit or latent) but nevertheless still very much part of the tool's reality. This exercise will also allow us to sketch out the bases of a classification of management tools.

Functional. The first dimension to take into consideration is *functional* (what is the tool's use?). For a management tool to exist, the designated object must serve management, that is, it must relate to the performance of the organisation, from the management's perspective.

We should point out that tools occupy a range of positions down the performance causality chain. Some of them, more upstream, enable the actions themselves; others, downstream, help to evaluate the effects of these actions. But whatever its position, the management tool has an organisational finality. In other words, it is closely linked to the organisational performance as the management of the organisation pursues it. Even when it seems to be interested only in the performance of individuals, these performances are conceived as being part of the organisation's performance as a whole. This finality is the expression of a control logic, contextualising the management tool within the logic of the formal system, concerned by questions of cost and efficiency. As we shall see later in this book, the official functions of a tool are not exhaustive of all its possible functions and only allow an imperfect anticipation of its real effects.

It is usual to distinguish between tools according to the functional domain in which they are deployed. For example, we talk about marketing tools (consumer panels, product life cycles, market surveys, etc.), human resources tools (support for annual performance reviews, training plans, recruitment tests, etc.) or strategic tools (development models, policy matrices, scenario methods, etc.). However, these groupings give only a general idea of the matter in hand.

A more interesting classification is according to the desired results and projects tools are intended to serve. Fayol (1949) outlines the principles of general administration, which can form the basis of this kind of classification:[5]

- planning (business plan, rules for purchasing and sales, standard contracts, budget, etc.);
- organising (flow charts, job descriptions, to do list, etc.);
- commanding (delegation of power, incentive systems, etc.);
- coordinating (project milestones, production operations, etc.);
- controlling (management charts, audit checklists, etc.).

---

[5] Peaucelle (2003) has proposed a modern translation of the Fayol-style administrative tools. Of course, most of the tools contribute to several principles: thus, a flow chart, which is considered a tool for organising, can also be used for commanding or coordinating.

Structural. The second dimension of a management tool is *structural* (what does the tool consist of?). Management tools have a visible structure and objective reality. They are localised. For example, a management chart, just like an evaluation grid, has structures and headings; in short it has a material existence. It is an object with a minimum of stability that can be used at the 'micro' level of the practices in the field. It is closely related to these practices without being the same thing: the tool used for the annual review is not the review itself; the balanced scorecard is not the performance management itself.

Here again it would be limiting to consider the structure of the management tool just from the point of view of what is most obvious: the entry screen, the form, the table of figures and so on. The management tool crystallises all the learned regularities and is made up of behavioural automatisms. It is, as the research stream opened by Berry (1983) would put it, an 'invisible technology'. In order to deal with the most pressing issues and to optimise the judgements of which they are the object, agents rely on the tool that is both familiar and legitimate. This then plays a part in setting up those organisational routines[6] revealed by the behaviourist theory of the firm (Cyert and March, 1963).

A second structural aspect is the material to which the tool is applied (what is it made of?). We could start from the nature of the information handled, which could concern:

- people (their skills, age, salary, debt capacity, tastes, etc.);
- things (volume of stocks of raw materials or products, etc.);
- elements considered as resources (budget, material, staff number, etc.);
- actions (number of customer visits, time allotted to activities, etc.);
- results of activity (turnover, margins, progress of a project, new clients, etc.).

---

[6] We will see later that routines are not ideologically neutral. They are associated with beliefs, social norms and conventions related to justifications.

According to Hacking (1999) there are different 'kinds', some indifferent, some interactive. A 'kind' refers to a category that allows the classification of individuals or objects. 'Indifferent' kinds are not affected by the classification and characterisation applied to them. On the contrary, the interactive kinds react to the information they help to produce. Quantifications concerning people are of this kind. Their mere existence produces reactive effects on the people who change their behaviour, which then impacts the information. Whereas statistics about stocks of spare parts or accounting statements do not directly modify the behaviour of the objects under study (they are indifferent), the dissemination of information about levels of payment or the spread of opinions (opinion polls) provoke a return – a *looping effect* (they are interactive).

Processual. A management tool also has a *processual* dimension, which is actualised while in use (how should it be used?). The use of a tool takes place within a tradition. The operating instructions for the tool ensure that this tradition will be passed on. However, these instructions for use are always incomplete because there is no operating knowledge outside specific contexts.

This dimension is that of technical action. Mauss (2007), for example, distinguishes between tools of weight and shock (mace, etc.), tools of friction (grater, file, etc.) and tools for making holes (knife, crankshaft, etc.). As far as management tools are concerned, a criterion could be that of mental operations: counting, quantifying, classifying, evaluating, making hierarchies (choice of investments, etc.); comparing (benchmark, budget control, etc.); reducing (balanced scorecard etc.); and modelling (strategic models, scenario methods, etc.). These different operations suppose that upstream there are formalisations, standards, classification rules and so on.

The reality of tools deployed over these three dimensions depends on their situation, because they are updated differently according to context. In his study of 'the social organism', Leroi-Gourhan (1993) highlights the link between social institutions and techno-economic devices and states that society fashions its behaviour with the tools that the material world proposes. In the same way it is no exaggeration to state that organisations build their behaviours on the tools that management offers them.

CONCLUSION

We take the spontaneous discourses of technique as our starting point and show their limits, noting that they are fated to remain within the reference framework of a determinist system. We try to go beyond these spontaneous discourses by seeking the bases for renewed thinking within the anthropology of techniques.

This detour, which is in fact a return to the sources of our reflection on technique and its objects, has allowed us to draw up a few rules in order to find a direction for the study of the instrumentation of management, to pinpoint its immaterial character and ultimately to arrive at a richer definition.

2 Traditional Approaches
Management Tools in the History of Organisation Theory

The diversion into the anthropology of techniques that we have just taken should not induce one to underestimate the contribution of authors more directly concerned with management and the tools it deploys. Such authors have left their mark in texts analysing the functioning, structure and development of organisations in order to improve their performance. Their work is brought together in a body of works called 'organisation theory'. Several lines run through this literature and various classifications have been put forward. We shall now examine two of the better known among them.

In his manual *Organizations: Rational, Natural and Open Systems*, W. Richard Scott proposes that an organisation can be seen as a closed or open system, and/or as a rational or natural system (Scott, 1981). This American sociologist argues that the history of organisations shows subsequent shifts from the closed rational system perspective to that of the closed natural system, and lastly to the open natural system perspective, which Scott maintains should become the dominant pattern, the most recent schools of his time being inspired by the 'open system'.

Instead of this reading of the development of organisational theory in terms of stages of development, we prefer Barley and Kunda's (1992) proposition. These authors maintain that management practices are influenced by the dominant ideology of the time.[1] They highlight an alternating movement between rational theories, that link efficiency standardisation and technical expertise, and normative

---

[1] Defined as 'a stream of discourse that promulgates, however unwittingly, a set of assumptions about the nature of the objects with which it deals' (Barley and Kunda, 1992, p. 363).

theories that advocate a less prescriptive management, relying on the shared values and involvement of the actors. The oscillation between normativity and rationality results more from the relative prominence of some ideas at some moments than from the complete substitution of one ideology by another. We will conduct our analysis of the conceptualisation of management tools in organisation theory relying on these two categories. And we will meet again the same viewpoints already highlighted in our analysis of the spontaneous discourses on technique: the technophile point of view, predominantly sustained in rational theories ('technique as a solution') and the point of view of resistance to technique predominantly sustained in normative theories ('between forgetting and minimising technique'). The technophobic position is largely absent from these classic approaches.

What contribution have these perspectives brought to the understanding of management tools? We propose to examine the literature from the end of the nineteenth century up to the 1980s. The idea is not to go through all the successive schools of thought, but to examine some classic texts, showing their contributions as well as their limitations.

RATIONALIST THEORIES OR TECHNIQUE AS A SOLUTION

For the so-called rational theories, which incorporate, as Barley and Kunda (1992) see it, the school of scientific management (F. W. Taylor, H. Fayol) and the school of rational systems (H. Simon, P. Lawrence and J. Lorsch, H. Mintzberg), management has to base itself on the technical application of scientific methods in addressing the problems arising in organisational life.

This idea emphasises the organisation as a formal structure with an economic purpose and throws the spotlight on a central character, the expert. The expert applies scientific principles to different areas of the business. Within the company he or she takes part in the activities of a technostructure that plans and controls work. Outside the company he or she takes on the role of consultant. Whether internal or external, experts take part in the development and renewal of management tools: information systems, decision-support systems, planning, time and motion tables, timekeeping, production management tools, pay schemes, organisation charts, etc. The manager takes on the role of an expert, a rational decision-maker who follows the rules and applies the methods that derive from them.

Management Tools from a Scientific Management Perspective

From the point of view of the school of scientific management, technology is a central factor for efficiency. It symbolises the rational and systematic process of industrial production, as distinct from modes of artisanal production, grounded in the producer's skills and judgement. Seen like this management tools appear as a vector of further rationalisation.

The history of organisational theory begins at the end of the nineteenth century with the works of Frederick W. Taylor (1856–1915) and Henri Fayol (1841–1925).[2] Both engineers, they are leading figures of this thought current. Their ideas and methods influenced, and still influence, the conduct of company managers. The Frenchman Henri Fayol drew from his experience general principles that are seen as the foundations of management (Fayol, 1949) and inspired the design of early management training as well as managerial practices (Wren, 2003). His work was destined to be known internationally, and his book *Administration industrielle et générale (General and Industrial Management)* was translated into more than ten languages.

The American Frederick W. Taylor was more 'computational': he worked by methodical observation and quantification (Taylor, 1911). Of course, one cannot reduce the origins of rational theories of management to the work of these two authors, but it was certainly their ideas that laid the foundations of the strongest programmes in

---

[2] There were precursors, but if the practices were ancient their codification was less so, and Bouilloud and Lécuyer (1994) remind us that without codification one couldn't talk of 'management techniques'.

this line of thinking. They were consulted, gave lectures and published, and they had followers who disseminated their ideas.

Taylor turned to science to replace old empirical methods. He focused on the organisation of industrial activities, and particularly those of the workers. Thus, he proposed rationalising workers' activity by systematically studying time and motion, in order to scientifically deduce a 'model' of the 'best way' of operating. This best method had to be suited to be taught clearly to the workers, who would then be asked to meet pre-established standards and production norms. One of Taylor's important ideas was the role of a special department dedicated to methods and organisation, responsible for defining optimal procedures and monitoring their use.

Administrative activities had become very extensive in large companies but they were not really taken into account by managerial practice. It was Fayol (1949), drawing on his own practice as director of a number of mining companies, who first drew up a set of rules relating to managing the organisations themselves and not only production. According to Peaucelle (2003) Fayol appears more than Taylor as the inventor of management tools. In fact, this term did not exist in Fayol's time; he used the term 'administrative tools'.[3] But he did shape the idea of them and their generic characteristics.

For Fayol, 'administrative tools' were the concrete means of putting his doctrine into effect: 'The day when the abstract idea of administrative doctrine is linked in the minds of state managers to the concrete notion of "administrative tools" we shall soon see appearing in the public service the action programmes, reports, conferences, and organisational diagrams which are of chief importance among these tools' (our translation, Fonds Fayol, HF5 Bis DR1, cited by Peaucelle, 2003, p. 207). Fayol's various writings are replete with information about tools, and he even offers a definition: 'They are a collection of documents that keep the manager informed and enable him to take informed

---

[3] Peaucelle (2003, p. 208) reveals that Fayol hesitated between several terms, including 'administrative procedures' before opting for 'administrative tools'.

decisions in all circumstances' (our translation).[4] Among the 'administrative procedures', the organisation chart, which Fayol calls the 'organisation table' (*tableau d'organisation*), along with the job description, are still useful guides in practice. These two tools obey the first general principle of administration, the division of labour, which, like centralisation, 'belongs to the natural order' (Fayol, 1949, p. 33). As Fayol explains, 'for social order to prevail in a concern there must, in accordance with the definition, be an appointed place for every employee and every employee be in his appointed place' (Fayol, 1949, p. 37).

The organisation chart, formally representing the interrelations of the personnel, is central among 'the organisation's administrative tools: managerial instruments'. It enables 'the building up and supervising of an organization' (Fayol, 1949, p. 78). Useful to organise the distribution of responsibilities, it enables at the same time reflecting on it and on the general direction given to decision-making processes by the special shape of the organisational structure. For Fayol, however, a complete picture of organisational geography is only achieved if the positions identified are covered by 'job descriptions'. These documents comprise a description of the works to be accomplished by the workers. They specify whom they work for, what they must do in general, and describe the principal operational outcomes that are targeted.

The name of Max Weber is often cited in managerial literature along with Taylor and Fayol because of his theory of bureaucracy. But the German sociologist is a different case, as his model of how bureaucracy functions should be seen above all as an analytic grid. Weber (1922) stresses that one should see in his characterisation of bureaucracy a methodological means and he uses the image of an 'iron cage', a rigid straitjacket that cannot be shed, to describe the loss of meaning induced by the techno-economic rationalisation that is reducing the possibilities by making the logic of technical means and impersonality prevail over the values of freedom.

---

[4] La réforme administrative de PTT, Fayol, Dunod, 1923. Archives Fonds Fayol, HF5 bis DRI, cited by Peaucelle (2003, p. 207).

Management Tools and the Rational Systems School

The rational systems school that evolved during the period 1955–80 updates the rationalistic orientation of the classic school. It is characterised by a description of rational managerial conduct established under the aegis of diverse techniques.

If for Simon (1947), an author central to decision-making theory, rationality is limited, as conduct within organisations is often more customary than rational, he strives nonetheless to minimise what he sees as the ill-effects of this limitation. To make the rationally-limited decisions converge towards the organisational objectives, Herbert Simon envisages a system of remote control based on a group of mechanisms (division of labour to frame attention, establishment of routines and programmes to standardise practice, and so on) structuring upstream individual conducts. As a good continuator of scientific management, Simon was interested in the possibilities offered by computers and took an optimistic position with respect to computing as long as its use is adapted to the types of decision concerned (see Table 2.1).

Table 2.1 *Decision-making techniques according to the types of decisions*

Types of decisions	Modern decision-making techniques
Programmed: Routine and repetitive decisions Organisations develop specific processes for handling them	1. Operations research (mathematical analysis, models, computer simulation) 2. Electronic data processing
Non-programmed: One-shot, ill-structured, new policies, Handled by general problem-solving processes	Heuristic problem-solving techniques applied to: • training human decision-makers • constructing heuristic computer programs

Source: adapted from Simon (1960, p. 8)

In Simon's work, the ways of seeing the organisation and of thinking about its rules for functioning have changed: the skills and the behaviours of individuals are now taken into consideration. But, like the classic authors of scientific management, the decision-making school of thought favours the formal and the conscious. The management tools considered incorporate more and more technique and the world of the office has also been invaded by a new type of machine: management computers.

Management Tools and the School of Contingency

Another current of thinking has marked and still marks organisation theory: the contingency theory school, which refines scientific management thinking. Authors in this field are against the idea of 'one best way', which is supported by the classic rational theory. For contingency theorists (Woodward, 1958; Burns and Stalker, 1961; Lawrence and Lorsh, 1967; Mintzberg, 1979), there is no unique ideal method; the types of approach or the solutions that are adequate always depend on context and situations encountered. According to them there should be a congruence, a 'fit', between external and internal factors. Although the authors sometimes deny it, the idea of 'fit' carries with it a rational project, that of the necessity to adapt to one's environment. The imprint of scientific management can still be found in contingency theory, as the organisations' structures and the corresponding tools are still rational means to reach the organisations' objectives.

For Joan Woodward, who is one of the most influential contributors to this line of thinking, technology is the prime contingency factor; she considers production methods a central factor in the specification of the organisation and the quality of human relations within enterprises (Woodward, 1958). Without saying that technology automatically determines the organisational structure, she claims that technology influences the type of structure and management that prevails in the organisation. For example, the structure complexity echoes the technical complexity. Thus, contingency theorists are still looking for general laws, which are now conceptualised as varying according to the characteristics of the case. In turn, Lawrence and Lorsch (1967) shed light on the role of environmental uncertainty and the importance of organisational differentiation (the degree to which the organisation is divided in sub-systems) to tackle it, whereas integration mechanisms give coherence to the whole.

Mintzberg (1979) generalises the idea of contingency by postulating that the efficiency of an organisation depends on the fit between the characteristics of the context and the means used to coordinate the work. The 'best fit' of the early authors of contingency theory cedes place to a 'getting it all together' principle (i.e., the need to consider all contingency factors together and to look for a coherence between the elements), which is just as important. This conception of contingency has given rise to extensions in different fields of management. Thus, according to two Belgian researchers, Pichault and Nizet (2000), there is a coherence between the organisational configurations defined by Mintzberg and human resources management (HRM). For each organisational configuration there is a corresponding HRM model[5] (see Table 2.2).

NORMATIVE THEORIES, BETWEEN FORGETTING AND MINIMISING TECHNIQUE

Since rational theories support the technophile point of view, normative theories find themselves more or less in the position of denial of technique, minimising its scope or simply putting it to one side, considering the technical object as something 'irrelevant'.

With the human relations school, from the beginning of the 1920s and until the end of the 1950s, a confident dialogue replaces the administration of strict and narrow control rules. Rather than advocating for new tools, writers like Elton Mayo, and later Abraham Maslow and Kurt Lewin, were committed to proposing more 'human'

---

[5] For the purposes of this demonstration we have simplified the works of the two authors who combine this contingency perspective with the political perspective of Crozier and Friedberg (1980).

Table 2.2 Correspondence between HRM and structural configurations

Structural configuration	Some contingency factors	Elements of internal context	HRM model	Characteristic HRM tools
Entrepreneurial organisation (characteristic sector: SME managed by an owner-entrepreneur)	Young, small-scale, unsophisticated technical system, simple and dynamic environment	Predominance of the strategic summit, direct supervision centralisation	Arbitrary model	Management relying on implicit criteria linked to the manager's ideology; few tools
Mechanistic organisation (characteristic sectors: large production companies or mass market services)	Older organisation, large-scale, non-automated regulatory system, simple and stable environment	Predominance of the technostructure; standardisation of work procedures; formalisation of behaviours; specialisation; action planning	Objectivising model	Abundance of uniform application tools: quantitative planning, classification grids, evaluation of personnel based on grading scales
Professional organisation (characteristic sectors: universities, hospitals, accountants' offices, social work organisations)	Complex and stable environment; unsophisticated technical system	Predominance of the operational centre; standardisation of qualifications	Conventionalist model	Tools in the hands of professionals; their development and application resulting from peer discussions

Innovative organisation (characteristic sector: cutting-edge technologies)	Complex and dynamic environment; young organisation; sophisticated technical system; fashionable structure	Predominance of support functions, in concert with the operational centre; mutual adjustment; selective decentralisation	Individualising model	Individualised tools: personalised timetables, retirement as desired, individualised salaries with a variable element, monitoring of skills, coaching
Missionary organisation (characteristic sectors: social economy, not for profit organisations)	Environment that is little studied in the literature	Standardisation of norms (system of values, beliefs); small units subjected to ideological control; conditional decentralisation	Value model	Management based on implicit criteria linked to values; few tools

Sources: after Mintzberg (1979) and Pichault and Nizet (2000) organisational models favouring commitment and personal development, participation and autonomy.

The mechanical and physical demands of work and the techniques of its regulation were deemed unimportant as compared to the social and psychological situation of individuals at work. One of the contributions of this school of thought is the distinction made between formal and informal structure. According to Roethlisberger and Dickson (1939), formal structure carries two kinds of logic: a logic of cost and a logic of efficiency, both of which are opposed to the logic of feelings, which expresses the values of the informal organisation.

The school for human relations remains rooted in the idea of one best way: there is one and only one good organisation. According to its authors, performance depends on working conditions (Mayo, 1933), motivation (Maslow, 1943; Herzberg, 1966), leadership styles (Lewin et al., 1939) or the general conception of the individual at work (McGregor, 1960). It is therefore a question of adopting 'good' methods in order to regulate functioning. But what determine the group performance are the informal aspects and its affective atmosphere. The school of human relations has relegated technology to the background, considering it as relatively unimportant compared to the psychological and social situation.

At the beginning of the 1960s, the expression 'human relations' became a burden for organisational psychologists. It carried connotations of listening and paying attention to the individual but not enough interest for the functioning of groups and performance. And so other labels were sought, such as 'organisational development' or 'organisational behaviour', which tried to convey the more global character of changes that this perspective implied. Authors such as Likert (1967), Herzberg (1966) and McGregor (1960) pushed for the design of organisational models favouring psychological growth, self-control, responsible autonomy and participation.

After a short time out of favour, the 1980s witnessed a revival of the critique of rational theories with the organisational culture theories. The Theory Z from Ouchi (1981), a cultural approach to management, suggests that productivity of large Japanese organisations results from an internally consistent set of norms, practices and behaviours which are grounded in trust and interpersonal intimacy. The idea that organisations could be approached via their culture took off in spectacular fashion following the publication of two bestselling works written by consultants: *In Search of Excellence* by Peters and Waterman (1982) and *Corporate Cultures* by Deal and Kennedy (1982). The latter, who are consultants at McKinsey, invite managers to identify the essential values that members of the company share. This was then taken up in academic fields, and by many psychologists, of whom Schein (1985) is the best known.

Peters and Waterman devote a chapter of their bestseller to an attack on the rational model of the classic school of organisations whose principles and concepts seemed to them to be opposed to the practices of the 'best enterprises'. Throughout their writings they are opposed to the excesses of the 'numerative, rationalist approach', advocate 'simplifying systems' and take issue with the misuse of tools such as organisation charts and job descriptions, which they believe 'transfix organizations' (Peters and Waterman, 1982, pp. 29, 121, 155).

THE PERVASIVENESS OF RATIONAL BELIEFS

The Rational Discourse Prevails Despite the Alternation of Theoretical Orientations

According to the analysis made by Barley and Kunda (1992), depending on time period, there is a succession of phases in managerial discourse with an alternation of normative and rational phases. We can link each of these periods with a specific manner of conceiving management tools (see Table 2.3).

If the alternation of rational and normative theoretical discourses is easily demonstrated, it seems to us that practices themselves always tend to favour rational beliefs. The technophile position remains dominant. So where does this pervasiveness come from? There are numerous explanations.

Table 2.3 Theoretical conceptions of management tools

Theory (and type)	Period	Reference authors	General characteristics	Conception of management tools (and point of view on technique)
Scientific management (rational theories)	1900–23	Taylor, Fayol	Theories based on formal elements structuring organisations and the way actions are led	Administrative tools equip the formal structure and guarantee the efficiency of management functions (technophilia)
Human relations (normative theories)	1923–55	Mayo, Maslow, Lewin, Roethlisberger and Dickson	Theories centred on satisfying human needs; the organisation includes the formal and the informal	The human factor and interactions between individuals within small work groups is more important than management artefacts (minimisation of technique)
Rational system (rational theories)	1955–80	(a) decision-making theory: Simon	Theory centred on the decision process, subjected to limited rationality	It is possible to compensate for the insufficiency of limited rationality by using appropriate methods (technophilia)

		(b) contingency theories: Burns and Stalker, Lawrence and Lorsh, Woodward, Mintzberg	Theory coupling management models with situational variables	There are not always good management tools, but there are tools that are more or less adapted (technophilia)
Organisational culture (normative theories)	1980s	Ouchi, Peters, Waterman, Deal and Kennedy, Schein	Theories centred on the organisation's culture as a regulatory and integration element	Organisational culture takes precedence over management artefacts and is a key factor of success (minimisation of technique)

The first is to be found in the fact that technophilia is comfortable. Faced with the complexity of the business world, its problems and its capacity for creating anxiety, technique reduces uncertainties. The tool is reassuring and it promises a certain predictability in the effects a practice will have: a 'good tool' is seen as a guarantee of 'good work'.

Technophilia therefore contributes to the manager's feeling of control over shifting realities. The movement of operational decentralisation and the growing distance between decision-making centres and those on the ground increase managers' need for control. The tool bolsters the action as it communicates certainties in the shape of operating modes and performance indicators.

Technophilia also proves to be a vector of professionalisation. The presence of a management tool legitimises experts' knowledge. In turn, this knowledge validates the experts' skills and the particular definition of the situations that they are promoting. As the tool offers a language as well as landmarks, it comforts professional identities. It facilitates communication between members of the same professional community and makes them less likely to be influenced by third parties who do not possess the codes.

Another advantage of instrumental thinking is that it is easy to teach. In a way, the extremely narrow technical vision of management constitutes the condition for learning it systematically. Brabet (1999) developed this idea very convincingly about human resources management underlying that in initial training, students are very keen to have tools and knowledge of an instrumental type. It is easier to satisfy them on this point than to evoke the relativity of the instrumental model and its insufficiencies, while the students still lack experience. Easiness lies in transmitting to them a vision of management that consists of using in an orthodox manner relevant tools having clearly identified rules and mechanisms.

Finally, the belief in the power of management tools legitimises the technostructure, because it valorises it as the main actor, as well as the consultancies that help and are paid to implement best practices and to set up standard devices. The strategic summit needs all of these: power is delegated to the technique, with which it is difficult to negotiate, and to the experts who possess the codes. Consultants are present upstream as well as downstream in order to check on the correct use of the tools that they themselves have pushed for.

The Rational Approach Is Reinforced by the Consultants

'Consultant thought' seems to be closely allied to the rational theory of organisation. Born at the same time, they are twins. Taylor is rightly considered as the first consultant in history (McKenna, 1995). Consultants and the theoreticians of the organisation theory classical school share the same conception of the decision-making process. Thanks to the experts who advise them, successful decision-makers are thought as having complete information on the problems they face and capacity to choose the best solution. Moreover, they are supposed to use efficient evaluation tools that help them to monitor its implementation and as a consequence to revise goals and the resources used in the solution or even the decision itself according to the achieved results.

Since the first consultant-engineers of the beginning of the twentieth century, organisations and ideas about what are the efficient models have evolved. The well-oiled gears of the Taylorist organisation have been succeeded by the network-enterprise, which by 'replacing paper processes with digital processes', creates 'the paperless office' and disseminates 'the Webwork style'.[6] But today, just as before, the consultant is there to persuade the most reticent to adopt the 'best practices' and to overcome resistance to change.

Here, experience and ideology often take the place of theory. Prescriptions are based on these and not on academic knowledge. Consultants' thinking is less informed by science than by shared beliefs and does not really pretend to rely on theory. Its legitimacy is to be found elsewhere, in common sense and in partially imagined

---

[6] Bill Gates on 'the company of the third millennium' (Gates, 1999).

locations: such and such a tool will be praised because it is used by 'the best companies', because it is inscribed in 'best practice'. According to Villette (2003, p. 49), the consultant is pushed into giving standardised services 'which often are just the almost mechanical application of formalised tools, matrices and schemes'. The affirmation that there are best practices means they can remain in universal mode in order to apply the same solutions to all companies, to blur any particularities, to propose standardised problem-solving schemes – sometimes called 'solutions'. For organisations, believing in these is functional: it allows a single vision to be imposed and to avoid considering any (always costly) specificity.

The world of consultancy is far from homogeneous. Between strategic consulting agencies that inspire structural novelties and organisational consulting firms that sell standardised solutions to small and medium-sized enterprises (SMEs), there is a lot of diversity (Maister, 1993). Nevertheless, they all participate in the dissemination of management tools. However, this does not mean that a globalised uniformity of practices is obtained. Even consultancies of international renown have to deal with 'societal effects' (Maister, 1993, p. 37), which means adapting their approaches and their tools to the specificity of the national context (Kipping et al., 2003).

Of course, there exist consultants who are more inclined to make use of normative theories. But they are both in the minority and overshadowed. Most of them are from a social sciences background and often do not work in the largest international agencies but in small, niche market consultancies. In accordance with the distinction identified by Henry (1992), they obey an 'intellectual logic' rather than an 'economic logic'. In any case, they often define themselves as 'interveners' rather than consultants, even if they limit their intervention to less profitable missions.

GOING BEYOND CLASSICAL APPROACHES

While rational theories may have shown their limits, the counter-theories ('normative theories'), as for example the ones of the Human

Relations school, have not really tackled the question of management tools. Whatever the diversity of the specificities of the periods in which they were formulated, rational theories have in common at least a kindly eye turned towards management tools, and at the most unbridled enthusiasm. We therefore recognise the technophile position here. As for normative theories, they bypass the question of management tools. They do not share the technophobes' hostility towards them but seek rather to put their scope into perspective. These theories therefore are better characterised by denial of technique.

In the end, whether they are basically rational or normative, most classical approaches to the theory of organisations do not really allow us to shed light on the main questions at the origin of this book. They remain dependent on common-sense epistemology, as in them we find reflected the oppositions that we discussed in Chapter 1.

However, in our opinion, two schools of thought have taken off in a new direction: on one hand the socio-technical approach to organisations that Barley and Kunda (1992) do not mention – maybe because of its European roots – and, on the other hand, the behavioural approach that constitutes a development in the research programme started by James March. It is partly under this latter influence that in France we have observed the development of a fresh look at management tools since the 1980s. These opened the way to a new kind of research on management tools that this book intends to give an account of.

The Socio-Technical Approach

This thought current started with E. Trist and F. Emery in 1950 at the Tavistock Institute of Human Relations in London. Along with the Human Relations school, it shares the axiom of technological non-determinism regarding the choice of organisation. But it is different in that it also affirms that seeking only to satisfy human needs and neglecting technology is to run the risk of inefficiency (Emery and Trist, 1960).

The socio-technical approach is based on the principle of con-joined optimisation of the technical and the social. It tries to show that any technology choice will result in modifications in social rela-tions and psychological working conditions. The opposite is true as well: it is not possible to change the psychosocial climate without changing the technological and cultural working conditions that are at its origin. In order to obtain better performance, action must be jointly undertaken to change the social and technical systems. The socio-technical approach is more than a theory; it is a way to resolve problems in the field. It describes carefully the obstacles encountered in each reorganisation experience that has been investigated. Its method consists less in fixing once and for all the ideal outlines of an organisation than in supporting and accompanying innovation processes. This approach is rooted in the principle that objects should not make decisions instead of people.

The socio-technical approach has provided a finer vision of the interactions between technique and the social. But on the one hand its conception of technique is limited in practice to the world of indus-try,[7] and on the other the proposed separation between two systems (technique and social) can be challenged. As the anthropology of techniques has shown, every technical object is social and every social fact includes technical elements.

The Behavioural Theory of Organisations

Richard Cyert and James March started with the model of limited rationality developed by Herbert Simon and took it further by study-ing its organisational consequences. They introduced a new perspec-tive to the theory of organisations, marked by the adoption of a descriptive point of view that breaks with the dominating prescriptive perspectives (rational or normative). According to this theory, formal routines (rules, strategies) and informal routines (beliefs, codes,

---

[7] Vaujany (2003) proposes extending this approach to the analysis of information technologies.

cultures) play an important role in decision-making. Decision-makers generally prefer to reproduce action plans (routines) that have been tried and tested in similar situations to those they are facing.

Cyert and March (1963) state that companies cannot be considered as a monolith because different individuals and groups have their own aspirations and conflicting interests. They propose looking at the enterprise as made of diverse coalitions with diverging interests playing political games and engaged in power relationships. They explain that conflicts arising from these relationships are essentially regulated through organisational routines, that is, systemised procedures set in place by the firm.

These early works influenced the shaping of the strategic actor theory (Crozier and Friedberg, 1980[8]) in taking rules into account as a source of power in organisations and in the study of their roles in the bureaucratic model. But unlike Michel Crozier, James March, whose reflections on decision-making processes were pursued throughout a long university career,[9] grants a great deal of importance to the analysis of processes in organisational functioning, and to the role played by formal rules and the problems created when they are changed (March et al., 2000). March's analysis of the organisation in terms of routines puts the emphasis on cognitive dimensions and on the role of rules intrinsic to any organisational phenomenon. What is interesting here for our reflection is that these routines are the very substance of management tools, as we mentioned in Chapter 1.

After the 1980s: Renewed Interest for the Instrumentation of Management in French Academia

The behavioural theory of the firm has allowed the management tool to be granted a status: it 'crystallises' routines and cognitive schemes that are taken for granted. It comes from routines but has its own effects. According to Aggeri and Labatut (2010), it is in this theoretical

---

[8] See in this book, Thesis 5 in Chapter 4.
[9] See Weil (2000) for an introduction to March's work.

stream that the work of Michel Berry, well known in France to have developed some original thinking on management tools, is to be situated. The origin of it is the publication of a collective report by a research centre (*Centre de Recherche en Gestion* – CRG) at the École Polytechnique of Paris on the role of management tools in complex social systems (Berry, 1983). This report challenged the vision according to which the behaviour of organisations is mainly a matter of will. Berry demonstrates that far from being a faithful servant, the tool is a central operator. Combined, tools form a technology that is all the more redoubtable as it is 'invisible' and not recognised as such. This invisibility is linked to the fact that the collective imagination grants too large a role to the will of managers and that managers try hard to make their will apparent. 'Invisible technology' can have negative effects – 'all the more so as it is allowed to roam free away from the light' (Berry, 1983, p. 5). It is therefore necessary to question the roles played by invisible technology, in particular its part in setting up behavioural automatisms that lead individuals to make choices that have little to do with their will or even their conscience. These automatisms have helped to reduce complexity, which can be seen necessary for action, and made this possible by some 'abstracts of the good and the true' (*abrégés du bien et du vrai*) which management tools provide.

Research carried out by another research centre (*Centre de Gestion Scientifique* – CGS) at the École des Mines of Paris (now Mines ParisTech) have taken this theme further. The book edited by Moisdon (1997) gives a wide overview of these studies (see also David, 1996, 1998). In these works, thinking about management tools is inseparable from intervening in the organisation: these authors perceive a 'coupling between management tool and intervention' (Moisdon, 1997, p. 283).[10]

While the interest for management tools seems to decline somewhat in management research handled by leading French engineering schools at the beginning of the 2000s, French sociologists turned their

---

[10] See Baumard (1997) for a critique of this stream of thinking.

attention to the subject, promoting a 'sociology of management devices' to develop some understanding of managerial practices taking into account the technical aspects of management (Benedetto-Meyer et al., 2011; Boussard, 2001; Boussard and Maugeri, 2003; Maugeri, 2001). Based on these first works and within the French Association for Sociology (*Association Française de Sociologie*) a network of researchers (RT30) was set up in 2004 in order to develop specific sociological work on management practices and tools in organisations and their dissemination outside the business world. Research production in this field has been particularly fruitful, largely due to the participation of the *Printemps* research centre at the University of Versailles Saint Quentin, where works about organisations' dynamics were developed. In her book entitled *Sociologie de la gestion* (*The Sociology of Management*), summarising this collective effort, Boussard (2008) distinguishes two levels in management: *logos* and 'techniques', which are assembled in 'management devices'.

In parallel, after having noted the importance of instruments for public action, French political scientists started a research programme about the conditions of choice of these devices or instruments, their uses and the effects they produce. With these works, it is recognised that reflection about the management tools should not only concern business firms but also address wider questions such as public policy or the functioning of the state (Halpern et al., 2014; Lascoumes and Le Galès, 2004a, 2004b, 2007).

Outside France, from the 1980s onwards, we also see the growth of innovative works developing an approach to management techniques inspired by sociology, especially in accounting, around the review *Accounting, Organisations and Society*.

CONCLUSION

The need to reflect more in depth about management tools is very clear from this survey of classical approaches to the theory of organisations. Until the 1980s reflection on the tools deployed in management was done piecemeal. Of the large number of theories advanced, those called above 'rational' are clearly technophile. Their main contribution is to highlight the central role of management tools and their importance in the functioning of organisations and the economy. On the other hand, while normative theories are not always in denial of technique, they often minimise its role considerably. They pay little attention to management tools, considering them as secondary or even despicable. Doubtless rational theories exaggerate the neutrality of management tools, which are considered as faithful servants of the managers' will. But normative theories fail to give an account of the importance of technique, which deserves to be approached as a distinctive phenomenon. Therefore, we have two kinds of incomplete views that meet in the same kind of theoretical project: producing general rules supposedly universally applicable.

However, the works referred to at the end of this chapter – both the socio-technical approach of the Tavistock Institute and the behavioural theory of the firm – have shown the way forward. More recently, work carried out in France by the management research in leading engineering schools, Sociology about management devices or Political Science about political instruments, has contributed to the legitimisation of social analyses that take a serious look at management tools. These works are essential landmarks as they send out strong signals about the importance of objects. Today, the literature in this field is quite abundant and diversified in terms of theoretical approaches, especially as other disciplines such as psychology and socio-linguistics have also taken up the theme.

The time now seems right to propose an initial ordering of these works as a typology of possible approaches to management tools in the form of stylised theoretical grids. This is the purpose of the second part of this book.

PART II Three Major Types of Social Science Approaches

In Chapter 2 we articulated our presentation around the classic works on organisation theory. In doing so we recognised the contribution of pioneering scholars, particularly Henri Fayol who underlined the importance of management tools. We also recognised how some of these early works opened up new perspectives. Now it is time to present the various theoretical currents that have addressed these questions related to management tools. This is the purpose of the second part of this book, which is organised according to the main theoretical approaches that are pertinent to our analysis and that share certain similarities with each other. These approaches are either schools of thought or works bearing more specifically on a particular concept associated with one or two leading authors. This spectrum is wide. But since our project is more of an anthology than an encyclo-paedia some selections have been made.

Our ambition here is to analyse organisations, enterprises or the economic system comprised of organisations, beginning with manage-ment tools and not, as is usual, with overarching elements (social superstructures, the general policies of enterprises, production systems, etc.).[1] This intention leads us to the presentation of a succession of 'representative theories', in the sense that they reflect upon technique, which shines a light, directly or indirectly, on management tools.

If there seem to be preconceived ideas in the choices made, the idea of novelty is certainly not among them, nor that of management orthodoxy. While some of the theories are quite recent, others are of an older vintage. Most of them were not formulated to give an account

---

[1] In some lines of thought, however, these can sometimes be reintroduced during the analysis of tools.

of management tools. In this overview, we have granted much importance to authors who did not remain at the surface of technical objects.
Rather, these authors have taken an interest in both the material and
ideational aspects that constitute tools – their 'inner life'. To different
degrees they have investigated the very substance of tools, beyond just
an analysis of their uses and of the conditions for their appropriation.

The selection and the analysis of these works are the result of a
three-step process:

1. Identify among existing theories those that seem the most pertinent,
   according to the principles outlined in Chapter 1.
2. Make an ordered anthology based on a small number of representative
   publications.
3. Make clear the main lessons of these theories by using the same framework
   in order to draw up a systematic description.

The works selected reveal a diversity of points of view. To
account for this diversity while avoiding a scattergun approach, we
needed to be able to classify and sort prior works according to satisfactory criteria. But what categorisation should we use? There are
many possibilities. Some works have a pragmatic orientation while
others are rather more critical. Sometimes the analysis is at a macro
level, interested in social phenomena, and sometimes it is micro and
focused on organisations or even on management situations. Some
research grants the technical object a central status while others
consider it more secondary. The disciplines mobilised by these works
(sociology, political economy, management, psychology, philosophy)
are varied. Each of these distinctions has its own point of interest.

Focusing on the ideas defended and their most common themes,
we finally decided to group these works into three thematic universes
that correspond to the following three chapters, respectively. Each
of these universes is subdivided into three to four 'theses' that link
those authors and texts with a certain theoretical proximity and
organise these works based on a common template. All in all, ten
theses are examined. Each thesis is presented on its own, focusing on

its key theoretical components (key concepts, behavioural hypotheses, and so on) and on the specifics of its approach to management tools. Then, we present different streams of studies that have built on each thesis. A synoptic table presents different studies that have addressed management tools through approaches that we thought resembled the respective thesis. One empirical study is developed at greater length in a box. Finally, we provide a summary sheet that recapitulates key ideas and presents reminders of the respective thesis.

In brief, the structure of Part II is as follows.

Chapter 3 will tackle *the critique of management tools as instruments of violence and domination*. In this part we present those works for which the implementation of management tools exerts forms of violence (economic, symbolic, political, psychic, etc.) and is complicit in establishing or maintaining states of domination or exploitation. Some works inspired by Marx (thesis 1) or Foucault (thesis 2) examine the role played by technical devices in societal functioning. Others, more clinically oriented (thesis 3), focus on the functioning of small groups (clinical sociology, psychosociology), or even on the individual psyche (psychodynamics, clinical activity).

The role of institutions in the formation and the development of management tools is addressed in Chapter 4. Central to this type of analysis are elements that relate to the social dimension of thinking and reasoning, such as interpretative schemes, norms, values, beliefs or social representations. It is these social objects that guide collective behaviour by leading organisations to adopt tools that correspond to them. These tools are produced by humans and they have an objective and an intersubjective reality. In this chapter the role of management tools is examined successively through the institutions that orient them (thesis 4), the conventions and categorisations that carry them (thesis 5) and, finally, the structuration processes of which they are enabling and constraining elements (thesis 6).

Chapter 5 considers *the interaction between management tools and actors*. Here actors' influence is central in the analysis and actors' roles are approaches from different viewpoints. For some (e.g., *actor-network theory*), human and non-human actors mingle together; there is neither subject nor object, only 'actants' (thesis 7). For others (e.g., activity theory), the artefact can only become an instrument from the moment when a subject-actor builds plans for its use (thesis 8). Yet others (thesis 9) focus on the communication dimension of management tools (e.g., *sensemaking*, semiology of management tools). A final group of works highlights the radical incompleteness of normal rules, routines and technical objects, subordinating their effects to those of the actors (theory of the strategic actor) (thesis 10).

In examining and presenting these works, our intention is neither to exhaustively present the theses of their authors nor to do justice to all their nuances. Rather, our aim is to clarify the core message of each thesis by making salient their most fruitful contributions to our project of unpacking the functioning of management tools. In simplifying and stylising the different approaches to management tools, our analysis has tended to leave aside important overlapping zones, underlying relationships and efforts of hybridisation between the different theses. We will consider these dimensions in the conclusion.

Some of these works do not give a lot of room to management tools themselves. The analytical category of 'management tools' is a category that we are building and which, in some of the texts studied, sometimes points to certain examples of tools or techniques present in the situations described (e.g., appraisal interviews, quality norms, coaching). But sometimes they point towards other notions (e.g., government technique, managerial model, devices) or even towards dimensions that seem quite adequate to us (e.g., routines, categories, calculation methods).

Focusing on the three thematic universes and the ten theses that correspond to them, this book aims to give an account of management tools. In this regard, it appears as the result of an attempt at elucidating and organising theoretically the empirical data that are proper to each of the theses examined and to the whole of the corpus under study.

The ensemble presented here will allow readers to further their understanding of whichever current they are particularly interested in.

3 Critical Perspectives on Management Tools

For the authors brought together in this chapter, social asymmetries, and the balance and relations of power are at the heart of the analysis. Management tools are caught up in these relations which they often mediate and facilitate, or sometimes moderate or regulate. Although these approaches allow the construction of a critique of management tools, showing how far they serve projects of domination and exploitation, participate in forms of oppression and violence and produce suffering, nevertheless the way in which the different theses construct their critique are diverse but complementary. Taken together, these approaches allow us to move from the most global social functioning and its systemic effects to the oppressed individuals in their subjective experience.

The authors of thesis 1 seek to relocate management tools either into an analysis of an economic system and its asymmetries, as far as the notion of capitalism will allow it, or a hierarchical social system with social groups in conflict. In order to be revealed, the truth about management tools has to be put back into this social structure, which largely determines the action that takes place within it.

The Foucauldian analyses of thesis 2 allow us to understand better how power is exercised over people in a concrete manner, how they are disciplined and oriented to conform to certain strategic goals, and how their subjectivity turns out to be produced by instruments of power in order to make them governable. This thesis not only allows very fine analyses of the techniques of control but it also attracts our attention to the role of expertise and knowledge for the production of social control, and to the intimate relationships between knowledge and power.

Finally, thesis 3 seeks to show the suffering and social dysfunctions that are created by such an exercise of power. Here, political and economic approaches give way to a clinical approach that looks at mental health.

Taken together, these three theses share an aim of emancipation and allow for understanding how the relationships of domination and exploitation are constructed on a daily basis, and how these relations manage to persist thanks to legitimation, social discipline, incentives and contracts or through the action of perverse personalities.

Thesis 1:

Tools Implicated in Relationships of Domination

The works brought together in this thesis share a vision of social life composed of social classes or social groups with divergent interests, some of which are dominant at a given moment and dominated at other times. The dominant groups hold on to power, resources and wealth in an unseemly fashion, trying all the while to remain in this position and to conceal the violence that lies behind the effort, while the dominated attempt to escape.

Management tools are caught up in these confrontational relational dynamics and can carry out multiple functions within them. First of all, beneath their apparent technicality they are likely to *legitimise social hierarchies* and the exploitation of one group by another. They may also be *active instruments* of exploitation and domination. More broadly, they could constitute a resource for different groups (not just dominant ones) and confer differentiated advantages in the struggle that opposes them. Finally, they can be seen as an *agonistic product* and, at a given moment, crystallise the state of the balance of power.

The general watchword of 'the non-neutrality of management tools', which is widely found in the literature, is still partly based on this thesis, which has been the first one to have underlined the political dimension inherent in these constructions (Boussard and Maugeri, 2003). The analysis mostly functions as a method of unveiling: far from their claim of mere technical efficiency, tools are *in fact* key elements and forces that allow some to dominate others, or weapons in an unfair fight.

Two main currents inspire these works – Marxist traditions on the one hand and the school of Bourdieu on the other. In the first case, social classes are defined according to the place they occupy in the system of production. In the second, the struggle does not take place solely on economic grounds; the differentials are cultural, relational or symbolic as well as financial. Let us remember that despite the similarities of their positions and their conditions, for these two traditions the people who make up these classes are not necessarily aware of their common situation and do not necessarily mobilise as a collective, although as individuals they are nevertheless caught up in these social structures. From the Marxist perspective the transition from the 'class in itself' to the 'class for itself' supposes a collective consciousness that encourages action and starts the class struggle. The works of Bourdieu partly sought to understand why this process rarely happened and looked for the answers in symbolic violence, the process of internalising one's place and the alignment of 'subjective hopes' alongside 'objective chances', that is to say the unconscious self-limitations of the masses. If (conscious) social classes do not exist, or only rarely, it is individuals who experience the daily struggle, linked to their position in the agonistic fields. Currents such as feminism, anti-racism, anti- and post-colonialism have extended the list of domination relations and have also produced critical analyses of management tools that we might associate with this thesis.

One of the key points of this thesis is that we cannot understand what is at stake with management tools if we do not situate them within a framework that goes well beyond the management situations where they are to be found or even the enterprises where they operate.

THE TOOL AS AN ELEMENT OF A SOCIAL AND ECONOMIC SYSTEM

From this perspective, an analysis of management tools has to incorporate an understanding of the wider social and economic system, one that is criss-crossed by domination relationships, power struggles between actors who have unequally distributed resources, and in which the state and the judicial system play a major role in fixing the rules of the game and producing both resources and positions. Tools must be linked to a capitalistic state that has a tendency to overdetermine their functioning. Lordon (2000), Capron (2005) and Vercher et al. (2011) respectively consider the EVA,[1] the international accounting standards or the codes of conduct imposed on suppliers as neo-liberal capitalist instruments.

Colette and Richard (2000) have argued that accounting choices, for example the calculation of the bottom line balance that measures the firm's profits, vary according to the nature of the dominant group in an economic system: the bottom line represented the share for the state in the Soviet system, the share of the personnel in the self-governing Yugoslavian system, and that of the shareholders in capitalist countries. In each case, it is the dominant group that is supposedly the recipient of the surplus made by the firm, once the other stakeholders have received their share. Accounting therefore presents as entirely natural the fact that the firm's profit, in capitalist countries, is the shareholders' profit.

Ezzamel et al. (2007), taking China as a case, have highlighted the role played by the dominant economic ideology in the choice of acceptable accounting practices: this is how the accounting principle of prudence – meaning the use of accounting provisions for risks and depreciations – was banished from accounting in the time of Chairman Mao Zedong. These practices of provisioning had in fact been targeted as a symbol of the dishonesty of capitalists who were reputed to be using them to conceal the level of real profits and hide the exploitation of workers. In a country converted to communism such practices could not be tolerated, for as exploitation was abolished, there was nothing to hide.

In these two cases the understanding of accounting practices gains depth if we refer to the functioning of the economic system as a whole and to the role of the state within it.

---

[1] *Economic Value Added*, a method for calculating an accounting balance that is supposed to measure wealth creation realised by an enterprise.

THE TOOL IN THE LEGITIMATION OF SOCIAL HIERARCHIES

The alleged technical neutrality of management tools has often been denounced as playing into the hands of dominant groups. Tools allow the gentle inculcation of a world favourable to certain categories without ever presenting themselves as ideological instruments. Thus Boussard (2001) shows us the centrality of the so-called 'stock-delay' indicator for those working at the *Caisse d'Allocations Familiales* (CAF), the French public administration in charge of delivering services and support to families. This indicator measures the number of cases that are backed up in the handling process and provides a very particular synthetic representation of the job carried out by the organisation. This indicator also designates the people in charge of the administrative handling of files (the *liquidateurs*) as the most important staff that carry out the CAF's missions. If these people are the most numerous and unionised, they are not the only important workers for providing good services to families. Social workers are attending personally families in need, and another group of people is in charge of paying social benefits. These two groups are not represented by the metric and criticise it bitterly. This kind of analysis could be extended to other kinds of performance measurements, which select *de facto* the best practices and valorise certain actors and behaviours to the detriment of others.

Reviewing what we know about the accounting of slavery in the USA and the Caribbean, Oldroyd et al. (2008) remind us that slaves were mentioned in accounts as assets, that is the property of estates along with cattle, poultry and agricultural machinery. Such practices – which conformed to the legal status of slaves – have added their own weight of unquestioned evidence and have helped reinforce the dehumanisation and transformation of human beings into merchandise.

Bourguignon (2005) relies on Lukács's concept of reification to analyse the effects of management tools. Through reification the 'relation between persons takes on the character of a thing and thus acquires an "illusory objectivity", which has a proper, rigorous, thoroughly closed and apparently rational system of laws, so as to conceal every trace of its fundamental nature: the relation between people', so much so that the reified world appears as 'the only conceivable world' (Lukács, 1971, p. 140). Bourguignon proposes to extract from this definition four fundamental components in order to describe reification as a process containing (1) a shift from subjectivity to objectivity, (2) resulting in the masking of the real subjective world and, further, its potential conflicts, (3) which prevents social dispute, (4) which finally aims at maintaining social order (Bourguignon, 2005, p. 358). Because they objectify only some representations (among the innumerable possibilities), management tools tend to hide the conflicts that exist. Thus tools that measure 'value creation' shine a light on consumers and shareholders and keep other stakeholders, notably employees, whose interests are partly contradictory, in the dark.

In a Bourdieu-type framework the notion of symbolic violence allows us to say similar things about management tools since they help make acceptable the meaning of things they focus on, a process that is all the more efficient since it is not recognised as violence (Benedetto-Meyer et al., 2011).

These different forms of concealment should also be understood as ways to hide the exploitation of the dominated by the dominant. This is what Boje and Winsor (1993) suggest when they denounce the 'masquerade' of *Total Quality Management* and its tools, which camouflage a revival of Taylorism whose goal remains, as in all Marxist literature, increased exploitation of the workers.

THE TOOL AS A LEVER OF EXPLOITATION

The management instruments and practices that accompany Taylorism were in effect the first to be criticised, particularly in the analyses of Braverman (1974). He showed that the fragmentation and mechanisation of work, the sources of deskilling, had robbed workers of the power that flowed from their skills and know-how in order to exert greater coercion over and profit from them. In this analytical vein, we could consider that all the devices that aim to improve productivity via the intensification of work or an increase in the scope of tasks and responsibilities, are exploitation devices. But as Taylorism is only one moment in the history of productive systems, Hopper and Armstrong (1991) invite us to revisit the whole history of management systems and cost calculation by considering them as successive responses to problems of mobilisation and control of the workforce that employers encountered.

Other mechanisms can be exposed, such as those that organise the debt levels of the dominated vis-à-vis the dominant and prevent the former from liberating themselves. We might recall grocery shops managed by employers in the paternalist or post-slavery world that, when associated with low wages, allowed the bosses to keep a hold on their freed workers because of the debts they were forced to contract at the store to feed themselves. Davie (2000) shows how the British obtained land free of charge from the natives in the Fijian islands by lending them money to pay off an alleged debt demanded by the USA, with gunboats in attendance. By acting as if the American debt was real, the British transformed it into a real accounting debt (via a loan that had to be reimbursed). Once the account had been established by force, the annual claim for reimbursement was thereafter only served up in the most neutral of legal and technical guises. Incidentally, the lands had been stolen from their owners.

THE TOOL AS THE RESULT OF POWER RELATIONS

A vision of social relations as conflictual can help nuance the argument and consider that management tools are not so much the tool of the strongest but rather emerge, at a given moment in a power struggle, particularly from resistance of the dominated to the will of the dominant, or even from their revolt.

Taking another look at the history of Taylorism, Linhardt (1983), encourages us to be wary of the dominant discourse of employers. In fact:

the real development happens in a way which is much more contradictory and conflictual than in the idealised version of a linear development of the organisation of work as a science [...] In the concrete organisation of work we meet a combination of different modes of organisation [...] a combination which is the result of employer policies, resistance and labour movements, economic factors outside the internal organisation of the work process, and diverse elements of the class struggle in society. (Linhardt, 1983, p. 10, our translation)

The rejection of timekeeping marked the first attempts to introduce Taylor's methods and pushed bosses into amending Taylorism by relying on psychology and sociology. 'These days, we can ask ourselves questions about the sometimes ambiguous roles played by ergonomics, occupational medicine, psychology, etc. Employers' policies often combine the direct reinforcement of exploitation and the intensification of work with an array of manipulations called "human", administered by specialists who, in principle, do not organise production directly' (Linhardt, 1983, p. 13, our translation).

Similarly, Burawoy (1983) encourages us to consider that the possibilities of coercion that weigh on the workforce vary according to period and place, to the system of professional relations, to labour law and to the level of organisation of workers' movements. Social security systems thus loosened food-related constraints by guaranteeing income in case of job loss, for example, and labour law limit an employer's discretionary power. The development of these institutions has meant that coercion has also been reduced but they have at the same time favoured workers' consent. That is why, according to Burawoy, it is necessary to pay attention to political devices that allow the reproduction of the production system thanks to a regulation of social struggles. At an intra-organisational level, Bourguignon and Chiapello (2005) show how a performance measuring system evolves according to the critique from people subjected to it.

Although it is possible to maintain that management tools favour domination by legitimising it, we can also observe that these tools may constrain domination and hence reduce arbitrariness. In some ways, it is the constraints tools bring to bear on this domination that make it legitimate (Boltanski and Chiapello, 2005). From this point of view, bureaucratic tools have a deeply ambivalent role: they are likely to facilitate the predictability of management action, favour equality of treatment between people and ensure a wider dissemination of information such as greater transparency in decisions and practices – all of which contribute to the reduction of hierarchical arbitrariness. The outlook of this thesis is that the state of instruments at any given moment should be analysed as the temporary and more or less institutionalised result of a fundamentally conflictual process.

THE TOOL AS A RESOURCE IN A STRUGGLE

Finally, tools may, at least in theory, also serve the cause of the dominated rather than the dominant: '"Accounting" and "emancipation" have typically been seen as contradicting each other, yet, as a social practice, accounting is deeply implicated in social concerns and should be evaluated in terms of its contribution to social well-being. Social analysis, seeing accounting intertwined in a wider social context, has reached a deepened appreciation of accounting's problematic character' (Gallhofer and Haslam, 2003, p. i). In practice, however, management tools only rarely play such an emancipatory role because they are the instruments of executives and managers, used at the strategic apex to control collective action.

Nevertheless, the study of the ways in which management tools evolve allows us to glimpse the fact that their history is often inseparable from the history of groups of actors who aim to gain more central or superior positions or to see their point of view taken into account. Xu and Xu (2008) illustrate this by pointing to how a project to standardise banking accounting in the 1920s affected the rise to power of new actors.

We must also recognise that many instruments or measurement approaches come not from the business world but from the laboratories of critical actors who want to see management practices evolve. This happened, for example, with instruments for measuring ecological footprints and various forms of social and environmental evaluation.

In summary: to interpret management tools, this thesis positions them in a more global economic and social system and tends to make them a revealing aspect of the system, of the power struggles that divide it and the forms that these struggles take. On this basis, two sub-theses appear. The first is predominant and deterministic and emphasises the properties of tools as *relays of power structures* that they facilitate on a daily basis by favouring and legitimising the exploitation of social asymmetries. The second is procedural and more contingent: it designates tools as being caught up in *a network of conflictual interactions* (whether they are considered as the result of power relations or as resources in a struggle) (see Table 3.1).

Table 3.1 *A selection of publications representative of the domination thesis*

Authors	Management techniques studied	Thesis defended
The tool as an indicator of a more global system		
Palpacuer et al. (2007)	Dismissal for personal reasons (a special legal method to dismiss personnel in France)	The increase in 'dismissal for personal reasons' coincides with extensive reorganisations in multinationals and should be related to changes in capitalism. The management of executives is increasingly centralised and individualised for those with 'high potential' – the executives the enterprise wishes to retain in the years to come if they accept unlimited mobility – yet more and more short-term for operational staff.
The tool as a relay of power structures: legitimise domination and exploitation		
Gaulejac (2005)	A matrix for quality scoring proposed by the EFMD (European	The quality discourse and ideal hide a much less glorious reality. 'Quality seems not so much a tool for improving production conditions but

Table 3.1 (*cont.*)

Authors	Management techniques studied	Thesis defended
	Foundation for Quality Management)	an instrument of pressure to reinforce the enterprise's productivity and profitability' (Gaulejac, 2005, p. 80, our translation).
Boussard (2001)	The 'prevailing indicators'. The example of the stock-delay indicator at the *Caisse d'Allocations Familiales* or CAF (Family Allowance Office)	The indicator reproduces a representation of the CAF's activity which valorises the politically dominant department by attributing to it the main responsibility for performance in the whole organisation. Those departments whose performance is not represented in the prevailing indicator feel denied and oppressed.
Lordon (2000)	Economic Value Added EVA™	EVA tends to naturalise the right of shareholders to receive a minimum remuneration for their capital input, contrary to the idea that shareholders carry the risks of the enterprise. The yield of the shares is also considered as given by the market, seen as external to the calculation of EVA, while in fact it is a political construct arising from the relations between economic forces. The calculation of EVA tends to reinforce the apparently factual character of these rates, which are not open to discussion, and so reinforce the favourable position of shareholders in the sharing of added value.
Vercher et al. (2011)	Codes of conduct and whistle-blowing systems	These contribute to increasing inequalities between actors in the global value chain insofar as they transfer the ethical responsibility – and with it, an increased part of the market risk – towards weaker actors,

Table 3.1 (cont.)

Authors	Management techniques studied	Thesis defended
		i.e., employees, workers and subcontractors. They contribute to the reinforcement and legitimisation of inequalities at the microeconomic level and of the neo-liberal regime at the macroeconomic level.
Pagès et al. (1998)	The appraisal and career development interview	A tool to mediate the contradictions of capitalism, between the firm's interests and those of the workers. An ideological self-persuasion tool. A 'gentle violence' based on the internalisation of constraints and the channelling of conflicts.

Tools found in the network of conflictual interactions

Authors	Management techniques studied	Thesis defended
Bessire and Onnée (2010)	Systems for measuring corporate social performance	In the recent fields of corporate social performance evaluation we can distinguish two different types of social rating agencies. One is non-profit, sees itself as arising from civil society and recruits militants; the other is the for-profit subsidiary of a credit rating agency and aims at extending its rating service for its investor clients. In rating practices and the recruitment of analysts, the ways in which these organisms see their actions differ. One is in a position of protest in order to bring about change; the other sees itself as functional.
Oakes et al. (1998)	Budget planning and performance indicators in museums	A control mechanism that changes workplace identities and in so doing increases the value of economic capital while reducing cultural capital as well as the autonomy of the museum field. A form of pedagogy that

Table 3.1 (*cont.*)

Authors	Management techniques studied	Thesis defended
Xu and Xu (2008)	Adoption of a classification and a uniform banking accounting terminology in 1920s China, starting with the Chinese translation of some Western concepts	introduces a new language and frames what is thinkable and acceptable. This adoption was promoted by one group of bankers in Shanghai, which had the habitus and the cultural capital (technical linguistics) to launch this standardisation project, which resulted in the devaluation of the capital of another group of bankers in the market, and modified the respective positions of actors in the banking world.

The Ideological Roles of the Sullivan Principles

(Arnold and Hammond, 1994)

The Sullivan principles were a voluntary code of conduct in operation between 1977 and 1987 that American firms working in South Africa could adopt at a time when apartheid was still in place. The companies that signed up committed to improving the situation of their black workers in terms of wages, access to training, working conditions, desegregation of spaces, and so on. Each year they were supposed to publish information about their policies, as verified by auditors, and the objectives to be reached, which increased year on year. This exemplary device was a way of using American companies to promote change in black communities. But we might also think that it was a kind of defence against the anti-apartheid movement, whose policy was to get companies out of the country and impose a general boycott. Arnold and Hammond show that despite the progress made by firms thanks to these commitments, they have also served to legitimise the pursuit of business in a segregationist state. After the creation of the Sullivan principles, investment funds that had previously been tempted to enforce the boycott policy regarding the shares of firms operating in South Africa eventually agreed to retain those companies in their portfolios that had signed up to the principles. The adoption of these principles has thus served to conceal the fundamental social contradictions underpinning South African society. In the end, social change took place thanks to the struggle led by the anti-apartheid movement and not because of company policies and the Sullivan principles. When the political situation became too tense in South Africa, enterprises began to withdraw from the country as business was no longer profitable. Through counter-expertise, the protest movements also disqualified the progress announced by companies that had applied the principles thereby contributing to make it recognised that signing the principles was not a sufficient guarantee for ethical investors.

Summary Sheet (Thesis 1)

The Axioms

Axiom of domination: the social world is layered, tiered between dominant and dominated positions and is associated with resources and the capacity to make more or less profits.

Axiom of social conflict: struggles (individual or collective) to accede to dominant positions or to fight against domination are present in all fields and are explanatory factors determining the behaviours observed.

Key Concepts

Domination: the social relationship according to which a person or a social group is in a position to exercise power over another person or another social group, and that is the source of advantages for the former and disadvantages for the latter.

Exploitation: dominant groups take advantage of asymmetries in power and escape degrading or tiring chores; they access comfort and the resources produced by the dominated who have only limited access to these privileges; the dominant accumulate monetary resources that give them power and ability to gain advantage from situations.

Ideology: a discourse serving the power interests and having political effects. Ideology can be in the service of the dominant, most often helping them to legitimise the situations of asymmetry that favour them, or in the service of the dominated, facilitating their struggle and perhaps allowing the constitution of collective movements.

Rules of the Method

General principle of analysis: the management tool is to be interpreted by placing it into the more general context of the balance and relations of power that are present in the economic field, and by questioning the roles it plays in the forms of domination active in the situation and acting on the dominated.

Posture: the constant search for a critical unveiling of all forms of domination and of everything that favours them even in the most banal daily situations.

Procedure: scrutinising how far the power asymmetries at work in the situations under study format or transform the management tool and its uses.

Figures of Speech

Naturalisation: technique and its tools tend to be taken for granted, which is the result of a power struggle.

Mask: the reality of exploitation and domination is covered by the management and technical discourse of efficiency, which obscures a deep understanding.

A Few Authors and Key Texts

Studies inspired by the works of Marx and Bourdieu belonging to *critical management studies*.

Thesis 2:

The Tool as a Technique for Discipline and Government

This thesis brings together some of the many works inspired by Foucault which analyse the role of instruments and management techniques (McKinlay and Starkey, 1998). Among the different management disciplines, these studies have been most developed in accounting because of the central role played by references to Foucault in the development of the journal *Accounting, Organizations and Society* (Gendron and Baker, 2005). However, this approach has also been used by sociologists and political scientists (Lascoumes and Le Galès, 2004a, 2007).

If we consider that the work of Michel Foucault is entirely devoted to the analysis of power, his approach consists in studying power not as something that some people or institutions have or wield but rather as something to which we are subjected. This is about studying power from its point of application and the mechanisms and techniques by which it operates, which explains why his work is interesting for the analysis of management tools.

Generally, Foucault's work is divided into three periods. The first, in the 1960s, is marked by works such as *Madness and Civilization: A History of Insanity in the Age of Reason* (1988 [1961]), *The Order of Things: The Archaeology of the Human Sciences* (1970 [1966]) and *The Archaeology of Knowledge* (1972 [1969]) and ended when he became a member of the Collège de France with his inaugural lecture 'The order of discourse' (1970). This lecture was about language, discourse and knowledge, which are indissociable from practices. The second period started in the 1970s with *Discipline and Punish: The Birth of the Prison* (1977) and his classes at the Collège de France, particularly those of 1977–8: *Security, Territory, Population* (2008) and 1978–9: *The Birth of Biopolitics* (2008). These are centred more directly on the practices of power and contain his analyses of the disciplinarian society and governmentality. The last period (the 1980s) was devoted to the practices of self and subject, with the publication of the three volumes of *The History of Sexuality* (1978).

MANAGEMENT TOOLS AS APPARATUSES OF KNOWLEDGE/POWER

Studying management tools as 'apparatuses' or 'devices'[2] means that a great number of heterogeneous elements are included in their study: material arrangements, information formats, procedures for use, moral representations on what is good, scientific theories, etc. It is therefore important to give an account of the correspondences and the network woven between these elements. If looking at the heterogeneity of management tools' components is not specific to this approach, focusing on how knowledge and power interact through the device is properly Foucauldian.

Power produces knowledge, which produces power. One must look behind each form of knowledge for the power it has produced and the power it allows, and also look behind every exercise of power relying on devices for the knowledge that these devices produce and are infused with. The classic example is that of psychiatric knowledge, which is produced because of a particular form of the exercise of power that is the shutting away of those who have been designated 'mentally ill'. This confinement is the condition for the development of knowledge that is based on a balance of power, which allows the justification of the asylum as an institution.

Most management tools, whose purpose is in effect to exercise power (to control profits, workflows or personnel), also suppose that there is production of ad hoc knowledge that cannot be dissociated from the way in which the question has been framed. Let us imagine a

---

[2] The French word is *dispositif*, which is sometimes not translated in Foucault-inspired literature.

warehouse: If the manager of the warehouse considers that her job is to manage the stocks, she will ask for information about the quantities she has in stock; if she reckons that her job is to manage the staff who work there then she will seek to measure the handling productivity; if, however, she sees her stock as wealth then she will need those elements concerning the value of the items in the warehouse. Whatever knowledge about the warehouse is thus built up, it arises from the desire to control. Yet, the identification of this strategic intent is not sufficient to understand the situation, since there are a great many possible practices in the management of this warehouse that cannot be dissociated from the different conceptions of control.

MANAGEMENT TOOLS AS A DISCIPLINARY TECHNIQUE

The practices of power are multiple: they evolve over time and shape historical periods. Foucault considers that the birth of heavy industry owes as much to new power technologies as it does to the steam engine. Among these technologies there is one, 'discipline', to which he dedicated numerous of his writings. Discipline is an individualising mechanism by which it is possible to reach the most tenuous parts of a social body. As the schooling system took the place of the over-costly tutoring model, it allowed both the management of the masses and an individualised follow-up and permanent surveillance of each and every individual within the multiplicity. This innovation was accompanied by the appearance of quantitative grading, exams and rankings.

In the third part of *Discipline and Punish* (Foucault, 1977) we find an analysis of a large number of disciplinary techniques. Among the techniques mentioned in the chapter on 'the docile body' we find 'enclosure', 'the distribution of individuals in space', 'strict timetable', 'a sort of anatomo-chronological schema of behaviour', 'the degree of precision in the breakdown of gestures and movements' and 'the best relation between a gesture and the overall position of the body'. Here, it is possible to recognise many of the principles of scientific work organisation – and indeed, the writings of Foucault have been used by various authors to give an account of factory management (Carmona et al., 2002; Miller and O'Leary, 1994; Sewell, 1998; Walsh and Steward, 1993).

Foucault also analyses the training process of individuals. Training is divided into stages, with organised progress and exercises according to the individual level, thus highlighting a link between the education system and the production system that has also been documented in the management literature (Hoskin and Macve, 1988).

In the chapter devoted to 'the means of correct training' Foucault (1977) reviews three mechanisms. The first is permanent hierarchical observation, which is made possible by certain architectural devices of which the Panopticon is the sublime example. But he also examines the personnel dedicated to this permanent surveillance (foremen, guards) who reinforce this activity. Then he talks about the systems of punishment and reward that aim at correcting any deviation from the norm. This 'penal system' does not work due to formalised law but from the normalising judgement, which then becomes the principle of coercion. The normalising judgement aims at homogeneity, yet individualises all the while by measuring discrepancies from the norm. Over the past few decades, the development of management standards (ISO 9000 for quality, ISO 26000 for sustainable development) and of accountability standards (in accounting or banking) explains why Foucault's work has been seen as relevant.

The last mechanism is 'examination', which is the knowledge/power device of the disciplinary regime par excellence. Examination supposes 'a fragile and highly detailed archive which is closely and continually constituted. The examination that places individuals in a field of surveillance also situates them in a network of writings; it engages them in a whole mass of documents that capture and fixate them. The procedures of examination were accompanied at the same time by a system of intense registration and of documentary accumulation' (Foucault, 1977, p. 189). If we consider the double impact of both generalised surveillance and record keeping in order to evaluate people, case by case, it is tempting to see in the development of new information technologies a lingering trace of the Panopticon disciplinary regime, or better, of what Deleuze named the society of control (Deleuze, 1992). Deleuze proposed this notion to take into account technical systems organising surveillance and the automatic recording of traces without imprisonment or at least organisational enclosure.

MANAGEMENT TECHNIQUES AS A TOOL
OF GOVERNMENT

Foucault took an interest in another group of power technologies – that of 'regulation' – which has developed a little later in the disciplinary family. These techniques 'do not aim at individuals as such but [...] aim at controlling the population [...] What does that mean: a population? It simply means a large group of humans but who are living beings, influenced by, ordered by, regulated by processes and biological laws' (Foucault, 2001 [1976], p.1012, our translation). This invention of 'regulation' goes hand in hand with the development of the political economy, which considers the necessity for the sovereign to regulate the flow of the population in quantity and quality and to direct it so that it generates through its own activity, encouraged and channelled, a greater wealth. The population is therefore conceived as a mechanism for producing wealth, goods, human beings, and so on. Different observation techniques, such as statistics, develop as do other organisms in charge of this regulation. This is the birth of a new concept of the exercise of power by those who governed throughout the eighteenth century, which Foucault contrasts from earlier forms and names 'governmentality'.

Miller and Rose (1990) and Rose and Miller (1992) started out from Foucault's work and then proposed a systematic framework for the analysis of instruments, identifying different levels. First of all, there is the discursive level of political practices, *political rationalities*. There we find the way that the exercise of power is conceptualised and moral justifications are deployed. These rationalities are also marked by a particular vocabulary that makes certain phenomena thinkable; they have an epistemological dimension in the sense that they presuppose the nature of the objects to be governed.

The second level of analysis is that of *programmes for govern-ment*. To govern presupposes a problematisation, a construction of the problems that need to be addressed, which goes hand in hand with the creation of knowledge about these problems. The social sciences are very useful to governors as they allow for the construction of spheres where governors can consciously establish well-calculated action plans.

The third level is that of *technologies for government* through which government programmes can be rolled out.

This framework was used by Peter Miller to produce different analyses of management tools as instruments of government. He turned his attention to the calculation of the discounted cash flow (DCF) in the 1950s (Miller, 1991), the development of standard costs at the beginning of the twentieth century (Miller and O'Leary, 1987) and activity-based costing (Miller and O'Leary, 1994).

Another interesting aspect of Foucault's analyses is the import-ance he gives to *strategic relations*. Of course, there are strategies behind the technologies of government, that is to say there are actors who use them to direct the behaviour of others. However, the ques-tion of liberties remains and the governed respond by trying to avoid having their behaviour dictated. Unlike the analyses of discipline, where the refusal of this leads to delinquency, exclusion, punishment and the reinforcement of policing, this power regime takes note of such acts of freedom and 'endogenises' them through mechanisms of government. Liberalism and neo-liberalism thus propose practices of government that are based on the freedoms of the actors, whose conduct is oriented and encouraged – but not prescribed in the smallest details as in the disciplinary mechanisms. Such a practice is envisaged by political economy theoreticians as the best means to yield the most productive population possible.

It is in fact a singularity of modern times that these two fairly different power regimes – disciplinary society and governmentality – cohabit. In the domain of management tools we find this cohabitation with two types of tools. On one hand we find a standardisation of behaviours, procedures and generalised surveillance. On the other there are motivational mechanisms that are based on the goodwill of the actors and aim at averaged results, recognising that there will be variations between individuals. For example, a public policy seeking to lower the death rate in a population aims at shifting the average indicator and not at lining up everyone to a standard age of death. But of course discipline also contributes to this global project by causing the internalisation of certain behaviours.

Foucault's works on governmentality are the sources of different contributions to the analysis of management tools. By governmentality we mean either a general relation between tools and politics or that very particular form of neo-liberalism to which Foucault devoted a whole year of lectures at the Collège de France (*The Birth of Biopolitics*) (Foucault, 2008b). These contributions include the following:

- any management tool can be analysed as the result of a strategic project formulated in the terms of a particular political rationality and a specific problematisation;
- it is possible to carry out such an analysis at the level of the organisation, but the tool in question can be analysed in a wider framework as 'carrying a specific conception of the politics/society relationship and supported by a conception of regulation' (Lascoumes, 2004, p. 7, our translation);
- there are different families of power technologies – discipline is not the same thing as regulation – but each one nevertheless produces knowledge and triggers resistance;
- Foucault's analyses of neo-liberal governmentality allow us to understand the new forms of action undertaken by states and the European Union as well as the new types of tools used, which are based on motivation, contractualisation and the building of regulated markets (Halpern and Le Galès, 2011).

MANAGEMENT TECHNIQUES AS TECHNOLOGIES OF THE SELF

In the last part of his work, marked by the three volumes of *History of Sexuality*, Foucault (1978) became interested in yet another group of techniques: the techniques of the self, by which he means those through which an individual shapes him- or herself.

This interest extends the question of subjectification that runs through all his work. Foucault does not believe in a free, pre-existing subject that is eventually oppressed by some kind of powers. For him, every subject is the product of a process of subjectification, the result of power practices and of the power struggles that shape it. Thus, discipline aims at shaping disciplined subjects and simultaneously produces outsiders (to use the words of Becker [1963]). The practices of power concern others but also oneself. Before it became an instrument of productivity, was not discipline a technology of the self, much admired by the ascetic movements?

Analysing management tools as techniques of subjectification is a trail that has been followed by different authors (see Table 3.2). For instance, Lambert and Pezet (2011) have examined intense moments (online auctions, or meetings held to analyse results) in the construction of professional identity for management controllers in an automotive equipment company. In the same way, Roberts et al. (2006) study the disciplinary consequences of regular meetings between finance directors and those responsible for investor relations with the representatives of institutional investors. Studies dealing generally with professionalisation may pay attention to this question of the production of subjects through the management devices to which they are submitted. As management tools display a heteronomous strategic intention towards the subject, analysis of them enables us to see the subjectification processes to which people are submitted. The reflexive and autonomous work done by the subject, meaning that a person constructs him- or herself as an ethical subject and to which Foucault attached great importance, is much less studied in the management literature. This would require studying the techniques of self-knowledge widely used in the teaching of management, or so-called 360° evaluation systems (Townley, 1995).

Techniques of Discipline and Care for the Self in Audit Firms

(Covaleski et al., 1998)

Over 15 years of enquiry and observation of the way major audit firms function have made Covaleski and Dirsmith very familiar with the world they study. For this work, they have cooperated with two colleagues working on two management practices, a disciplinary one (Management by Objectives or MBO) and a technology of the self (mentoring). MBO ensures that individual objectives are fixed according to the firm's global aims. This allows for hierarchical control to be replaced by a kind of self-control. Individuals are thus led to make the company's goals their own. Regular review procedures allow for performance comparisons between colleagues and for the discussion of any non-achievements, as well as ways of rectifying them and thus recalling the power of the norm. As for mentoring, this assumes personal discussions between mentor and mentee, which are an opportunity for the latter to be guided towards greater conformity to the expected norms in order to climb the hierarchical ladder of the audit firms. During these discussions, financial performances are not the only thing to be examined because topics such as behaviour, dress and people's private life are also touched upon. Depending on the mentors, the norms of MBO are either reinforced or eased. This easing might be made because of the requirements of the job and in the quest for 'customer service', which establishes the reputation of the autonomous professional. As for mentees, they are not necessarily more at ease with less quantified norms of professionalism that are transmitted during mentoring and could be considered more arbitrary. Whereas MBO lays out a power network that tends to separate the partners who are responsible for clients from those who are in charge of running the firm, mentoring designs another power network according to the ability of certain mentors to place their protégés in various positions in the hierarchy. The appearance of these two power techniques reveals the power relations within audit firms as well as their capillarity and heterogeneity, just as it reveals the many possible ways they can be resisted.

Table 3.2 *A selection of publications representative of the Foucault-inspired thesis*

Authors	Management techniques studied	Hypothesis defended
Knowledge/power		
Hoskin and Macve (1988)	Management accounting and its development in the 20th century especially in railway companies (calculation of costs, various ratios, and forms of reports)	The invention of certain management practices must be connected to a pedagogical revolution in the education of elites, in this case in the West Point military academy, a system imported from France's École Polytechnique. It is about a general change in the knowledge/power relation with the appearance of a grammatocentric and panoptical system organising a demanding visibility (*accountability*) of human beings (extensive written reports and evaluations using mathematical grades).
Loft (1986)	System of cost accounting in Great Britain at the start of the 20th century	Methods of cost accounting developed when Great Britain sought to combat the excessive profiteering of some suppliers during the First World War. Knowledge about the cost of products is inseparable from a power relation. Other actors working on different strategic projects also contributed to post-war development of such techniques (socialists who thought they might have to manage the economy, industrial leaders who rationalised their production with Taylorism, cost accountants who wanted to found a profession on a corpus of knowledge, etc.).

Table 3.2 (cont.)

Authors	Management techniques studied	Hypothesis defended
Discipline		
Hopper and Macintosh (1993)	Responsibility centre's reporting at ITT during H. Geneen's tenure as CEO	H. Geneen was a highly disciplined individual. At ITT he set up a disciplinary system where we can find most of the principles or practices outlined by Foucault: enclosure with enclosed responsibility centres, discipline through numbers; body efficiency with dressage-like training; disciplined body with hierarchical surveillance, ranking systems, examinatory practice and self-normalisation.
Townley (1993)	System for the evaluation of individual performances in British universities	This system constitutes a kind of Panopticon that allows permanent and anonymous tracking. Although the action may be discontinuous, its effects are permanent.
Sewell (1998)	Computerisation of production processes and new organisations of work in autonomous teams	These two devices increase vertical (via information systems) and horizontal (through team members) surveillance. Together they favour the development of self-discipline which follows the same mechanisms as the Panopticon.
Governmentality		
Miller and O'Leary (1987)	Standard costs and budget	These techniques should not be viewed as a new stage in the development of technical precision and refinement. Rather, these calculating practices are part of a larger array of power devices (with the scientific organisation of work, industrial psychology, and so on) aiming to make individuals manageable and efficient.

Table 3.2 (*cont.*)

Authors	Management techniques studied	Hypothesis defended
Aggeri (2005)	European environment programmes since 1973, and their main modes of action	Identification of three environmental governability regimes: restricted pollution and regulation; widespread pollution and traceability; global pollution and exploratory cooperation. Characterisation of the regimes through four elements: objects of government; targets of government; regime of visibility; forms of government.
Lenay (2005)	The PMSI programme for the medicalisation of information systems (programme set up in French hospitals in 1982)	The hospital system is in fact host to several 'forms of governmentality': regulation (based on the PMSI); planning (based on objectives and means contracts); and a new form called 'organisation' (whose object of government is the patient's journey). Because of the competition between these forms the effect of PMSI is not homogeneous across hospitals and regions.
Care of the self		
Dambrin and Lambert (2017)	The practice of care of the self among members of a marketing team in a cosmetics firm	The marketer is obliged to work on his/her appearance and image. He/she keeps a permanent watch on his/her body (weight, body posture), clothes, hair, make-up, perfume, as well as the way he/she speaks of him-/herself or others. Employees develop self-control in order to conform to their idea of the company's expectations and in order to incarnate in the best way possible the brands or the products they are responsible for. The firm has changed techniques of the self into an instrument of control in the service of the company.

Summary Sheet (Thesis 2)

The Axioms

Axiom of analytical entry by practices and techniques: refusal of any essentialist approach of institutions (of the state, for example). These can be better understood through the study of the practices of power and the devices implemented.

Axiom of the microphysics of powers: the technologies of power can be analysed according to their effects or their points of application, their relations with the production of knowledge or truths, or the process of subjectification that affects individuals submitted to these regimes of knowledge/power.

Axiom of subjectification: there is no subject in the way the term is usually meant (the author of proper reflection and producer of actions and free decisions). Rather, subjects are constructed through subjectification matrices and produced by techniques of power over oneself and others.

Key Concepts

Device: devices are 'material operators of power, that is to say, of techniques, strategies and forms of subjection put in place by power' (Revel, 2002, p. 24, our translation). This concept designates an assembly of heterogeneous elements, said and non-said, material and discursive (discourse, architectural arrangements, rules, etc.) that has a dominant strategic function, 'which supposes that it is a question here of a certain manipulation of power relations [...] That's what a device is: strategies of power relations supporting some kinds of knowledge and being supported by them' (Foucault, 2001 [1977], p. 299, our translation).

Discourse: this designates 'a group of statements which may belong to different fields but which nevertheless obey all the common rules of functioning' (Revel, 2002, p. 22, our translation). The discourses are infused by 'orders' that are produced by identification procedures, prohibitions and exclusions. The devices are inseparable from the discourses that underpin them.

Disciplinary power: this is characterised by a certain number of coercion techniques that set up and organise a systematic individualised control of times, spaces and movements and that exercise influence on behaviours and bodies in particular. Each person is controlled and followed individually so that he or she will become obedient, adopt certain behavioural norms and respect them.

Governmentality: unlike sovereignty which concerns territories, and discipline which is exercised over bodies and individual behaviours, the object of governmentality is the population and it is based on a particular power technique, 'regulation', that is a 'conduct of conduct' (Foucault, 2008a). It supposes other techniques of observation, like demographic statistics, which aim to give an account of the state of the population. The population is not submitted but governed. The government does not aim at absolute and total control and does not seek to normalise each person individually. It relies on a certain conceded freedom that itself becomes a technique of government.

Techniques of the self and care of the self: the techniques of the self (Martin et al., 1988) are exercises, rules and behavioural schemes by which an individual constructs his- or herself and establishes a certain relation with him-/herself. The individual exercises these techniques on him-/herself, through which he or she produces him-/herself.

The society of control: this concept was proposed by Deleuze (1992), commenting on Foucault. Societies of control succeed disciplinary societies. In disciplinary societies, the individual moves ceaselessly between different closed environments: first, the family, then school, the barracks, the factory, sometimes the hospital and finally the prison, which is the closed environment par excellence. Enclosure is necessary for discipline by means of controlling the body. The control society relies on other kinds of discipline and is open and fluid, but the movement of individuals is coded and tracked permanently, thanks to information technologies.

The Rules of the Method

General principle of analysis: the study of any phenomenon has to be done via its *genealogy*. It is important to reconstitute the conditions of how it emerged, also paying attention to the voices that have been silenced and the breakdowns that have made it possible. There is always a certain kind of arbitrariness and power relations behind any institution and it is important to locate these. For a given period of time, work has to be done in an archaeological manner using archives and not just relying on common discourse. This should be done by bringing different dimensions (philosophical, economic, scientific, political) into play and by showing that they respond to each other and constitute a coherent configuration of knowledge and power.

Posture: a critique of the essentialist approaches of institutions and ideologies in favour of a study of devices and the discourses that support them.

Procedure: describe the devices, the manner in which they exercise power over people (the practices of power), identify the discourses that give them meaning, the historic context in which they are found and the various pieces of legitimating knowledge they produce.

Figures of Speech

Power/knowledge: this expression, born of the collage of the two elements that Foucault analyses as inseparable, emerged from his commentators – probably from the work coordinated by Gordon (1980).

The Panopticon: Foucault devoted a chapter of *Discipline and Punish* to this construction, which is the archetype of disciplinary power. In the architectural model proposed by Jeremy Bentham, prison inmates are self-disciplining and incorporate the norms of behaviour that are expected of them because they can never know when they are being observed. The Panopticon relies on continuous individualised surveillance. It is also a power that is exercised over the body.

The disciplined subject: individuals who conform perfectly to the norms and have accepted and incorporated their permanent and individualised tracking via a system of grading, indicators, etc. They are themselves the product of an education and a process of sub-jectification. They tend to reproduce these forms of subjectification to which they have been subjected. Disciplined subjects make des-potic bureaucrats.

A Few Authors and Key Texts

Starting from the work of Foucault, see Hoskin and Macve (1988), Lascoumes and Le Galès (2004a), Miller and O'Leary (1987, 1994), Miller and Rose (1990) and Rose and Miller (1992).

Thesis 3:

The Tool Alienates and Dehumanises

Although it is rooted in social sciences, and sociology in particular (Enriquez, 1997b; Fritz, 2007), the clinical approach on which this thesis is based has mainly developed in the French-speaking world and in South America. This is no doubt due to the firmly established socio-psychological critical tradition in these countries. In France, the thesis of alienation associated with a criticism of instrumental reason has been richly nourished both by clinical sociology (Gaulejac, 2008) and by the psychopathology of work (Dejours, 2006). Following the legacy of Gabriel Tarde (1969), these works rely on the undefined boundaries between the psychological world of individual emotions and the sociological world of collective events. The management tools are then perceived as inhabited by these two worlds.

CLINICAL APPROACHES

Being located at the intersection of sociology and psychology, most of the authors who are attached to this thesis share the same clinical approach, which views the management tool as a means of dehumanising work and alienating people.[3] Domination is examined mainly through the psychological (or psychosociological) lens. These works also agree on a primacy of the field, both of a physical field in which the clinician must move to grasp the concrete human behaviours, but also of a 'mental ground', corresponding to a lived experience. Two main streams can be identified in this literature.

---

[3] Lévy (1997, p. 15, our translation) defines the clinical approach as 'the approach to a subject or some subjects in a group or organisation, struggling with some suffering, a crisis which concerns them entirely'.

The first stream belongs to the *psychosociological* movement (social psychology and clinical sociology), which is characterised by the attempt to establish links between interpretative sociology and clinical psychology. Borrowing from psychoanalysis and Marxist analyses, it has developed a critical questioning of the meaning of collective actions and produced knowledge about change in organisational and institutional fields.

The second perspective is more centred on individuals, and on how they commit themselves and their subjectivity to work (Dejours, 2007; Dejours and Deranty, 2010). Although today this perspective cannot be reduced to the *psychopathology* of work, it is in fact what underlies it. Springing from within psychiatry, this movement has little by little moved away from its strictly medical foundations and centres its analysis on work practices and the psychological process by which subjects mould themselves in their work, gain advantage from it or suffer from it.

Although the levels of analysis are different, the two schools of thought strongly converge in their attitude to management tools. Psychosociology is focused on small groups and analyses structures and organisational devices in their relation to individuals. The second stream focuses on the individual but is nevertheless sensitive to the collective dimension of work and organisational systems. Both streams of research agree on questioning the technicity of management tools and their seeming objectivity. Tools are accused of being in the service of an insidious exercise of authority that plays down the subjective dimension of work. It is possible to identify two streams of criticisms towards management tools in this literature (see Table 3.3):[4]

---

[4] For a number of psychosociologists, the critique of modern forms of management goes hand in hand with a critique of the social world based on Marxism and psychoanalysis (Gaulejac, 2005; Pagès et al., 1998). The organisation is seen as a system of mediations of the contradictions posed by the development of capitalism (cf. thesis 1).

Table 3.3 *A selection of publications representative of the clinical critique thesis*

Authors (reference discipline)	What is at stake?	What is criticised?	In the name of what?
Critique of the manipulative project			
Enriquez (1982, 1989, 1997a) (psychosociology)	The enterprise as a power structure dreaming of control over the psyche of individuals	Management bluff to make workers marvel at accounting statements; ideology of rationality; control of minds	Autonomy and the liberty of individuals
Aubert and Gaulejac (1991) (clinical sociology)	Perversity of management as an ordinary regime; disorder of the dominant	The tool as a rational façade. Contradictory movement: decentralisation versus measurement	The complexity of socio-affective relations; the deconstruction of dominant ideologies
Beauvois (1994, 2005) (social psychology)	The liberal split between the political field and social existence	Psychologising ideologies ('naturalising') and the illusions of freedom they hold	Experimental analysis of how influence and manipulation work
Critique of technicism			
Dejours (1990, 1995, 2006, 2007) (psychosociology of work; psychodynamics)	Human suffering in organisations	Action reduced to instrumental activity; resurgence of work-related pathologies	Psychoanalysis; the psychic mechanisms that link work and mental health
Dejours (2003) (psychosociology	A top-down vision of work	The limits and the damages of evaluation;	Psychoanalysis: the reality of

Table 3.3 (*cont.*)

Authors (reference discipline)	What is at stake?	What is criticised?	In the name of what?
of work; psychodynamics)		symbolic domination	work; the ideal of justice
Clot (1995) (psychosociology of work; clinical approach to activity)	The rationalisation of work	The illusion of work without the individual	Psychosociology of development (Vygotsky); taking subjectivity into account as a component of the reality of work
Amado and Enriquez (2006) (psychosociology)	The alienation of individuals by organisations and institutions	Critique of positivist and technicist thought	Complexity; the unconscious dimension of processes

- the critique of a manipulative project: according to this critique, management tools are lures used by deeply perverse managers whose project, hidden behind an appearance of rationality, aims at better subjugating individuals;
- the 'critique of technicity', which sees in management tools a terrible simplification that ignores elements of reality and takes no notice of the complexity or the subjectivity of people.

CRITIQUE OF THE MANIPULATIVE PROJECT

For many clinical sociologists, a manipulative project is inherent to management techniques. The invocation of excellence thus conceals the intentions of the dominant: a project of influence in which management tools only come into play as a means of rationalisation. This line of thought has run through the psychosociological literature for years. The critique of the manipulative project is largely based on the idea that the apparent complexity of management tools is justified above all by their effect as a lure, aiming at making people impressed in order to better subjugate them by emphasising their apparent complexity. Each form of organisation promotes a technology that is adapted to it. Management tools of bureaucracies claim to be founded on science. Modern organisations move away from the prescriptive Taylorist model to entrap individuals through subtly reinforced mind control. These organisations seemingly offer more autonomy to their staff but at the same time increase their control through the use of modern technologies. Decision-making tools, information and communication systems are the new locus of power.

Praising the merits of individual responsibility and inviting salaried workers to 'be themselves', organisations endow the submission of workers with individualised meanings that are beyond political analysis. The workers pay for greater liberty from which, in the end, they do not really benefit, by an uncertainty linked to organisational contradictions. They have to face these contradictions by making their behaviour conform to the ideal norms that they have partly internalised: satisfaction of clients, zero defaults, profitability, prescriptions regarding behaviour, etc. These constraining situations foster the appearance of stress states that are not 'collateral damage' but the inbuilt consequences of a new mode of the productive activity regulation.

Following on from La Boétie (1975), psychosociology has taken an interest in the enigma of voluntary servitude and the unconscious influences that lead us to find justifications for our obedience (or even our rebellions) by convincing ourselves of their rational nature. More specifically, the psychology of commitment[5] teaches us that an act commits us even further since it gives us the feeling that we decided

---

[5] A theory developed by Kiesler (1971), who supplies an explanatory framework for certain manipulation techniques (Joule and Beauvois, 2002).

on it ourselves. This is the basis of the 'liberal illusions' that drain workplaces of any political consciousness by propagating the ideal of a free and responsible individual (Beauvois, 1994, 1997). This framework explains very well the development of a 'behavioural technology' aiming at some sort of social training (Brunel, 2004). These technologies appear as a form of delegation, helping individuals to become responsible for dealing with the stress created by organisational contradictions.

THE CRITIQUE OF TECHNICISM AND THE DISCARDING OF SUBJECTIVITY

Because they are interested in what links the individual subject with others, clinical approaches to work take technique seriously. But this recognition does not come without a critique of technicism and its philosophical attachments (positivism, rationalism). The critique concerns management insofar as it assumes workers' unwavering devotion to notions like efficiency, constructed as a supreme value, and change, seen as the inescapable march of reason.

In its exclusive service to economic rationality, management does not take into account what is real: it appears to be completely subjugated to instrumental action. This kind of action is deployed in the world of the states of things, an objective world rooted in the values of truth and efficiency. Postulating a continuity between technical systems and reality, management tools reduce human activity to performance indicators, subtracting subjectivity from reality. They are therefore closed to reality and its complexity, especially to the unconscious dimensions of organisational processes and the issues of power. This closing down could be interpreted as a pathology, that of 'quantophrenia',[6] or measurement pathology,

---

[6] The expression used by the American sociologist Pitirim Sorokin (1956) in his critique of the excessive recourse to figures, and recently taken up again by Gaulejac (2005).

which consists of wanting to translate all human phenomena systematically into numerical data.

The unawareness of effective work, 'denial of the real' and the ideology of transparency have negative effects on both work execution and workers' health. The rationalisation of work removes the human dimensions and engenders exclusion. The monitoring of individual performance, which is a device that carries an 'economicist' view, is in fact too remote from real work and causes suffering through 'pathologies of overload' that lead to depression and even suicide among workers (Dejours, 2003).

The Instrumentation of Social Training

(Brunel, 2004)

Companies use personnel development techniques (NLP,[7] transactional analysis, etc.) in order to inculcate the codes of behaviour that are most useful to the firm. These neo-behaviourist techniques have aims in common: develop self-confidence, learn to know oneself, manage one's emotions and interactions with others. For these techniques, the psyche is a 'manageable' object that can be 'reprogrammed' in order to allow the 'liberation of potential' and 'to become a better performer'. The tools deployed are easy to use. Their operational nature and their insistence on personal efficiency make them very seductive to managers. Collective conflicts are erased and power struggles become irrelevant: if anything, such conflicts would reveal psychological communication problems that emerge from personal deficiencies. These techniques imply that it is the task of the individuals to use appropriate tools to manage and adapt themselves to the organisational realities.

---

[7] Neurolinguistic programming.

Summary Sheet (Thesis 3)

The Axioms

Axiom of the subjective constitution of reality: subjectivity (impulses, fantasies, emotions, subconscious forces) is part of the reality of work.

Axiom of the perversity of the dominant: power is pathological, infused with narcissism, perversion and death wish: 'To have power is to have blood on one's hands' (Barus-Michel et al., 2003, p. 221).

Axiom of management reductionism: by reducing human activity to performance indicators, management tools negate subjectivity. They therefore seal themselves off from reality and engender suffering and pathologies.

Axiom of organisational control: organisational control is based on the colonisation of inner life relayed by a managerial ideology and management tools that conceal relations of domination.

The Key Concepts

Submission: gaining subjection in the psychological field (domination of minds). By reducing their capacity for autonomy, management tools subjugate individuals.

Manipulation: action that aims at making people do something they would not have done spontaneously, without those people noticing it. Manipulation relies on management techniques and tools.

Reification: a cognitive and political operation of abusively giving human entities a character of things. As management can only be exercised over objects, management tends to be concerned with the reification of individuals and groups to be managed.[8]

Subject: the human being, complex and conflictual, whose lived experience is considered.

---

[8] Also see Bourguignon (2005) on this notion (cf. thesis 1).

Rules of the Method

Principle of general analysis: subjectivity must be reinstalled in the analysis of collective phenomena.

Posture: both clinical and denunciatory. The clinical posture is inherited from medicine: one must listen to the subject's complaint, which is of a being who suffers. In order for the subject to regain health one must identify the problem and apply a remedy. To denounce is to consider that management constrains subjects via the false neutrality of its tools; it is appropriate to fight against forms of oppression by revealing them.

Procedure: two possible entries: either through individual symptoms and the signs of suffering at work (stress, pathology, of over- or under-activity, fatigue, burn out, suicide); or via collective symptoms (social conflict, managerial problems, organisational dysfunction).

Figure of Speech

Moral harassment: for example, scorecards as a means of bullying. 'Up or out' ('Progress or leave').

A Few Authors and Key Texts

Beauvois (1994, 2005), Dejours (1990, 1995, 2003, 2007), Enriquez (1982, 1989, 1997a), Gaulejac (2005).

4 Institutionalist Perspectives on Management Tools

In this chapter we look at the role of institutions in the formation and development of management tools. In this type of analysis those elements relating to social cognition (interpretative schemes, norms, values, beliefs, social representations) take a central role. The theses reviewed in this chapter have in common to centre in their analyses on habits of behaviour or thought, or rules that are more or less taken for granted and more or less formalised (customs, morals, rights). Being somewhat stable, these elements impose themselves on individuals in a given social world. They are called 'institutions' by the neo-institutionalist authors of thesis 4, 'conventions' by the conventionalists of thesis 5 and 'social structures' by the structurationists of thesis 6.

And yet the nature of the questions handled by each of these analyses differs: the neo-institutionalists (thesis 4) study the role of institutions at the level of institutional fields composed of groups of organisations that interact regularly. Their analyses allow us to interpret the movements to adopt management tools as processes of isomorphism within the same field but also question the nature and the degree of these adoptions. Institutions form a kind of force field that structures organisational behaviours. The actual content of institutions is not of central importance for this literature and is not often described in the respective works.

However, this is what conventionalists (thesis 5) seek to do because they are sensitive to the normative content of institutions, the behaviours and the forms of judgement they prescribe and their arbitrary nature – i.e., that other conventions could do just as well. Conventionalists are interested in management tools because they embed and carry conventions that orient behaviours and social cognition, which would have different effects if other conventions were adopted.

The structurationists (thesis 6) are no less sensitive to the structuring character of management tools in which the institutions can be encoded (structures of meaning and legitimisation) than conventionalists. However, they are less concerned with the content of these institutions' interests and more reserved about the real weight they represent. Their attention is directed towards the dynamics of social transformation that management tools accompany or organise. Their analysis is as much concerned with the constraints organised by the tool as with the margins for manoeuvre that it leaves and the possibilities it presents. The effects of management tools should be analysed according to a double causality that takes into account both the social structures that they bear as well as the possibilities for action that they open up and the unexpected effects that flow from them.

Taken together, these three theses allow us to understand in detail the role of institutions in the composition, development and effects of management tools.

Thesis 4:

Management Tools Influenced by Institutional Strategies

The neo-institutionalist approach is based on the idea that organisational and individual rationality is embedded in beliefs and in scripts that define what is collectively considered as efficient discourse or behaviour. According to this perspective, organisations that interact frequently with each other (which are part of the same field) tend to converge in the display of organisational forms or even practices because they seek to gain legitimacy by conforming to dominant models of what is socially acceptable or valued. The concepts upon which this approach relies will be presented first. Then, we explain how the perspectives that concern management tools more particularly have evolved over time.[1]

THE FOUNDING CONCEPTS: FIELD-LEVEL INSTITUTIONS AND ISOMORPHISM

Neo-institutionalism emerged in the late 1970s and 1980s through the study of how organisations unquestioningly adopt institutionalised practices and procedures. The first revelation of this research was that organisations are influenced by their environment, and that they choose one organisational form or another for reasons of *legitimacy* rather than efficiency. In other words, social pressure is a strong driver of managerial choices of organisational structure, and questions of efficiency are left up to the operational staff whose actual practice differs from official policy. Actual organisational operations are not based on publicly displayed organisational forms but on a principle

---

[1] Thesis authored by Carine Chemin-Bouzir (Associate Professor, Reims Management School).

of *trust* between internal players and *good faith* (Meyer and Rowan, 1977). The adoption of institutionalised organisational structures may be ceremonial and *decoupled* from actual operations (Meyer and Rowan, 1977).

These forms spread throughout *institutional fields*, which are defined as all of the 'organizations which, in the aggregate, constitute a recognised area of institutional life: key suppliers, resource and product consumers, regulatory agencies and other organisations that produce similar services or products' (DiMaggio and Powell, 1983, p. 148). These fields are characterised by 'an increase in the extent of interaction among organizations in the field; the emergence of sharply defined inter-organizational structures of domination and patterns of coalition; an increase in the information load with which organizations in a field must contend; and the development of a mutual awareness among participants in a set of organizations that they are involved in a common enterprise' (DiMaggio and Powell, 1983, p. 148). Research in the 1980s stressed that interactions flow from the propagation of the most legitimate organisational forms.

Later, this propagation was extended to all the practices and behaviours making up institutions, and this central concept, the *institution*, is defined as 'a more or less taken-for-granted repetitive social behaviour underpinned by normative systems and cognitive understandings that give meaning to social exchanges and thus enable self-reproducing social order' (Greenwood et al., 2008, pp. 4–5). Institutions exist at the individual level (shaking hands in Western societies), the organisational level (adopting a particular type of management control), the field level (conforming to a social hierarchy to recruit staff or form alliances) and the overall societal level (basing the legal system on judicial procedures considered appropriate), even if research is focused on institutional fields.

The institutional field is made up of organisations that adopt the same institutions because they interact extensively with each other. This phenomenon is called 'isomorphism'. Institutional isomorphism was initially defined by DiMaggio and Powell (1983, p. 149) as 'a constraining process that forces one unit in a population to resemble other units that face the same set of environmental conditions'. They distinguish between competitive isomorphism and institutional isomorphism. Competitive isomorphism involves the process of searching for efficiency in a given context. Institutional isomorphism is based on three interlinked dynamics: coercive, mimetic and normative isomorphism.

- *Coercive isomorphism*, or political influence, results from the formal and informal pressure an organisation undergoes from other organisations it depends upon (the government, for example through law, foundations that finance non-profit organisations, or holding corporations that impose reporting mechanisms on their subsidiaries).
- *Mimetic isomorphism* is the process by which firms adopt standard responses when faced with uncertainty. When the link between their objectives and the means necessary to attain them is poorly defined, when objectives are ambiguous, or when the environment creates symbolic uncertainty, organisations may copy from each other to reduce uncertainty. These models spread through staff transfers, consulting firms or employers' associations.
- *Normative isomorphism* comprises professionalisation processes that aim to establish a cognitive base and the legitimacy of professional autonomy. In-service training, networks and organisational socialisation drive this kind of isomorphism.

The concept of isomorphism was revised by Greenwood et al. (2008). They highlighted several studies reporting that organisations can respond to institutional processes in different ways. Their 2008 definition proposed that isomorphism refers to the relation between the organisation and its institutional context, and that this relationship varies and does not necessarily lead to homogeneity. Since the beginning of the 1990s, institutionalist scholarship has provided more nuanced analyses of power relations, trends and the imitation of prestigious players. In the process, a new field of institutionalist research has developed in northern Europe (for example Czarniawska, 2002) alongside North American research. This evolution in neo-institutionalism provides a broader account of the diversity in institutional fields.

FROM SIMILARITY TO VARIETY: RESEARCH BETWEEN 1990 AND 2000

Since the 1990s, the notion of multiple *institutional logics* existing in different fields has led to the idea that fields are not all homogeneous. *Institutional logics* are symbolic and practical systems, which include the presuppositions, beliefs and values that underpin these institutions (Alford and Friedland, 1985; Friedland and Alford, 1991; Thornton and Ocasio, 1999, 2008).[2] They are historically situated, and they appear at several analytical levels, especially the societal, organisational and individual (Thornton et al., 2012). Actors may confront multiple and contradictory logics, which introduces an element of agentic choice to the theory (Greenwood et al., 2011).

In 1991, Powell and DiMaggio considered the multiplicity of institutional logics and revealed that various actors struggle within fields for the dominance of either of these logics (Powell and DiMaggio, 1991). Their book presents numerous empirical studies in support of this idea, and they call for more research to consider the political and power dimensions of such struggles. Soon actors, particularly organisations, were given a much more active role, and research became more interested in the notion of the *institutional entrepreneur*. Institutional entrepreneurs are actors who attempt to institutionalise a practice or a model. Particularly Scandinavian institutionalism developed such notions of active institutionalisation and de-institutionalisation processes (Djelic and Quack, 2008). Alongside Powell and DiMaggio's work (1991), Oliver (1991) analysed different strategies that organisations can adopt when facing institutional pressure: these range from passive acceptance to outright resistance.

---

[2] Thornton and Ocasio (1999, p. 804) define an institutional logic as 'the socially constructed, historical patterns of cultural symbols and material practices, including assumptions, values, and beliefs, by which individuals and organizations give their daily activity meaning, organize time and space, and reproduce their lives and experiences'. Based on Aristotelian philosophy, Friedland (2009, 2011, 2013) proposes that logics are troikas of subjects, objects and practices, linked together by a 'substance' that constitutes the content of the logic.

The institutional entrepreneurship approach led to better understanding of the strategies of both internal and external organisational actors, and it has brought 'neo-institutionalism' closer to the 'old institutionalism' of 1940–60 (Greenwood and Hinings, 1996), which, using qualitative studies of micro-phenomena in and around organisations, had shown the importance of such strategies as well as power (Blau, 1955; Gouldner, 1954; Selznick, 1949, 1957).

Neo-institutional analysis distinguishes between *emerging fields* and *mature fields* (Powell and DiMaggio, 1991). Mature fields show higher institutional stability because their logics are less numerous or less contradictory, or because their cohabitation is organised. For example, Lounsbury (2007) shows that the practices and beliefs of fund managers in Boston differ from those of fund managers in New York. However, these two kinds of institutional logics may coexist when they are distributed spatially. Mature fields differ in their degree of fragmentation (the number of non-coordinated actors who support different logics), formal structure and power centralisation or concentration (e.g., Pache and Santos, 2010; see Greenwood et al., 2011 for a review of the literature).

Fields are increasingly being studied at the international level. The term 'transnational' (Djelic and Sahlin-Andersson, 2006) underlines the fact that national influences and the actions of nation-states interact in complex ways with global governance exercised by transnational actors and 'soft' regulation (i.e., based on non-mandatory rules). The influence of social movements, for example regarding environmental protection, is also a rich research avenue (Hoffman, 1999).

This general presentation highlights three important contributions of institutionalism to the study of management tools. The strong distinction between legitimacy and efficiency (Meyer and Rowan, 1977) and the notion of decoupling raise the question of why firms adopt a practice or management tool, and of the consequences of a ceremonial adoption of practices targeting efficiency. The introduction of the notion of 'agency', or active behaviour, raises the question of 'power' (Powell and DiMaggio, 1991, pp. 27, 31) in both institutional fields and institutionalised organisations. Finally, research on transnationalisation is of particular interest, since it documents the effects of soft regulation, where standards and other written norms play an active role in structuring fields.

THE DISTINCTION BETWEEN LEGITIMACY, EFFICIENCY AND DECOUPLING

Meyer and Rowan (1977) distinguish between legitimacy and efficiency. They advance the idea that formal rules are adopted to achieve legitimacy, or social acceptance. Efficiency, by contrast, relies on staff's ability to *operate a logic of trust and good faith* that goes beyond formal rules. The two levels interact and both are necessary for the organisation to survive.

The question of the interaction between formal rules and actual practice has been widely studied. For example, Erlingsdottir (1999), and later Erlingsdottir and Lindberg (2005), distinguish between *isomorphism* (adoption of the same organisational forms), *isonymism* (adoption of the same labelling or names) and *isopraxism* (adoption of the same practices). They describe processes of homogenisation and 'heterogenisation' of names, forms and practices in a study of several hospitals and medical laboratories implementing quality procedures. Based on a field study of five years, they argued that the propagation of names (isonymism) does not necessarily lead to that of associated procedures (isomorphism), and that isomorphism does not necessarily lead to the propagation of corresponding practices (isopraxism). A hospital may claim to adopt *Total Quality Management* (TQM) without necessarily implementing its associated procedures. But even if the procedures are set up, this does not necessarily translate into a change of organisational practices.

To explain these different levels of implementation we need to remember that early neo-institutionalist scholarship stressed that those organisations being the first ones in a given field to adopt specific management tools often do so by view of efficiency. By contrast, those organisations adopting the tools later do so to attain legitimacy, that is, social acceptance. Tolbert and Zucker (1983) illustrate this process by studying a public authority recruitment procedure. Kennedy and Fiss (2009) further research this idea. For them, the first organisations adopt a management tool (here, TQM) to seize opportunities, whereas those who copy them do so to ward off a threat. Meanwhile, Westphal et al. (1997) argue that these two waves are key to understanding whether or not tools are tailored to the organisation: while the first adopters 'customise' the tools, the followers adopt the tools as they are, without adapting them to the local context.

The role of internal actors is crucial for distinguishing between levels of imitation. Actors in the firm undergo institutional pressure to earn legitimacy, particularly senior managers (Liang et al., 2007), and they then influence their companies' practices. The distinction between adopting a procedure to gain legitimacy (i.e., without influencing practices) and adopting it to improve efficiency is relative insofar as setting up procedures usually influences practices in the long term, even if internal actors are initially reticent (Siti-Nabiha and Scapens, 2005).

POWER, CONFLICT AND INSTITUTIONS

Beginning in 1985, calls were made to take the role of agency and power more into account in neo-institutional scholarship (Perrow, 1985; Powell, 1985). Covaleski and Dirsmith (1988) studied how a budgetary procedure was the subject of intense negotiation between internal and external actors in a US university, and how the dominant social expectations for the budgetary system – that is, its legitimacy – evolved, competed with one another, and were defended by internal and external actors in a debate infused with power struggles. The state, which financed the establishment, demanded transparency and rationality, and at first, the university accepted these demands. In a period of budgetary restriction, the university then proposed a qualitative approach to justifying budget demands. This approach was accepted by the person negotiating directly with the university, but rejected by the tax office, which controlled spending and advised the state governor, who was responsible for the final decision. Later, rivalries appeared over budget attribution: should the university or the state government be responsible for research on local economic or technological development? The analysis shows how the development and naming of budget lines influenced politicians' decision to reduce university funding, and how intense negotiations and power struggles accompanied the debate over the method used to calculate the university budget.

Following the call by Powell and DiMaggio (1991), institutionalism has since the 1990s studied these dimensions of agency and power in increasing detail, particularly through empirical studies of management tools. These works include studies of accounting techniques (Carruthers, 1995), performance indicators in Swedish universities (Modell, 2003) and the spread of accounting norms (Carpenter and Feroz, 2001). Townley (1997, 2002) also contributed to this line of research: she shows how British universities resisted an institutional logic based on a performance assessment scheme imposed by the state, and how in return, the state changed the budget rules to impose its vision of faculty management.

Research focusing on institutional logics investigates the assimilation processes (Thornton et al., 2012) of a logic as it begins to challenge the dominant logic in a given field. Most of these studies focus on the introduction of management tools, such as patents in an academic logic (Murray, 2010), or detailed specifications leading to public funding for the development of cooperation between British biology researchers and local businesses (Swan et al., 2010). Currie and Spyridonidis (2016) studied the introduction of a managerial guide entitled NICE in a hospital where a medical logic dominates. Bijan (2017) focuses on taxation regime changes, stressing that a new institutional logic is implemented through the alignment of symbolic and material aspects of identities and practices.

TRANSNATIONALISATION AND INTERNATIONAL STANDARDS

Scandinavian institutionalism has developed yet another approach to these phenomena. One of the features of this approach has been the study of transnational phenomena, and how public management models are created, propagated, and subsequently adopted beyond national borders. One of the major lessons of this line of research is the fact that adopting the same model does not necessarily lead to uniform practices, because of significant local variations (Czarniawska and Sevon, 1996, 2005). Thus, numerous studies have focused on transnational phenomena of market economy governance (Djelic and Sahlin-Andersson, 2006), and on how international standards[3] influence this governance (Brunsson and Jacobsson, 2000).

Standards are set up by particularly active organisations (such as the European Union, OECD, FIFA, WWF and ISO). These organisations operate in worldwide institutional fields. For example, the field of financial accounting includes not only firms that produce accounts but also parliaments, governments and international standards organisations that create and disseminate compulsory or optional rules and standards. So, at a time when sovereign states are losing their importance in transnational governance, the importance of voluntary standards is increasing. Studying international standards includes investigating the organisations that create and adopt them.

---

[3] 'Standards' are formal, precisely codified international norms.

Standards can be set up by public organisations for the purposes of regulation, or by private organisations that benefit from the emergence of standards in various ways. A company might wish to see its manufacturing process become the international norm, giving it a competitive advantage. A sport that is not yet nationally recognised might create an organisation to standardise its rules. So doing, the organisations behind this standardisation may present themselves as an elite, thereby granting them access to public funding, and allowing them to get other organisations to adhere to their rules, thus furthering their dominance (Ahrne et al., 2000).

ISO standards also aim to be adopted by a large number of organisations and to be applied to all. Researchers have studied the type of knowledge – rational and built by professionals rather than academics – on which ISO standards are based (Furusten, 2000), how ISO standards are created in the organisation that promotes them (Halström, 2000), but also how they are 'sold' to ensure widespread adoption (Henning, 2000).

Although they enjoy a degree of autonomy, actors adopt standards when they believe in them or consider themselves similar to other actors who have already adopted them. Such free choices can be a stronger source of homogeneity than centralised power and decision-making. Apart from the phenomena of decoupling and organisational hypocrisy (Brunsson, 2002), heterogeneity may arise from the fact that several standards are in competition, or that these standards only apply to one area of organisational life. For example, although all football clubs play according to the same rules, each team has its own style of play, and football league rankings reveal differences much more than similarities. Finally, fashion can play a significant role in the adoption of standards, and variations appear not only in space but also over time (Brunsson and Jacobsson, 2000).

Table 4.1 presents a list of representative neo-institutionalist publications.

Table 4.1 *A selection of representative neo-institutionalist publications*

Book or article	Type of management tool studied	Principal contributions
Decoupling		
Tolbert and Zucker (1983)	Recruitment procedure	The first organisations that adopt a management tool are looking for efficiency, while those that adopt it later are looking for legitimacy.
Westphal et al. (1997)	Total quality management	The first organisations that adopt a management tool adapt it to the local context, while those that adopt it later do so without adapting it.
Kennedy and Fiss (2009)	Total quality management	The first organisations that adopt a management tool do so to seize opportunities, while those that adopt it later do so to prevent a threat.
Siti-Nabiha and Scapens (2005)	'Value-based management' and performance indicators	Management tools can be decoupled from real practices at the time of their adoption, but eventually they influence actual behaviour.
Erlingsdottir and Lindberg (2005)	Quality procedures	Similar names for adopted procedures (isonymism) do not necessarily lead to conformity with the standard model in terms of applied procedures (isomorphism) and practices (isopraxism).
Power and heterogeneity		
Covaleski and Dirsmith (1988)	Budgetary category	Methods of calculating university income and expenditure are the subject of power struggles to establish the legitimacy of respective calculation methods.
Carpenter and Feroz (2001)	Accounting standards	Institutional pressure relayed better within organisations when decision-

Table 4.1 (cont.)

Book or article	Type of management tool studied	Principal contributions
		makers stick to the proposed management tools.
Townley (1997)	Performance evaluation procedures	Local actors can resist institutional pressure by diverting management tools from their original purpose. In return, institutional pressure can change form to ensure that actual use aligns with the spirit of the tool.
Transnational governance		
Djelic and Sahlin-Andersson (2006)	International standards	Fields are structured by five forces: commodification, democracy, scientisation, the tendency towards organisation and rationalised moralisation. There are three international methods of regulation: creating rules and standards, accompanying implementation and initiating reflection.
Brunsson and Jacobsson (2000)	International standards	International standards structure global fields; they are created by organisations in the field and are actively promoted so that the greatest possible number of actors adopts them.
Drori et al. (2006)	ISO norms	The spread of organisational forms in the modern world differs from Weberian bureaucracy since they combine quasi-scientific formalisation with the autonomy of the actors.

The Role of Business Schools Rankings: A Partial Isomorphism

(Wedlin, 2007)

This article reminds us that rankings – business school and university rankings in particular – contribute to the structure of organisational fields by setting up distinctions regarding the status of organisations. Rankings affect organisational identities, and are themselves derived from the institutional logics that permeate the field. These logics show themselves in the criteria used to rank the schools and universities, criteria whose weights vary between rankings.

Two of the three schools studied in the article are internationally oriented; the first one defines itself as having a research orientation, the second one is geared more towards the business world. The third school has a national or even regional vocation, and develops both research and corporate relations. All three schools focus on some of the ranking criteria, such as graduate monitoring, and they attempt to improve their performance in this area, thus contributing to isomorphism. However, this isomorphism is only partial, because each school remains faithful to its own identity and chooses to concentrate on only some of the other criteria. The first school is interested in criteria that reflect academic excellence, given its research orientation. The second one is interested in criteria that involve corporate relations and publications aimed at students and professionals. The third school concentrates on setting up its MBA programme. They all agree on the importance of these rankings and analyse them in the same way, but the identity of each school remains deeply rooted in its specific characteristics while the rankings do not create complete isomorphism. The criteria are sufficiently general, abstract, and therefore ambiguous, to leave room for heterogeneity.

Summary Sheet (Thesis 4)

The Axioms

Axiom of the search for legitimacy: organisations that adopt the most widely recognised practices and procedures increase their legitimacy and chances of survival, independently from the efficiency of these practices and procedures.

Axiom of embedded agency: the rationality of actors is limited as they are embedded in one or more institutional logics. Certain actors can initiate change because they operate at the intersection between potentially conflicting institutional logics, which leave room for choice and change dynamics.

Key Concepts

Institutional field: all organisations that interact more with each other than with others. The concept therefore goes beyond the notion of sector and includes suppliers, clients, contractors, subcontractors, partners, etc. The field is characterised by the emergence of inter-organisational structures of domination and patterns of coalition, as well as the development of a shared consciousness among participants that they are committed to a common enterprise.

Institutions: the definition of the central concept of institution appeared quite late, and it is still not settled. One handbook of organisational institutionalism proposes the following definition: 'A more or less taken-for-granted repetitive social behaviour, underpinned by normative systems and cognitive understandings that give meaning to social exchanges and thus enable self-reproducing social order' (Greenwood et al., 2008, p. 4). Other authors (Phillips et al., 2004) anchor institutions in discourse rather than action. Actions would therefore be the product of institutions comprising dominant discourses.

Isomorphism: DiMaggio and Powell (1983) have defined isomorphism as a constraining process that forces some actors to resemble others who face the same set of environmental conditions. In recent years, this definition has been extended to include processes that yield homogeneous or heterogeneous organisational responses.

Institutional logics: this is a recent but rapidly expanding concept, defined as 'historically and socially constructed models of cultural symbols and concrete practices, including the suppositions, values and beliefs by which individuals and organisations give meaning to their daily activities, organise their time and space and perpetuate and reproduce their lives and experiences' (Thornton and Ocasio, 1999, p. 804). More briefly, we may suggest that they are the models on which institutions are based.

Rules of the Method

Principle of general analysis: organisations must be studied in relation to established, taken-for-granted models in a given institutional field.

Procedure: analysis of fields and of individual organisations situated in fields. Field-level studies generally measure the dissemination of institutionalised models. Recently, researchers have begun to consider that organisations themselves are multiple entities, and that different interest groups within organisations support different institutions or institutional logics. The analysis of power games between these different groups improves our understanding of the isomorphism microprocess.

Figures of Speech

Decoupling: a foundational concept of neo-institutionalism that is concerned with the fact that the search for legitimacy makes organisations distinguish between the adoption of legitimate organisational forms and the search for efficiency. This concept is debated today, because efficiency itself is a social construct being part of what is an institutional logic.

Hybrid organisations: these combine different institutional logics in an original manner via cooperation between the supporters of each logic, the recruitment and socialisation of such supporters, or the partitioning of practices aligned with different logics.

A Few Authors and Key Texts

DiMaggio and Powell (1983), Greenwood et al. (2008), Meyer and Rowan (1977), Powell and DiMaggio (1991), Thornton et al. (2012).

Thesis 5:

Tools as Investment in Forms

The expression 'investment in forms', coined by Eymard-Duvernay and Thévenot, designates a collection of tools (norms, standards, regulations, etc.) that are necessary to any production and which should be considered as 'investments' in the same way as machinery (Thévenot, 1984). Setting up these tools is costly but brings about greater yields by allowing for time savings (many choices have already been made in the set-up and are therefore no longer questioned) and a fluidity and regularity of action. After re-reading the works of F. W. Taylor they identified the 'slide rule', the 'chronometer', the 'formula', the 'measure', the 'task', 'written instructions', the 'rate', and many others as investments in forms. Management tools are obviously part of these.

This approach draws attention to the work of 'formatting', to the many choices made between alternative possibilities, and to the way of coding and framing things and people in order to make their management easier. All these operations are establishing new conventions that are incorporated into the management tool via investments in form. These conventions are productive because they allow the reduction of uncertainty.

THE CONVENTIONALIST APPROACH

The notion of convention, put forward by the economics of conventions (*Économie des Conventions*, the school of thought to which Eymard-Duvernay and Thévenot's research belongs), actually includes two different accepted meanings (Biencourt et al., 2001). According to one, the convention allows the resolution of a problem concerning the coordination of action in a context of uncertainty (e.g., choosing which side of the road to drive on).[4] To this *strategic* perspective (elaborated by game theory), conventionalist economists have added an *interpretative* and *cognitive* perspective. According to them, the convention allows the coordination of both behaviours and representations. Key to coordination is actors' agreement over the characterisation of situations and the things and people engaged in situations. In both cases we can refer to 'conventions' because, as different ways to act are possible, there is a plurality of evaluation models and ways of getting people to agree (Boltanski and Thévenot, 2006).

The judgements are expressed through 'reality tests' that allow the worth of the beings involved to be established (Boltanski and Thévenot, 2006; Wagner, 1994). When these tests are formalised they presume investment in forms and, the wider their validity, the more it will be said that they are 'instituted'. Their institution means that they are accepted as legitimate. They are supported by a system of justification that incorporates a definition of the common good ('polities' in the models of Boltanski and Thévenot (2006)). We can consider that certain management tools, e.g., performance evaluation systems, equip the reality tests of the business world (Bourguignon and Chiapello, 2005).

Numerous works have studied economic phenomena from a conventionalist perspective (Diaz-Bone and Salais, 2011; Eymard-Duvernay, 2006a, 2006b; Karpik, 2010). Although the plurality in market functioning and the multiplicity of enterprise types have been made visible,[5] this approach has rarely taken an interest in

---

[4] 'Lewis type' conventions are typical examples. These are coordination conventions that satisfy five propositions: (1) almost everyone conforms to the convention; (2) almost everyone anticipates that almost everyone else will conform to the convention; (3) almost everyone prefers general conformity with the convention; (4) there is at least one alternative to the convention; (5) the four preceding propositions form '*common knowledge*' (Lewis, 1969).

[5] Diverse typologies have been produced, insisting on the existence of different 'quality conventions' organising the markets for goods and means of production (Eymard-Duvernay, 1989; Gomez, 1994; Storper and Salais, 1997), different 'financing conventions' relative to the financing of businesses (Rivaud-Danset and Salais, 1992) or even diverse 'salary conventions' (convention of productivity or unemployment for Salais, 1989) organising the relation between employment and the job market.

management tools themselves. This is because, with their background in economics, conventionalist authors have sought above all to develop an alternative concept of markets as opposed to 'standard theory' (Favereau, 1989). A notable exception is the work by Eymard-Duvernay and Marchal (1997) who were looking at the different ways of evaluating workers in the job market, just as Eymard-Duvernay (1989) had earlier sought different models of quality for products. They found that tools and devices for personnel selection were equipped with diverse 'skills conventions'.

Management tools sometimes appear as the means to disseminate a convention and to frame its interpretation. In the view developed by Gomez (1994, 1997), management tools are (along with other elements) part of 'material devices' that ensure the dissemination, understanding and repetition of the convention. Mercier (2003) studied the transformation of the forms of management at the RATP (Paris region transport authority). Particularly through the setting up of performance contracts and individual interviews, a double transformation emerged regarding the 'convention of effort' that regulates the employment relationship and the 'quality convention' that concerns production.[6] The definition that predominates in these analyses is that of a convention that is rarely formulated or formalised but does in fact regulate behaviours and decisions.

The works inspired by this perspective are most interesting for the study of management tools as they deal with formats and formatting of information (accounting, indicators, classifications), which are not themselves management tools but are frequently found in their composition (see Table 4.2 later in this chapter for a list of representative publications).

---

[6] See other examples of work on management inspired by the perspective opened up by Gomez (1994) in the publication edited by Amblard (2003b).

THE SOCIOLOGY OF QUANTIFICATION AND CLASSIFICATIONS

Desrosières, whose work is devoted to these questions, differentiates the notion of 'quantification' from that of 'measure', which 'inspired by the traditional epistemology of natural sciences, implies that something exists in an already measurable form according to a realistic metrology, like the height of the Eiffel Tower'. However:

> the immoderate use of the verb 'to measure' leads us into error by leaving in the shadows the conventions of quantification. The verb 'to quantify' in its active form (making numbers), supposes that a series of conventions of equivalence should be drawn up and explained beforehand, thereby implying comparisons [...] inscriptions, encodings, codified procedures that can be replicated and calculations leading to the same expression in numbers. Measurement properly speaking comes afterwards, as an implementation of conventions. (Desrosières, 2008, pp. 10–11, our translation).

This sociological approach[7] was applied very early to the different classifications used by the statisticians of the INSEE (French National Institute of Statistics and Economic Studies), whether it was industrial classifications (Guibert et al., 1971) or those of socio-professional categories (Desrosières, 1977). Desrosières and Thévenot (1988) show that drawing up a classification of socio-professional categories was informed by categorisations developed in other social arenas. Several classifications, depending on different representations of the social space, have been produced over the years. For example, the dichotomy between salaried and unsalaried workers appears only relatively late as a determining criterion and could only be drawn up thanks to the

---

[7] In the past few years, several French journals have devoted special issues to the sociology of quantification: *Genèses* (vol. 58, 2005); *Revue française de socio-économie* (vol. 5, 2010); *Sociologie et Sociétés* (vol. 43, no. 2, 2011). See in English Diaz-Bone and Didier (2016).

establishment of labour laws that allowed such a distinction. In fact, the oldest classifications, distinguishing between trades, tended to put bosses and workers into the same category. Identification of a hierarchy among salaried workers came along even later and is linked to the development of collective agreements and internal devices within personnel management (identifying several levels of employment in the public sector just as in companies, with a hierarchy of workers, supervisors, executives). These categories were subsequently fixed by law according to professional agreements (collective bargaining).

The conventions that are the foundation of the classifications are therefore fed by political and social processes surpassing them and result in compromise. Desrosières and Thévenot (1988) also show that the classification under study is propelled by the search for a triple representativity (statistical, political and cognitive). This trio suggests that any form of quantification should be analysed systematically from these three points of view. The production of a number aimed at describing the state of a group of things, people or events, or the creation of a classification that does the same by using a system of categories, arises first of all from a desire for *statistical representation* (are things said about what is to be described and qualified? Is the table representative?), *political representation* (how are the spokespersons of groups[8] chosen? What are the groups or entities represented in the classification?) and *cognitive representation* (what ideas do we have about what is to be described and what needs to be selected to be displayed? What are the underlying social or political philosophies?).

Eyraud (2004), on the transformation of accounting practices in Chinese firms, and Chiapello (2005), on the accounting norms of businesses in Europe since 2005, have pursued this perspective. Their dissection of accounting rules and layouts has revealed many

---

[8] On this question of spokespersons, see the study by Didier (2009) on the evolution of agricultural statistics in the USA.

quantification conventions.[9] The change in accounting conventions accompanies a profound transformation of the definition of the enterprise and its role. Accounting brings into existence conventional and historically situated definitions of the enterprise. Representations of the economy are thus embedded into accounting – not just business accounting but also national accounting, as Gadrey (2006) shows by examining debates about the measurement of gross domestic product (GDP). More generally, it is the conception of the economic entity whose accounts are to be established that is at stake in the conventions chosen.[10] The spread of the investment in forms that accounting rules represent favours the circulation of the ideas behind them. Suzuki (2007) tells how Japan adopted a Keynesian economic model after the Second World War under the influence of American occupation at the same time as it adopted national accounting formats developed in Britain. This was done despite the predominance of very different economic concepts among the Japanese academic community. The conventions contained within the tool and which permit its construction are thus spread with the diffusion of the tool. And these conventions influence those who use the figures produced with their use, but nevertheless without total determinism. Bezes (2004), who also studies a quantification tool arising from a Keynesian project,[11] shows how this same tool and its statistical categories can be reinterpreted within a neo-liberal framework at a later date.

The study of classifications and modern systems of categories prolong an old tradition in sociology and anthropology, which took

---

[9] Amblard (2004) shows that accountants cannot act without using a multitude of conventions that allow them to find the answers to numerous uncertainties that weigh on their work. This enquiry shows that, generally, reflexivity about the rules applied is weak and their character as an 'arbitrary' convention goes unquestioned, to the point that accounting conventions satisfy the five criteria of a Lewis-style convention (Lewis, 1969). See Chiapello (2017) for an English presentation of accounting conventions.

[10] See also Eyraud (2011) on the accounting reforms of the French state.

[11] This is a system for calculating the total salary in the public sector, originally designed to measure the state's impact on the economy by the salaries paid out.

one of its main instruments of analysis[12] from the study of language and systems for the naming and classification of natural and cultural universes of 'natives'. Durkheim and Mauss (1963) had already high-lighted the existence of commonalities between 'primitive classifica-tions' and those of scientists.[13] The perspectives and research programmes that were opened up more than a century ago still seem to be strikingly relevant today:

> A class is a group of things; and things do not present themselves to observation grouped in such a way. We may well perceive, more or less vaguely, their resemblances. But the simple fact of these resemblances is not enough to explain how we are led to group things which thus resemble each other [...] Every classification implies a hierarchical order for which neither the tangible world nor our mind gives us the model. We therefore have reason to ask where it was found. [...] These facts lead us to the conjecture that the scheme of classification is not the spontaneous product of abstract understanding, but results from a process into which all sorts of foreign elements enter. (Durkheim and Mauss, 1963, p. 4)

The sociology of classifications supposes taking an interest in the processes of categorisation, which means the operations that allow the creation of classes and categories of analysis or thought. Starting from the idea that things or entities to be classified are made up only of particular cases, this sociological perspective examines the steps neces-sary for two singular entities to be brought into a certain relation. This operation can be understood as 'putting into equivalence' (Boltanski and Thévenot, 2006). By making such a connection, the classifier ignores taking account of those properties that might oppose such a

---

[12] This tradition has been incarnated in recent times by the British anthropologist Douglas (1986) who defines culture as a system of shared classifications and is interested in institutions as a process of influence on these classifications.

[13] Boltanski (1970) relied on this same tradition to justify precursory work on the classification systems used in consumer surveys, which should be studied with the same perspective as that developed for studying indigenous taxonomies.

relation. Thus, a classification according to job titles does not consider age, gender, geographical origin, personality traits, place of work, etc.

The study of categorisation should allow an understanding of what enables entities to be grouped into the same class. We are used to distinguishing between 'prototypical' classifications (organised around a typical, particularly outstanding example and around which other entities are assembled by resemblance), and 'logical' or 'Aristotelian' classifications (where the boundaries are guarded by precise criteria that supposedly allow the separation of entities into different classes).[14] While the former belong to the vernacular and the latter to the scientific world, scholarly classifications are often hybrid. This is because many different factors count in the establishment of classes, as has been shown by Bowker and Star's (2000) analysis of the International Classification of Diseases (ICD). This can be explained by the fact that some investments in forms aim at coordinating very different people, contexts, and strategies. For example, the ICD is used in many countries, and by actors as different as doctors, social security organisations or statisticians drawing up mortality tables. This makes such classifications 'boundary-objects' (Star and Griesemer, 1989; Trompette and Vinck, 2009) whose contours are also shaped by the need to ensure coordination between spaces and groups that are very different.

Moreover, the categories are constantly at risk of imploding under the weight of the heterogeneity of the elements they assemble. This heterogeneity hidden behind the constructed equivalence threatens to rise up at any moment, to such an extent that it is necessary to shift attention to the largely political work to make things that do not spontaneously form a whole hold together.[15]

The detailed study of categories also reveals beings that are difficult to classify, a phenomenon that deserves attention because it provides insights about the implicit frameworks that organise our

[14] See the work of the American cognitive psychologist Eleanor Rosch.
[15] See Boltanski (1987), which is devoted entirely to these questions about the category of 'Cadres'.

representations. Being difficult to classify also has fairly serious consequences for the fate of these beings and the way in which they are understood. Thévenot (1979) described in detail the classification problems posed by young people:[16] using the 'apparently more unambiguous' age criterion conceals in return the heterogeneity of the group and the fact that any evolution does not have the same meaning depending on the social origin of the young. Bowker and Star (2007) expose more clearly the ethical questions posed by the existence of 'residual categories' in which 'atypical' cases that do not 'deserve' to be distinguished are brought together.

The creation of equivalence through the application of an 'equivalence convention' does not occur only when categorising or classifying. It also occurs when things are 'commensurated'. Commensuration is a process that entails the comparison of the qualities of different entities according to a common measure (Espeland and Stevens, 1998). Cost–benefit analyses, utility calculations, price, voting procedures and the calculations of scores are all examples of this. It is a technique of inclusion, because disparate qualities are taken into account and compared. But it is also a technique of exclusion, because whatever is not 'commensurated' (i.e., taken into account; for example some costs in a cost–benefit calculation) does not exist. Commensuration neglects certain pieces of information and reorganises the rest in a new form. It can thus produce new entities, just like administrative practices that create what they claim to describe (professional categories, the beneficiaries of welfare payments, and so on) (Hacking, 1999). Commensuration is very useful for action because it allows the combination, hierarchical ranking and arbitration of contradictory elements. Because of this, it is the basis of all management tools that help in decision-making and performance evaluation.

---

[16] 'The young frustrate the plans of statisticians. When it is not just a question of simply avoiding counting because they do not belong to any household, for example young workers living in hostels or youth placed in special institutions, they do not fit easily into classes, even into the most tried and tested grids. They do not respect the active/inactive opposition and they move from one intermediary status to another, such as that of family help, military service, internship or even as unemployed' (Thévenot, 1979, p. 3, our translation).

The perspectives reviewed here have proven a rich ground for the research of management tools, including examinations of the conventions, classifications and systems of categories that underpin and are contained within these tools.

ANALYTICAL PERSPECTIVES ON MANAGEMENT TOOLS

A first group of studies can be carried out aiming, like in the works on classification discussed above, to identify the different kinds of convention (political, cognitive, statistical) that accompany the management tool, either because these conventions were directly inscribed in the tool's format during the investment in forms, or because they accompany its instructions for use. Besides uncovering these conventions, it is appropriate to wonder what 'maintains' them and in particular what links can be made with other devices, including legal ones, or various initiatives that promote certain conceptions of the phenomenon to be managed.

Particular attention ought to be paid to the judgement and evaluation models incorporated in the tools in order to make the underlying value systems stand out (Boltanski and Thévenot's 'polities' (2006)). From this point of view, a detailed analysis of the judgement devices ('tests') could also allow to detect the differences between the claimed judgement models and their actual implementation. These devices incorporate not only judgement conventions on 'worth' but also many other conventional choices, some of which are said to be 'technical' and are discovered by following the operations of quantification in great detail.[17] Multiple disputes and controversies have enmeshed the process of choosing and incorporating conventions, and the end result has become consistent and autonomous from the original judgement models.

---

[17] See, for example, Didier's (2009) highly detailed analysis of the multitude of operations necessary in order to be able to produce a table of figures on agricultural yields. Or Chiapello (2015, 2018) for the work of creating new circuits of funding and the changes of valuation techniques.

Because they are only conventions, they are always likely to be challenged, paving the way for a dynamic analysis of conventions (Amblard, 2003a) and, beyond this, of tools. Such discussions may trigger a transformation of tools (Bourguignon and Chiapello, 2005), measurement conventions (Gadrey, 2006), or the statistical 'expressions' (Didier, 2009) that they contain. The detailed examination of these dynamics could make up a research project. The different following elements could then be examined. One could seek to understand whether the tests that organise the judgements are criticised, and why: because they poorly implement the judgement principles they claim to represent (reformist critique) or in the name of other principles (radical critique) (Boltanski and Chiapello, 2005). In return, these critical moments call for the justification of these conventions. This justificatory work in response to critics makes conventions and judgement principles more visible. Because of the controversy, each party is indeed required to clarify the normative assumptions upon which their judgement is based. This 'justice regime' is opposed to a 'regime of correctness'[18] (*justesse*), in which conventions are largely not thought out because they are taken for granted and not disputed (Boltanski, 2012). The critique may be sufficiently insistent as to destabilise the reality test. It is then interesting to understand the nature of the transformations that follow: do the test's organisers choose to 'stretch' the test (to make it conform more to the project), to change the conventions that are incorporated in it, or even to move the judgement away to spaces that are less controlled by the critique (*displacement*) and towards less formalised tests (Boltanski and Chiapello, 2005)? The institutionalising nature of the controversies (Lemieux, 2007) can then also be illustrated in the case of management tools.

---

[18] *Justesse* is translated by fairness in Boltanski (2012) but a closer translation would be correctness as this regime does not suppose consciousness and also concerns unproblematic relations between things as in a well-oiled machine.

The approaches presented in this thesis also allow certain effects of management tools to be clarified. Because of the forms of designation, classification and judgement that they incorporate, management tools have an effect on the cognition of the people who use them and contribute to institutionalise certain representations (Eyraud, 2004).

However, their effects go beyond the cognitive dimensions insofar as people act according to the judgements and classifications produced by management tools while others act according to how they have been treated because of the classifications or according to the treatment of topics that concern them (Espeland and Stevens, 2008). This is what Espeland and Sauder (2007) show in their study of law school rankings in the USA. In particular, they highlighted the effects of 'self-fulfilling prophecies'[19] as a high ranking of a school reinforces its reputation and its image and therefore its ability to raise funds, obtain subsidies, attract the best students, ensure that they get good salaries when they graduate, etc. The rankings of schools therefore tend to maintain or even to reinforce the positions of those at the top of the list. Espeland and Sauder also showed the effects of the rankings on the schools' policies: the development of scholarships (to attract the best students who will help improve the ranking position) at the expense of grants on social criteria; the standardisation of programmes and the suppression of specific missions that are not taken into account in the rankings; the transformation in the work of student placement services that try to 'slot' their students in somewhere rapidly at the highest salary, rather than helping them to find a job that would suit them; the considerable increase in staff numbers and external communications budgets at the expense of other kinds of

---

[19] A prophecy that modifies behaviours in such a way that it causes the prophecy to be fulfilled. This is one of the ways in which people react to judgements and forms of categorisation that concern them. This expression was coined by Merton (1949) and it applies to all kinds of judgements and prejudices about people, going well beyond those mediated by management tools.

investment; strategies aimed at gaming indicators (for example by enrolling students with poor results in standardised tests in specific programmes that allow the schools to circumvent negative effects on the rankings, or the frantic search for applicants in order to artificially increase selectivity rates).

Two types of effects can be distinguished.

First, the use of tools has consequences for the treatment of people, things and situations that are affected by them. Certain 'tests' produce evaluations that cannot be dissociated from access to certain resources (salary, budget) or certain places (positions and titles). Because of this, it is worthwhile to look at the role of tools in fabricating social hierarchies. More broadly, even simple classifications not associated with a project to evaluate respective worths can engender discrimination, stigmatisation or exclusion, as has been shown in many studies, starting with typical classifications of race or mental illness (Bowker and Star, 2000; Starr, 1992). The effect of categories in their interaction with public policies aimed at one or another category of people whose lives they transform has thus been well documented. Eymard-Duvernay and Marchal (1997) renewed this type of analysis by showing the effects of exclusion from the job market produced by certain selection tools.

Second, the people and organisations concerned by these classifications and judgements react to them because they are 'interactive kinds' according to the expression used by Hacking (1999) (as opposed to 'indifferent kinds'). In other words: 'The courses of action they choose, and indeed their ways of being, are by no means independent of the available descriptions under which they may act' (Hacking, 1999, p. 103). The auto-conformation of law schools because of the rankings in the study mentioned above is a typical example. Some public policies that are based on benchmarking, such as those arising from the European Union's 'Open Method of Coordination' (OMC), rely on these effects of 'reactivity' to conform the practices of multiple actors (Bruno, 2008).

Putting a Value on Nature

(Fourcade, 2011)

In her comparative case study of two oil spills, the Amoco Cadiz
in France in 1978, and the Exxon Valdez in the USA in Alaska in 1989,
Marion Fourcade has studied how monetary value is calculated for
losses sustained by nature (as opposed to losses incurred by commercial
and tourist activities), where claims regarding damages and
compensation were made against shipowners and oil companies in the
subsequent lawsuits. She shows how the different economic valuation
methods used should be interpreted as the results of different
judgements on the value of nature and on the reasons why nature has an
economic value in the first place.

These judgements are founded on the two countries' different view of
nature. While the large open spaces in the United States allow Americans
to grasp the idea of nature easily, the whole landscape of France has been
shaped by human activity and nature is inhabited and exploited by
humans everywhere in the country. Nature's value is therefore much
more strongly linked to human activities than it is in the USA.

The definition of the victims of the two oil spills, in part, arises from
this. In France, the victims were principally those who used the coast,
while in the USA it was the whole nation that has lost something due
to the destruction of natural seashores in Alaska (the number of people
directly concerned by the Exxon Valdez spill was very low). The
valuation methods in France stressed the cost of cleaning up and
restoring nature so that it could be accessed again by its users. In the
USA, an evaluation was carried out to estimate the subjective loss of
value felt by the American people. As humans can get back on their
feet more quickly than nature – its biodiversity and dynamic
ecosystem – the two countries had very different perceptions of the
necessary restoration period, which had important consequences on
the levels of compensation. Compensation was very high in the USA,
enabling protected areas and advanced ecological research programmes
to be put in place. In France, by contrast, it took ten years for
compensation to be paid and even then only reimbursed local villages

for their clean-up costs. If in both countries 'nature is priceless', then in one case this resulted in huge claims for compensation, while in the other, it was a refusal to see money as an equivalent and thus implied a refusal to put a price on nature hence yielding almost symbolic compensation claims.

Table 4.2 *A selection of publications representative of the conventionalist thesis*

Authors (principal thesis)	Techniques studied	Principal results
Origins and types of conventions		
Desrosières and Thévenot (1988, chapter 1) (Link between conventions and external legal devices which support them)	The history of the socio-professional categories at the INSEE (French National Institute of Statistics)	Comparison of several classifications over time. Identification of what changes in classification methods and highlighting links between these changes and the appearance of institutions concerned with labour (labour law, collective agreements, works committees).
Isaac (1998) (Link between conventions and the nature of the activity they are organising)	Code of conduct in the services sector	Codes of conduct only appear in professions where the client/service provider relationship makes the construction of the quality complex. Their content needs to be analysed as does the quality convention in these professions. Other quality conventions could explain the recourse to different tools (such as quality assurance standards or certification).

Table 4.2 (cont.)

Authors (principal thesis)	Techniques studied	Principal results
Bidet (2005, 2010) (Link between conventions for measurement, the state of production and construction techniques, and management problems)	The history of ways of measuring, managing and setting tariffs for telephone activity	A variety of metrics associated with various forms of economic optimisation reasoning, concrete technical problems and management practices have been identified. Attention has thus historically been paid to the management of lines and telephone operators, optimisation of traffic on a saturated network, the profitability of an existing network in financial terms, and the retaining of the best customers in a competitive context.
Gadrey (2006) (Link between measurement conventions and temporary social compromise on what is the source of wealth)	The way of calculating GDP, its evolution and current discussions	The history of national accounting and its controversies should not be seen as 'one of continual scientific progress where, because of scientific debates, methods and concepts have not ceased to improve a tool that is both theoretical and practical' but rather as 'largely determined by politics and its vision of power and wealth' (our translation).
Kletz et al. (1997) (The weight of meta-conventions	The jobs classification grid at the Paris	The choice of a particular layout, which here was a grid with columns (sectors)

Table 4.2 (*cont.*)

Authors (principal thesis)	Techniques studied	Principal results
on the concrete content of adopted conventions)	Museum of Sciences and Industry	and rows (levels) as well as relying on a few classification criteria to 'weight' the jobs (a choice that can be considered as meta-conventions) had structuring effects on the result obtained. The grid was drawn up twice following different processes but nevertheless came to similar results.
Furusten (2000) (Quality norms incorporate conventions on the forms of the action and the nature of organisations more than on the quality)	ISO 9000 standards on quality management	These standards are based on hypotheses about the functioning of organisations and the role of management, celebrating the virtues of the clarification of processes, the use of quantified aims and permanent managerial control. The norms incorporate a managerial doctrine that is a reminder of the Taylorist dream. But they are in contradiction with what we know about the effective functioning of organisations and the actual work of managers.
Gilbert and Leclair (2004) (Despite their adaptability and	The SAP software package (ERP)	This software package comes from material requirement planning (MRP) systems used for the

Table 4.2 (cont.)

Authors (principal thesis)	Techniques studied	Principal results
customisability, software packages are based on particular organisation models)		calculation of needs in terms of components in the German mechanical industry. The structure of this industry, the organisation methods it applied in the 1970s and its production methods are inscribed in this software package, which makes it much less well adapted to flow industries where the number of elements to be supplied is low, or even to service companies to which it introduces complications they do not need.

Life and the effects of conventions

Eyraud (2004) (Conventions have a performing power)	The accounting framework in Chinese firms and the budgetary accounting framework of the French state studied in the way they evolve	Accounting conventions cannot be dissociated from a definition of the entity that they describe, stage, produce and reproduce. In a context of change, new categories are introduced little by little and transform the actors' representations, educate their judgement and carry the construction of new management reflexes.
Espeland and Sauder (2007) (Actors react to	The classification	The scores tend to homogenise the schools' practices and to develop

Table 4.2 (cont.)

Authors (principal thesis)	Techniques studied	Principal results
classifications and categorisations)	of law schools in the USA	strategic management practices of indicators in them. The cognitive effects on funders, recruiters and students are considerable. Because of the decisions that stem from them, these effects tend to reinforce the positions adopted.
Bezes (2004) (The conventions that form the foundation of the tool can be reinterpreted and serve different aims)	System for calculating salary costs in the French public sector	Originally conceived as an instrument for knowing and planning the state's total expenditure on salaries following a Keynesian economic policy paradigm that sees salaries as policy levers. In the end, it was used to rationalise the state's spending on personnel and to frame negotiations with unions.
Eymard-Duvernay and Marchal (1997) (Conventions change the destinies of people who are judged by them)	Selection methods used by recruiters	'Competences' are 'configured' through devices (words, objects, procedures) by which candidates are perceived. There are several 'skills conventions' that open up different 'value' judgements of the candidates. Some of these conventions are more likely than others to promote long-term

Table 4.2 (*cont.*)

Authors (principal thesis)	Techniques studied	Principal results
		unemployment by associating in a simplistic way people's incompetence to variables such as age, gender, level of education or lack of experience.
Beunza and Garud (2007) (Conventions influence the construction of prices on financial markets)	Reports of financial analysts on Amazon between 1998 and 2000 (period of the internet bubble)	Financial analysts are seen as 'framemakers': people capable of making conventions of judgement to resolve a situation of uncertainty. In this case, there was uncertainty about the categorisation of the firm (internet company, bookseller, distributor?) and thus the definition of firms to which it could be compared and the choice of pertinent financial indicators for its evaluation.
Barraud de Lagerie (2009) (The institutionalisation of a classification system does not mean the end of controversies)	Business Social Compliance Initiative (BSCI) standard allowing the social audit of suppliers	This standard has been constructed as a rigid process around a long questionnaire giving the auditor very little latitude and including a grading system that allows no compensation between items. Its set-up gave rise to discussions and questioning from all parties, including the auditor who administered it, the person

Table 4.2 (*cont.*)

Authors (principal thesis)	Techniques studied	Principal results
		who commissioned it in order to use the results, and the unions. However, none of these have succeeded in preventing its use.
Chiapello and Godefroy (2017) (Valuation conventions mediate relationships between actors)	Social Impact measurements used by Impact Investors	The form of the indicator cannot be separated from the relational configuration between investors and investees that gave rise to it and give it its relative coercive force. Investors can be more or less involved in the actual functioning of the social enterprise and be financially interested in social impact or only in financial results.

Summary Sheet (Thesis 5)

The Axioms

Axiom of the conventional nature of social life: life in society and humans' ability to coordinate with each other is based on the existence of conventions that allow agreements to be reached on the quality of things and people, the way to act, and the choices to be made in situations.

Axiom of the plurality of conventions: not only is the choice of a convention arbitrary, in the sense that another convention would also have been possible, but in any social situation several conventions coexist and compete over the interpretation of situations. This forms balances that are continuously unstable.

Axiom of the productive and interactive nature of conventions: the conventions adopted have effects on the functioning of groups and on the individual beings to whom they apply.

Key Concepts

Convention of coordination: in the context of a relative uncertainty about the choice of the action to be taken, the coordination convention is a recurrent problem solving procedure. The convention may be non-formalised ('we have always done it like that') or it may be hardened and incorporated into devices.

Convention of evaluation or judgement: certain conventions coordinate not only behaviours but also representations because they are accompanied by a valuation model.

Classification (or nomenclature): a collection of 'boxes' in which 'things' are classified. This system is organised according to coherent principles; the different categories are mutually exclusive and the classification is complete, that is, it must be able to take in the whole collection that it claims to classify.

Categorisation: process by which different objects are perceived as similar and through which different classes of objects are constructed. All designation is a form of categorisation. All formalisation is a process of categorisation.

Commensuration: particular form of 'equivalence work' that uses quantification and brings different qualities into a common metric (Espeland and Stevens, 1998).

Test: social device through which people, things and diverse elements are valued. Its outcome is the production of an order and the establishment of a judgement. Tests enact judgement devices (Boltanski and Thévenot, 2006; Karpik, 2010).

Dynamic of tests: study of forms and the effects of the critique of the reality tests that organise judgements; cycles of critique and justification; controversies making conventions of judgement apparent; change or displacement of tests; recuperation of the critique (Boltanski and Chiapello, 2005).

Rules of the Method

General principle of analysis: management tools rely on a great number of conventions, such as socio-technical conventions that allow the translation into technical or quantified language of the designers' preoccupation, or socio-political conventions that relate to the choice of finalities, representations of policies to be carried out or the functioning of the system to be managed. The analysis aims to shed light onto these different conventions.

Posture: constructivist. What has been constructed must be deconstructed in order to reveal its arbitrary nature.

Procedures: the comparison of conventions adopted to resolve similar questions in different economic universes (companies, sectors, different countries) or at different moments in time; the study of moments of conventional uncertainty, of critique or debates where the actors hesitate between several conventions or look for new ways of taking action; the updating of categories of thought incorporated in the tool and the analysis of classifications that it utilises as a system of representation.

Figures of Speech

Investment in forms: the effort and expense relating to perfecting a new way of acting, analysing or evaluating and its increasing rigidity in tools, procedures and measuring systems must be considered as investment in forms. Once the form is acquired, it allows the production of a regularity and a capacity to relate automatically to other standard forms (Thévenot, 1984).

Classification struggle: originally a notion developed by Bourdieu to describe the symbolic struggles about the definition of social classes, their boundaries and respective position. By extension, any disagreement about definition and the delineation of categories, no matter what is classified and qualified (people, objects, organisations, events). This dispute should be interpreted in the light of the interests at stake and the categorisation's multiple consequences for the actors.

Boundary-object: an object (a category or an archetypal case) that is interpreted differently according to the 'community of practices' that uses it. It allows cooperation between these communities (e.g., a classification of soils usable by botanists and geologists) (Bowker and Star, 2000; Star and Griesemer, 1989).

A Few Authors and Key Texts
Various works of Alain Desrosières, Ève Chiapello, Wendy Espeland, Luc Boltanski and Laurent Thévenot. Boltanski and Chiapello (2005), Boltanski and Thévenot (2006), Espeland and Sauder (2007), Espeland and Stevens (1998, 2008), as well as Bowker and Star (2000), Karpik (2010), Diaz-Bone and Salais (2011); Eymard-Duvernay (2006a, 2006b).

Thesis 6:

Technology Is Both Constraining and Enabling

The works of the British sociologist Anthony Giddens have inspired research about the social effects of 'technology', which is defined as both a *material* artefact and a *social* object with many uses.[20] This type of research considers technology–user interactions and analyses their repercussions at different levels: for individuals, teams, and organisations. Two distinct perspectives can be identified from the study of this literature. Before summarising them, we first schematically introduce a few central concepts.[21]

STRUCTURATION THEORY (ST): SOME OF THE CENTRAL CONCEPTS

According to Giddens (1984), individual behaviours, practices, intentions and discourse, otherwise known as 'social *systems*' cannot be understood independently from the 'social *structures*' that give form and shape to them (and even condition them to some extent). Social structures, in turn, result from human activities that carry on in space-time and acquire a systemic character when they are routinised. This process of recursive co-structuration is known as 'duality of structure'.

By emphasising the *process* of structuration, Giddens (1984) considered the conditions for the reproduction of social systems at three levels: (1) the structure known as *signification* refers to

---

[20] This thesis is authored by Marion Brivot (Université Laval, Québec, Canada).

[21] Englund et al. (2011) show that only structurationist research in information systems has really made a conceptual effort to appropriate and extend Giddens's (1984) work. Authors in other fields, including management and accounting, typically combine structuration theory with other theories, including actor-network theory (e.g., Jones and Dugdale, 2002) or neo-institutional theory (e.g., Dirsmith et al. 1997; Jack, 2005).

interpretative frames, by which meaning is created and shared collectively; (2) the structure known as *domination* refers to material and symbolic resources thanks to which power can be wielded; and (3) the structure known as *legitimation* refers to the means by which norms and moral rules are laid down.

In his founding works on ST, and in his later writings on modernity, Giddens pays little attention to the role of technology,[22] specifically. According to him, nothing distinguishes it from other structuring elements: 'Language is [constraining]; yet language is the means of doing all sorts of things one could not accomplish without it. Although it has a physical presence, technology is no different. *It is constraining and enabling*' (Giddens and Pierson 1998, p. 83, emphasis added). Nor does he spend time on the business organisation as a particular social system. This does not stop ST from being used in management,[23] accounting and information systems research.

According to some authors, technology is a *bearer* of structures (perspective A);[24] technology therefore possesses a potential for structuration that is fully expressed if it is used in accordance with the 'spirit' in which it was designed. Others, in contrast, hypothesise that social structures are neither present in technology nor in individuals (perspective B). Based on this understanding, the role of technology in the structuration process is only an indirect one but it remains important, because technology mediates, constrains and enables human practices that, themselves, are the sources of structuration (see Table 4.3).[25]

---

[22] In his work on 'the consequences of modernity' (Giddens, 1990), the author comments briefly on the role of 'expert systems', but elsewhere he specifies: 'Technology does nothing except as implicated in the actions of human beings' (Giddens and Pierson, 1998, p. 82).

[23] See Whittington (1992) for a critical analysis of these usages by Giddens.

[24] See for example Caglio (2003) or Jones and Dugdale (2002).

[25] The studies in Table 4.3 have been selected because their operationalisation of ST is very clear.

Table 4.3 *Research representative of the structurationist thesis*

Authors	Technology studied (field)	Dimensions of the structuration process influenced by technology (explicit or implicit in the work)	Social effects of technology noted
Orlikowski (1992)	Computer Aided Software Engineering, CASE (a North American IT consulting firm)	**Domination**: CASE makes new bureaucratic controls possible, with a bearing on productivity and the efficiency of IT developers. **Signification**: CASE transforms the way in which developers resolve problems. **Legitimation**: CASE becomes the only legitimate way of developing large-scale programmes in the firm.	The work of developers becomes more standardised and the firm's control system more bureaucratic.
Barrett and Walsham (1999)	Electronic Trading System, LIMNET EPS (the London Insurance Market)	**Domination**: EPS leads to a perceived loss of control and autonomy by underwriters and brokers. **Signification**: EPS triggers an evolution of the meaning of brokers' and underwriters' roles. **Legitimation**: EPS weakens the legitimacy of traditional risk placement methods and introduces new, better ways to manage risk exposures.	Productivity in risk placement increases. Surveillance work is facilitated. The role and identity of brokers and underwriters are redefined (among other things).
Jones and Dugdale (2002)	Activity-Based Costing Method (ABC)	**Domination**: ABC 'facilitates new patterns of domination by opening up	Managerial accounting knowledge and

Table 4.3 (*cont.*)

Authors	Technology studied (field)	Dimensions of the structuration process influenced by technology (explicit or implicit in the work)	Social effects of technology noted
	(worldwide diffusion networks of ABC)	the activities of "staff" personnel to the scrutiny of "line" managers, and offers means to control the costs of these' (p. 152). **Signification**: ABC allows the identification of products that are to be cut and clients that are to be dropped. **Legitimation**: ABC 'legitimates the detailed examination of certain activities by identifying some as "value-adding" and others as "non-value adding"' (p. 152).	practices evolve.
Ahrens and Chapman (2002)	A formal performance measurement system (PSM) focused on 'food margin' (a UK restaurant chain)	**Domination**: PMS leads to questioning extant power relations, e.g., 'could an operational area manager order a restaurant manager to reduce a food margin percentage deficit when, at the same time, the restaurant was exceeding its budgeted cash margin?' (p. 167). **Signification**: PMS facilitates new interpretations of financial performance,	The responsibility of local restaurant managers is redefined.

Table 4.3 (cont.)

Authors	Technology studied (field)	Dimensions of the structuration process influenced by technology (explicit or implicit in the work)	Social effects of technology noted
		e.g., a higher than budget cash margin might be attributed to variables other than the skills of the restaurant manager, including a lax budget. **Legitimation**: PMS leads to questioning the legitimacy of imposing certain head office norms (e.g., at what level of profit should one turn a blind eye to violations of brand standards by a local restaurant?).	

THE PLACE OF TECHNOLOGY IN PROCESSES OF STRUCTURATION: TWO DIFFERENT ONTOLOGIES BUT COMPLEMENTARY EMPIRICAL RESULTS

Perspective A postulates that technology carries interpretative models, resources and norms that are encoded in it by its designers. Its repeated use leads to the institutionalisation of these structures but in non-identical ways, depending on the organisational context in which it is employed (Barley, 1986). In fact, there can be interference between the new structures conveyed by the technology and the organisational structures that existed prior to its adoption.

Starting with this idea, Orlikowski (1992) proposed a triadic model of the organisation, individuals and technology. Users and technology are mutually structured since technology is both an *output* of human activity (conception and development) and an *input* that is more or less enabling and constraining for human activity; this is what the author calls the 'duality of technology', an echo of the expression 'duality of structure' (Giddens, 1984). This microprocess creates a dynamic of reinforcement (or transformation, depending on the situation) of existing organisational structures. Although it is causal, Orlikowski's (1992) model is not deterministic because the changes brought about by the technology-in-use are unpredictable: thanks to the 'interpretative flexibility' of the technology, individuals can alter the way they use it at any moment.

'Adaptive structuration theory' (AST) (DeSanctis and Poole, 1994), including 'adaptive structuration theory for individuals' (Schmitz et al., 2016), is for the most part a more detailed reformulation of the above proposition. In our opinion, the main nuance it introduces has bearing on the notion of the 'spirit of technology', which is the official line for its use,[26] jointly defined by designers, sponsors and agents of deployment. The idea that such a spirit exists allows researchers to accentuate the existence of several kinds of appropriation, including creative appropriation, which does not conform to the spirit of technology and is the source of unplanned structuration episodes.

Researchers who subscribe to perspective A[27] have distinct methodological preferences, including, predominantly, interpretative approaches, enquiries of the 'grounded theory' type, socio-ethnographic procedures and action-research. Empirical studies that test causal structuration models quantitatively[28] are much less frequent and, arguably, are less compatible with an orthodox interpretation of Giddens's (1984) structuration theory.

Some researchers moved away from perspective A, adhered to perspective B's view, and eventually abandoned both to embrace a

---

[26] Schmitz et al. (2016) prefer to define the spirit of technology as a user's understanding of that technology's capabilities and affordances.

[27] See Pozzebon and Pinsonneault (2005) for a review.

[28] See for example Schmitz et al., 2016.

socio-material approach instead. Wanda Orlikowski's work is representative of this gradual conversion.[29]

Studies linked to perspective B, including Barrett and Walsham (1999), Orlikowski (2000) and Orlikowski and Barley (2001) stand out in three different ways. They argue that perspective A is not consistent with Giddens's anti-materialist stance on structure. Structure cannot be encoded into technology and most social effects of technology are unpredictable, *not* because of creative appropriations by users but because any action (even one that conforms to prescription) has consequences that escape human intention.[30] Studies that support perspective B concede that technologies-in-use (i.e., different ways of using the technology) can be a trigger for change in organisational routines, or that it can provide the opportunity for a change that is already germinating elsewhere.

Moreover, since technology is increasingly customisable, reconfigurable and reprogrammable, the frontier between conception and use is more and more fuzzy and it actually seems reasonable to postulate that most users diverge from the official line of use (where there is one). The problem, thus, is to understand what new, *emerging* structures are enacted by technologies-in-use, and *not* whether users faithfully or unfaithfully appropriate a given technology or whether they adopt or fail to adopt the structures encoded by developers into the technology. For those who hold this view, a longitudinal study of the effects of technology on social life is not desirable because technology is flexible and constantly evolves, thus the object of the research is not stable over time. Hence, we have to content ourselves with 'taking snapshots' of ephemeral technology–human interaction situations.

---

[29] As attested by the evolution between Orlikowski (1992), Orlikowski (2000), Orlikowski (2005) and more recently, Scott and Orlikowski (2014), and Barrett et al. (2016).

[30] The example used by Giddens (1984) is that of someone who switches on the light when s/he gets home and sending fleeing a burglar who was in the house at that moment (the unintended consequence of an intentional act).

Perspective B does not constitute a less rigorous application of ST than perspective A – on the contrary – but it is closer to the later works of Giddens on modernity (Giddens, 1990) where he examines instability and the rapid evolution of contemporary social practices. Studies adhering to perspective B were intended to redress perspective A's tendency to see technology as *embodying* structures. Yet these studies ended up being criticised, too, for focusing excessively on human agency and leaving little room, if any, for examining technology's material dimension (Barrett et al., 2006). Essentially, ST seems unable to properly render the fluid interchange between the material agency of technology and the human agency of computer programmers and users (Orlikowski, 2005). This important limitation is probably the chief reason why ST-informed research on technology has progressively given way, since the mid-2000s, to studies informed by various theories of 'socio-materiality' (Leonardi, 2011), including Bruno Latour's analysis of socio-technical change (Bijker and Law, 1992),[31] and Karen Barad's (2007) notion of 'entanglement'[32] (see for example Scott and Orlikowski, 2014).

These two perspectives – A and B – diverge ontologically on whether or not structure can be embedded into a technological object. However, they seem compatible in their empirical results: certain tools are rigid and not very adaptable. They thus impose stiffer rules on human–technology interaction and at the same time deliver fewer opportunities for unforeseen structuration episodes than flexible tools. It is therefore quite logical that the first type of technology should lead to the institutionalisation of the structures expected (or, if preferred, 'encoded into the tool') while the second type, which is less constraining, should lead to the institutionalisation of fortuitous structures.

---

[31] For Latour and the other actor-network theorists cited in this book, human agency should not be given priority over material agency. People and technologies use each other and form associations.

[32] For Barad, a theoretical physicist by training, reality is the quantum 'entanglement' of matter and meaning. Based on this view, materiality is not a 'thing' that mediates practice. Practices are 'material-discursive' and the world is 'enacted', or made real, in ongoing practices (Scott and Orlikowski, 2014).

The Use of a Centralised System of Knowledge Management Helps to Transform the Social Structures in a Lawyer's Office

(Brivot, 2008)

Before the introduction of a formal system of knowledge management, the lawyer's office studied was organised along classic lines for a professional services firm: a structure of democratic domination between the equity partners, a structure of signification marked by a quest for technical excellence and devotion to the client's cause, and a structure of legitimation defined by professional norms on the one hand and performance indicators – including the number of hours personally billed by each lawyer– on the other.

The use of a centralised system of knowledge management aiming at promoting standardised models for legal and tax opinion letters when dealing with recurring client questions caused a partial evolution in the existing organisational routines. Tensions between users and the authors of codified knowledge in the database came to the surface (domination). Professional values became hybridised with bureaucratic values: a 'good opinion letter' is a letter that is technically valid but also not too costly to produce, thanks to the reuse of organisational knowledge in the database (signification). Finally, the diktat of 'hours billed' gave way to a more qualitative evaluation of performance where the originators of 'best practices' enjoyed a new legitimacy while those whose consultations, made visible in the knowledge base, were judged as non-valid or poor quality by their peers were discredited (legitimation).

Summary Sheet (Thesis 6)

The Axioms

Mediating role of technology in the structuration of social systems: the structural properties of social systems are both the conditions and the results of human action. Human–technology interactions can play a mediating role in this process by helping institutionalise or deinstitutionalise existing structural properties.

Duality of technology: human practices and the material properties of technologies interact with one another, each mutually affecting and transforming the other. Technologies are not only structured by their designers but also by their users who appropriate them, customise them, and give them meaning in their own ways. However, technologies are only malleable up to a certain point and necessarily *constrain* users' choices by limiting what it is possible to do. Nevertheless, they also *enable* action by providing readily available interpretation models, resources and norms (perspective A) or by allowing the construction of emerging models, resources and norms (perspective B).

The role of technology in generating structure: this topic is subject to ongoing debate. Some authors consider that tools are bearers of structures. Studying their appropriation therefore comes down to studying the institutionalisation of the structures that they convey (perspective A). Others reckon that the structure cannot be reified and emerges during human activities, which are continuously mediatised and redefined by technology (perspective B). In both cases, the structuration process may be catalysed by technology but cannot be fully anticipated.

Key Concepts

Structural properties: these are collections of rules and resources that enable social practices to endure over time and space by giving them a systemic character. We can distinguish in particular a 'signification structure', which is the vision of the world shared by the members of a group; a 'domination structure', which is the result of the distribution of material and symbolic resources among the group members; and a 'legitimation structure', which is related to the group's norms and moral rules.

Structuration episodes: technology usage events where new structures emerge, or where old structures are reproduced/adjusted.

Rules of the Method

General principle of analysis: ST-inspired research typically separates the effects of technology on human practice and vice versa, but does so only *analytically* because materiality and agency are often imbricated empirically.

Posture: interpretative flexibility. Individual users interact with technology in their own way; technology's structuring effects on human activity cannot be modelled *ex ante*, are often unintentional and are above all provisional. If causalities are postulated, they should be treated with the utmost circumspection because human agents can at any moment alter the cycle of development, use and institutionalisation of technology's use.

Procedure: three procedures can be distinguished, including (1) the diachronic longitudinal approach, which consists of studying the evolving use over time of a given technology by a group of users; (2) the diachronic parallel approach, which consists of analysing the use of the same technology by distinct groups of users; and (3) the synchronic approach, which compares different human agent–tool interaction situations.

Figures of Speech

Figures associated with perspective A: 'encoded structures', 'agency', 'spirit of technology', 'appropriation of structures', 'structuration episodes', 'expected and unexpected consequences'.

Figures associated with perspective B: 'enactment' or 'instantiation' of 'emerging structures' and 'technology-in-use' or 'technology-in-practice'.

A Few Authors and Key Texts

Ahrens and Chapman (2002), Barley (1986), Barrett and Walsham (1999), DeSanctis and Poole (1994), Jones and Dugdale (2002), Orlikowski (1992, 2000), Orlikowski and Barley (2001), Orlikowski and Robey (1991), Poole and DeSanctis (1992, 2004), Pozzebon and Pinsonneault (2005) and Schmitz et al. (2016).

5 Interactional Perspectives on Management Tools

The notions of actor (although not all the theories discussed here use this exact term) and interaction are central for the authors of the theories reviewed in this chapter. It is not the properties of the humans that are prominent in these works but the interpersonal positioning that guides their relations, the way in which they interact in complex surroundings (network, action system, activity system, sign system, etc.) and the social dynamics that result. The four theses examined here are alike in many ways. Unlike critical approaches and certain institutionalist approaches their analysis does not include the effects of social superstructures. In these cases there are no external determinants, no overarching social influence. The accent is on the autonomy of the actors who have the means (construction of meaning, power to act, strategic capacity) that grant them the free space they exploit.

These approaches are interested in situations of specific, localised interaction. They recommend the description of the singular characteristics of these situations, particularly in terms of interaction. These analyses rely on a significant amount of direct observation, *in situ*, which requires taking in the actors' perceptions and opinions. Description is very important here because it is necessary to examine the concrete elements or situations and describe problems in detail in order to understand the dynamics of the interactions between the different objects, tools and actors present. The elements of the analysis (human and non-human) are seen in motion. The authors of the theses examined here are all interested in the pathway, the action, in 'things that are happening'. This perspective is derived from the notion of interaction, which implies confrontation, positive or otherwise, twist and surprises coming together with the possible transformation of human and non-human elements.

The status of the management tool is variable, depending on the thesis in question. In actor-network theory (thesis 7), technical objects have the status of actors and have political weight. Here, tools help to define the space in which people move and to structure the relations they maintain between themselves.

In activity theory (thesis 8), the tool is an unfinished entity. To become an instrument it needs arrangements and plans for its use. When it becomes an instrument, the tool mediates individual activity and intervenes in the construction of collective learning.

Thesis 9 is derived from different sources and is the most composite in this group. Through different means, it attempts to establish reversibility between the tool as language and language as a tool.

Finally, strategic actor theory (thesis 10) has the most reservations about the direct influence of management tools. They are considered part of the universe of formal rules and their effects are always contingent and subordinate to actors' strategies.

In all these works, the management tool constitutes an element in the organisation of relations between human beings and their environment, and there is an inter-structuration between the management tool and social practices.

Thesis 7:

The Tool Is a Human/Non-Human Arrangement

Actor-network theory (ANT), also called the sociology of translation, is the basis of this thesis.[1] ANT was developed at the beginning of the 1980s by researchers at the Centre for the Sociology of Innovation (CSI) at the École des Mines engineering school in Paris, notably Madeleine Akrich, Michel Callon, Bruno Latour and John Law (Akrich et al., 2006; Callon, 1984; Latour, 1987, 1991; Law, 2003).

THE SYMMETRY BETWEEN HUMANS AND NON-HUMANS

Researchers at the CSI were originally interested in the conditions for the production of science and the diffusion of technical innovations and they wanted to break with extremist positions that consider science to be outside of society, political passions, cultural prejudices and personal feelings, or that consider scientific facts to be merely the result of power games. They reject this dual vision because, for them, society and technique, humans and non-humans, do not belong to two distinct worlds. They are closely linked and they interact with each other. In order to understand better the way in which humans and non-humans act mutually upon each other, let us pause for a moment to consider Latour's (1991) example of the key. How can a hotel owner make sure that guests return their key to the reception before leaving the hotel? One solution is putting up a notice saying 'Please return your key to the reception.' This often fails to work for a number of reasons, such as absent-minded guests,

---

[1] Thesis authored by Bénédicte Grall (lecturer at the Conservatoire National des Arts et Métiers, CNAM, Paris).

or a lack of public spirit. A second solution consists in the use of a heavy and cumbersome key ring. This seems to be more successful as guests want to get rid as soon as possible of an object that deforms their pockets. Here, the human acts on the non-human (the hotelier modifies the key ring) and the non-human acts on the human (the key ring changes clients' behaviour).

In short, ANT is 'a disparate family of material-semiotic tools, sensibilities, and methods of analysis that treat everything in the social and natural worlds as a continuously generated effect of the webs of relations within which they are located. [. . . It] describes the enactment of materially and discursively heterogeneous relations that produce and reshuffle all kinds of actors including objects, subjects, human beings, machines, animals, "nature", ideas, organizations, inequalities, scale and sizes, and geographical arrangements' (Law, 2009, p. 141). Understanding society is achieved by re-establishing the symmetry between humans and non-humans: non-humans are neither neutral nor all-powerful. To understand society means understanding the interactions that exist between humans and between humans and non-humans.

NETWORK AND THE TRANSLATION PROCESS

For the authors of ANT, any person, object and even society itself should be seen as the ever-temporary result of a network. The network is a meta-organisation gathering humans and non-humans (knowledge, people, organisations, machines, management tools, institutions) that are linked to one another. To arrive at this temporary result, it is necessary to overcome controversies within the network and make the network intelligible, that is, give each human and non-human element of the network a particular role. This is possible thanks to the translation process defined by Callon (1984, p. 214) as 'the mechanism by which the social and natural worlds progressively take form. The result is a situation in which certain entities control others.' These ideas have been developed at the beginning to understand processes of innovation. The capacity to construct a network successfully is decisive to support and stabilise the innovation.

The translation process passes through four pivotal moments (Callon, 1984): problematisation, 'interessement', enrolment and mobilisation of allies. Problematisation is the starting point of any project and it should allow problems to be formulated, define the actors concerned, and the alliances to be made. Any project gives rise to controversies because, most of the time, it is impossible to determine what is certain and what is uncertain. These controversies cannot be resolved by invoking some kind of natural order and thus give rise to many negotiations within the network. It is through interessement and enrolment of human and non-human allies that these discussions can be settled. Interessement is 'the group of actions by which an entity [...] attempts to impose and stabilize the identity of the other actors it defines through its problematization' (Callon, 1984, p. 203). 'Interessement achieves enrolment if it is successful' (Callon, 1984, p. 205). The actions of interessement and enrolment allow the network to be stabilised, which means that they act so that all actants[2] in the network are firmly linked and work as one – that is, they are 'punctualised' (Latour, 1987). Their aim is also to mobilise an ever-increasing number of allies and spokespersons in order to extend the network and make sure that the innovation is being used by the greatest possible number of actants. Innovation is therefore considered as a 'black box', something taken for granted and no longer questioned by those enrolled.

OBJECTS AS HUMAN/NON-HUMAN ARRANGEMENTS AND THE NOTION OF PERFORMATION

Considering that any person, object and even society itself are always the temporary result of a network led the authors of ANT to define technical objects as socio-technical devices or human/non-human

---

[2] Actant: designates what or who acts within a network, has weight and may be a human, non-human or a human/non-human arrangement.

arrangements.[3] This definition pinpoints the fact that objects are a mix of the social and the technical and that they are true actors because 'devices do things' (Callon et al., 2007, p. 2).

This approach has been used in the field of economic sociology and it puts the accent on *calculative devices* and *market devices* in the construction of markets. Here again it is a question of showing that objects, which are often overlooked, are true actants. 'They articulate actions; they act or make others act' (Callon et al., 2007, p. 2).

Advocating for the active role of socio-technical devices that 'convey or lead to a certain way of acting', Muniesa and Callon (2009) talk about 'performation'. Borrowed from the pragmatics branch of linguistics, the notion of 'performativity' comes from the verb 'to perform' which means to provoke, to initiate, to constitute, to act so that something happens (Muniesa, 2014). The notion of 'performativity' is transformed into 'performation' to 'insist on the fact that to perform is an action, a work'. The analysis of devices' performation allows a better understanding of market construction and, more generally, the role of economics. 'It is because it intervenes in the drawing-up of socio-technical arrangements that economics, seen in the widest sense, takes part, like all sciences, in setting up power relations. It is because it produces modellings and representations which imply proof tests that [economics] can intervene, with an efficacy to its own, in these arrangements and draw lessons from the experiences that it organises' (Muniesa and Callon, 2009, p. 319, our translation).

UNDERSTANDING THE IMPLEMENTATION AND ROLE OF THE MANAGEMENT TOOL WITHIN AN ORGANISATION

ANT opens up new perspectives with regard to management tools, redefined as socio-technical devices or human/non-human arrangements,

---

[3] The notions of 'device' and 'arrangement' are borrowed from Foucault and Deleuze respectively (Callon et al., 2007).

and proposes a method for understanding them. They appear as black boxes, complex tools, the result of a network composed of a multitude of heterogeneous actants. The ordinary user does not understand these complexities and does not need to know them in order to use the tools.

In order to understand how and why a particular management tool is adopted within an organisation, one must either study the tool as it is being made or 'open the black box' after the implementation phase. It is a question of reconstructing the translation process set up in order to arrive at this result, rediscovering the controversies and negotiations that took place between humans and also between humans and non-humans. It might therefore be interesting to ask a number of questions: What human and non-human actors were present? What were the different points of view? What roles did the actors play? What different technical solutions were possible? What enrolment and interessement actions were performed?

ANT allows a different understanding of the diffusion of management tools and the adoption process. The classic diffusion model is based on the presupposition that the technique does not have to be questioned and that consequently it is the users who have to adapt. In ANT, this is substituted with the interessement model, which, conversely, implies co-construction such that objects and users are united by a number of links. For a management tool to be implemented successfully, it is necessary to find multilateral adaptations, and to search for a compromise implicating humans and non-humans (Briers and Chua, 2001; Muniesa, 2005; Preston et al., 1992).

ANT invites us to look at the role management tools play in an organisation and the ways in which they work. We can thus try to understand the behaviour of buyers in a hypermarket through the study of merchandising devices (shelves, display, positioning of products, etc.) and the way in which these non-humans interact with humans (Barrey, 2007; Cochoy, 2007). One may also choose to focus on the performance indicators most used by organisations to illuminate their dynamics (Boussard, 2001).

Some management tools also seem to extend the range of business companies' activities by facilitating 'action at a distance'. For Latour (1987), this expression denotes the possibility of acting on events, places and people that are not present by inventing means that render them mobile but keep them stable (as 'immutable mobile') (Dechow and Mouritsen, 2005; Preston, 2006; Robson, 1991, 1992). When applied, for example, to software packages for the management of customer relations, this perspective allows us to envisage tools as devices that increase companies' ability to act at a distance, for example via information about clients shared by different actors in the arrangement, remote purchasing, controlling the sales team from a distance, and so on.

Table 5.1 presents a representative sample of works in ANT and the sociology of translation literature.

Table 5.1 *A selection of publications on ANT/sociology of translation*

Authors	Objects studied	Approach to management tools	Most significant contributions
Robson (1991, 1992)	The way in which accounting and social context are interconnected.	Numbers and accounting data are not neutral representations, faithful to reality.	Numbers facilitate certain actions, especially action at a distance. Accounting is the translation into numerical data of the way a company functions. This translation allows an image of the company's

Table 5.1 (*cont.*)

Authors	Objects studied	Approach to management tools	Most significant contributions
			functioning without being present. It is a form of control at a distance.
Preston et al. (1992)	Setting up a budgeting process in British hospitals.	The definition of the tool and its implementation are not two linear, independent and consecutive processes.	The budgeting process is not a clearly defined technique that can be set up in the same way in all organisations. Rather, it is a construct dependent on context and the network to which it belongs.
Briers and Chua (2001)	Setting up a new accounting tool within a company: activity-based costing (ABC).	The management tool is a black box that has to be 'opened' in order to understand how it has been implemented.	Setting up a new management tool is the result of numerous interactions between humans and non-humans. In order to be implemented, a management tool must be sufficiently malleable to adapt to needs and local

Table 5.1 (*cont.*)

Authors	Objects studied	Approach to management tools	Most significant contributions
			constraints, while at the same time it needs to be sufficiently robust to maintain its identity.
McGrath (2002)	The adoption of a tool to help with dispatching in the London Ambulance Service in 1996, after an initial resounding failure in 1992.	The new management tool can be a source of fear and anxiety.	Proposal of the 'golden circle' method, which involves identification of the people directly affected by the new tools in order to enrol them, by acting on their fears and anxieties.
Dechow and Mouritsen (2005)	Analysis of the implementation of Enterprise Resource Planning (ERP) software in two companies.	The management tool acts on users' behaviour and on their way of working.	It is important to understand the technical logic of the ERP chosen: what it allows and especially what it does not.
Preston (2006)	Historic account of a programme to reduce herds of Navajo native inhabitants.	Accounting documents played a determining role in the three main phases of the programme:	The accounting documents played a triple role: they allowed action at a distance when the decision was

Table 5.1 (*cont.*)

Authors	Objects studied	Approach to management tools	Most significant contributions
		decision, implementation, evaluation.	made to implement this programme, they helped during implementation, and they finally served as a justification when the programme failed.
Sarker et al. (2006)	The study of the failure of a business process change (BPC) project.	The management tool plays an active role in the company.	In the classic literature, strategic vision, implication of the top management and communication are often presented as key elements in the success of a BPC project. This study shows the importance of redefining the role of humans and non-humans so that the new network is coherent.
Barrey (2007)	The historic study of the	The management	The concepts of translation,

Table 5.1 (*cont.*)

Authors	Objects studied	Approach to management tools	Most significant contributions
	conditions for the emergence of merchandising in France.	tool can be a means to control profit.	interessement and enrolment help describe the conditions of the emergence of merchandising. They also allow better understanding of how the control of this market device has been a contested issue between suppliers and distributors.
Cochoy (2007)	Study of the role of merchandising devices in purchasing actions in supermarkets.	The management tool plays a mediating role in the commercial relationship.	In a supermarket, merchandising devices like shelves, labels, etc. are actants. They perform the act of purchase.
Cho et al. (2008)	Study of the implementation of an information system in a Swedish hospital.	The management tool can be a source of betrayal.	Technical insufficiencies can slow down the adoption of the tool.

Setting up the Continuous Electronic Quotation System at the Paris Stock Exchange

(Muniesa, 2005, 2007)

Through his study of the implementation of the electronic quotation system at the Paris Bourse, Muniesa became interested in the process that made it possible to introduce a new technical device at the heart of an organisation.

This required a translation process that takes into account, within the new network, the different power relations and the implementation of actions of interessement in order to enrol the different parties concerned.

In the case of the automation at the Bourse, the translation of the interests of the various affected parties was accomplished by maintaining stockbrokers' filter function and by setting up real-time access to information about the order book for bankers. The success of the project depended greatly on stockbrokers, which is why they had to be enrolled. To gain their acceptance, the automation project needed to ensure they would have a lasting role. With this in mind, a complementary tool, the 'filter', was introduced into the new device. When an order did not pass the filter, the stockbroker treated the operation manually and checked that the client wanted to maintain the order. This 'filter' meant that the role of stockbrokers was confirmed and also satisfied the bankers' main concern, which was to have access, at any time, to the same level of information as stockbrokers. Other actions took place that aimed at 'associating' the stockbrokers with the new device in a sustainable manner, such as the organisation of training sessions for those identified as the most influential or even installing computers outside Palais Brongniart, the Bourse building. The training programmes meant that the project's promoters could be used as allies. As for the location of computers in the offices of stockbrokers, and not at the Palais Brongniart, it has favoured the abandonment of old practices and the introduction of new habits.

> The translation process facilitated the introduction of a new technical device within an organisation by retaining some traces of the past (the role of the stockbrokers as filters), removing others (open outcry trading in the Palais Brongniart), and enabling new forms of organisation (continuous quotation, bankers' real-time access to order books).

Summary Sheet (Thesis 7)

The Axioms

Axiom of symmetry: in order to understand society, the symmetry between humans and non-humans, strong and weak, macro and micro, must be re-established. No single point of view should be privileged; no point of view should be censored.

Axiom of controversies: conflicts, tensions and power relations are at the heart of all activity.

Axiom of society being made: society does not constitute a framework inside which the actors mobilise. Society is the transitory result of ongoing actions (Latour, 2005).

Key Concepts

Network: a meta-organisation bringing together humans and non-humans that are in relation to one another.

Actant: designates something that acts within a network, has weight, and may be human, non-human or a human/non-human arrangement.

Translation: the process by which the network is made intelligible, that is, giving a role to each human and non-human within it to put an end to arguments. There are four stages to this translation process: problematisation, interessement, enrolment and the mobilisation/extension of the network.

Spokesperson for the allies: designates the actants involved in the network's negotiations.

Action at a distance: possibility of acting on events, places or people not present, by inventing means that render them mobile, keep them stable and are combinable (Latour, 1987, p. 223). For example, cartography is a way of acting at a distance: 'By coding every sighting of any land in longitude and latitude (two figures) and by sending this code back, the shape of the sighted land may be redrawn by those who have not sighted it' (Latour, 1987, p. 224).

Performation: 'The process whereby socio-technical arrangements are enacted, to constitute so many ecological niches within and between which statements and models circulate and are true or at least enjoy a high degree of verisimilitude. This constantly renewed process of performation encompasses expression, self-fulfilling prophecies, prescription and performance' (Callon, 2006, p. 25).

Rules of the Method

Principle of general analysis: thinking of objects, actors and society as the temporary result of a network.

Posture: re-establishing symmetry between all actants (humans and non-humans) within the network. Considering their actions and their discourses in the same way.

Procedure: either studying the management tool 'as it is being made' or 'reopening the black box' after the implementation phase. In both cases, it is important to study closely the arguments and different stages in the translation process.

Features of Speech

Black box: designates a complex object that results from a network composed of a multitude of heterogeneous actants, where the ordinary user does not know the functioning and has no need to know it in order to make use of it.

Centres of calculation: designates the place within the network where knowledge is accumulated and decisions are made (Latour, 1987, p. 232).

To punctualise: designates the work done within the network so that all the actants remain firmly linked and work as one (Latour, 1987, p. 235).

Map and territory: expresses the difference between the representation (the map) and what is represented (the territory), which tend to be confused in some interpretations of objectivity.

A Few Authors and Key Texts

Starting with the works of Latour and Callon, see Cochoy (1999, 2007) and Muniesa (2007) in economic sociology, Briers and Chua (2001), Dechow and Mouritsen (2005) and Robson (1991, 1992), in management studies.

Thesis 8:

The Tool Is Nothing outside the Activity System

This thesis is based on Cultural-Historical Activity Theory (CHAT), developed by the Soviet school of psychology. In the 1920s, Lev Vygotski (1896–1934)[4] proposed a reformulation of psychological theory along Marxist lines. From Marx he borrowed the principle of the transformation of self and of mankind through material and language tools, which he considered a major psychological fact. Social factors play a central role in this theory: the genesis of the psyche happens through activities carried out with others and the technical mediation of these activities. To analyse an activity is to analyse a system that includes the individual, the material or conceptual tools the individual uses, the individual's relations with the surrounding community, the product the individual intends to make and the interactions and transformations that happen, all the while maintaining a global vision of the system. In this case, the tool has become an instrument representing what is used in the transformation process.

FROM TOOL TO INSTRUMENT

The originality of Vygotski's position, and that of those who continued his work, in particular his pupil Leontiev (1978) who extended the theory by considering the individual in a collectivity, consists of seizing on the notion of the instrument to widen the field. Similarly, human action on nature is carried out through the mediation of the tool, which is an intermediary between the organism and the physical world. The action of individuals on their and others' behaviour is mediated by a system of signs that Vygotski termed 'psychological

---

[4] For a synthetic overview of his work, see Vygotski (2012).

tools'. This is a very broad notion in which he includes language, different forms of calculation, patterns, diagrams, plans, etc.

Continuing Marx's line, which states that the means used to work modify 'the natural nature' of man, Vygotski states that their appropriation restructures the development of the psyche. Instruments are therefore not just simple auxiliaries that maintain the human psyche by leaving mental functions unchanged. On the contrary, they transform its development and therefore have a central role. But they are nothing outside the activity system. They only produce effects via an internal reconstruction by the subject which supposes social cooperation.

Vygotski was key to advancing a developmental psychology that is not restricted to childhood, unlike Piaget (1952) to whom he is often compared, and he established a new perspective on activity. This theory is applied in various fields (psychology of education, psychology of work, ergonomics, didactics, information technology and so on). Having strongly influenced modern psychology,[5] this theoretical framework has excited some interest among researchers in organisation sciences and its application has been extended to the analysis of management problems and understanding the dynamics of work. It is currently the inspiration for two approaches of management tools.

Like the pragmatic theory of habits with which CHAT shares important convergences, as Lorino (2018) has pointed out, the theory of activity approaches social situations in a dialogical and processual perspective. Management tools are not considered in isolation, but through the mediations they establish, acting in the same way as architecture does: 'Architectural instruments, such as building architecture, enterprise resource planning (ERP), and accounting models are "architectural" (they frame collective activity) because they are

---

[5] Jérôme Bruner, American psychologist, the pioneer of the cognitive revolution who was inspired by the work of Vygotski, was the first to attempt the partial translation of *Thought and Language*.

"architextual" (they convey narrative architextures and instantiate them in day-to-day activity)' (Lorino, 2013, p. 63).

INDIVIDUAL ACTIVITY MEDIATED

The first approach stems from the work of activity-based ergonomics, which emphasises cognition as opposed to the traditional physical and physiological ergonomics of *human factors* (Montmollin, 1995).

This approach is detailed by Rabardel and centred on the psychological subject (Béguin and Rabardel, 2000; Rabardel, 2001, 2002, 2003; Rabardel and Bourmaud, 2003). It covers a conception of the tool that is closely linked to that of learning processes. To use a tool, one must appropriate it and this appropriation brings about a change in the user. That kind of learning allows the eventual resolution of problems or autonomous production. Therefore it influences the subject but also changes the structure of the activity and may even give rise to new goals to be met. The tool participates in shaping the aims of the subjects who use it, because it carries in itself implicit goals and a cultural heritage incorporated by its designers.

Rabardel was devoted to broadening the conceptualisation of the instrument, underlining the fact that the artefact (material or symbolic) – anything casually termed a 'tool' – does not constitute the whole instrument. To be an instrument, it would require arrangements and plans for its use that organise the action. These arrangements are either specific to the subjects or the result of their appropriation of social schemes. Rabardel has also proposed modelling activity situations using instruments, the Instrument-Mediated Activity Situations (IAS) model (see Figure 5.1).

Some ergonomic research on the management of dynamic environments and aimed at optimising existing work systems, such as in urban transport systems, is very directly interested in performance and the indicators that report on it. An example is the work of Zanarelli (2003). Building on an observation of activities in two professions of regulating the Paris Metro (head of control at the

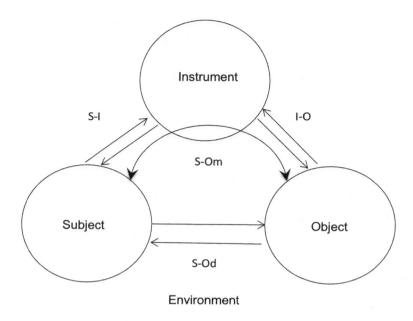

FIGURE 5.1 **The IAS model: the characteristic triad of instrument-mediated activity situations**
Note: The IAS model adds interactions mediated by the instrument (S–Om) to direct subject–object (S–Od), subject–instrument (S–I) and instrument–object (I–O) interactions.

centralised command centre and departures manager at a terminus), she proposes ergonomic recommendations for the development of the organisation but also performance indicators to evaluate the regulation strategies in both roles.

In parallel, instrument-mediated activity has recently emerged in management sciences (Lorino, 2013; Teulier and Lorino, 2005) as a unit for the analysis of management practices. This incorporates a set of ideas that contribute to rethinking the appropriation of management tools. This makes it possible to go beyond the opposition between design and use as the design continues with usage (Mitev and Vaujany, 2013; Vaujany, 2006), but also to mark the conditions and limits of the transfer of tools from one organisational context to another, and particularly revise claims about the universality of tools that pilot performance.[6]

ACTIVITY AND COLLECTIVE WORK

The second approach is more global and applicable at the level of the whole organisation (Engeström, 1996, 2001; Engeström and Middleton, 1998). For Engeström, activity is collective from the outset, because the individual is not isolated; the individual is part of a community that brings together all of the subjects who share the same object of activity. Applying Vygotski's ideas to the study of interactions and communication at work, Engeström, who is the leader of a very active line of research, has attempted to broaden and develop activity theory by taking a more direct interest in collective activity and the way in which it is structured. This has led him to develop the initial triangle (subject–artefact–object), by introducing new concepts that allow the analysis to be extended.

The individual is not an isolated *subject* but is part of a *community* that represents all the subjects who share the same *object* of activity (the task to be done, the goal to be reached). The individual's activity cannot be described outside this context. When new members arrive in a community, they have to appropriate some distributed knowledge. Relations between individuals and community are regulated by *rules* (norms, conventions, shared work practices) that are implicit or explicit and that maintain and regulate actions and interactions inside the system. The activity is carried out by means of *instruments* according to a *division of labour* (distribution of actions among the subjects) and is part of a *production*, real or abstract, that has to be achieved (Figure 5.2).

Ardichvili (2003, p. 11), applied this model to a collaborative adult education programme and obtained the following analytical breakdown:

---

[6] See Benzerafa's (2007) thesis on the implementation of the *Balanced Scorecard* in state administrations.

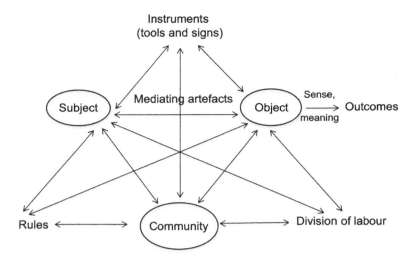

FIGURE 5.2 **Basic structure of an activity**

- *Object*: the area of practice in which participants in the training course try to develop their skills (for example, a new process of product development).
- *Subjects*: participants in the training programme, learners and a variety of other individuals or groups depending on the object under study.
- *Rules*: codes by which the learning and the application of knowledge are carried out.
- *Instruments*: conceptual models and learning methods (for example a product/market analytical grid used during an internship in the development of new products).
- *Community*: the extended learning network, including subjects as well as those who have access to the knowledge produced by training or who interact with the subjects.
- *Outcomes*: not only the individual learnings but also the associated organisational knowledge about new modes of learning for people to be trained in the future.
- *Division of labour*: in the most usual case, those responsible for the programme are distinguished from those being trained. The latter are responsible not only for acquiring knowledge but also for generating new knowledge and sharing it with other members of the organisation.

Activity theory gave Ardichvili a basis for the organisation of pedagogical situations. The experience that he investigated is structured around business ideas borrowed from real life and made available by several *start-up entrepreneurs*. The aim for the learners who work in a team is to think up propositions that would make these ideas viable and to evaluate their feasibility. Engeström's model has made it possible to analyse the dynamics of the social interactions in a team learning activity.

Table 5.2 presents a representative sample of works in activity theory.

Table 5.2 *A selection of publications on activity theory*

Authors (reference discipline)	Approach to the tool	Objects studied	Most significant contributions
Mediatised individual work			
Rabardel (2001, 2002, 2003), Béguin and Rabardel (2000) (Cognitive ergonomics)	The tool (artefact) does not constitute the whole of the instrument.	The interactions between instrument, subject and object.	Duality of the instrument: • a material or symbolic artefact; • one or multiple associated plans for use.
Zanarelli (2003) (Cognitive ergonomics)	The instrument as an organiser of the activity based on the operators' conceptualisations.	The activity of regulating the Paris Metro in relation to situations of disturbance.	Interpretation of the management of residual traffic in terms of instruments. Showing that several instruments can ensure the

Table 5.2 (*cont.*)

Authors (reference discipline)	Approach to the tool	Objects studied	Most significant contributions
			same function, for example the evaluation of punctuality.
Collective work			
Engeström, (1996, 2001), Engeström and Middleton (1998) (Psychology)	The instrument as a social construction and mediator of multiple interactions	Mediated collective activity	The tool both allows and limits the activity.
Lejeune and Harvey (2007) (Management sciences)		The Quebec health system in a reform context (application of the law on agencies developing local health service networks and social services).	An alternative to the re-engineering of processes (radical reconception of work) by a collaborative approach, better anchored in the situations.
Ardichvili (2003) (Management sciences)		Dynamics of the interactions in an MBA course for adults in employment.	Renewal of the conception of training programmes.

The Limits of the Use of the Balanced Scorecard in Public Administrations

(Benzerafa, 2007)

In the application of public policies, public administrations increasingly apply management tools used by commercial organisations. This is the case of balanced scorecards (or BSC) developed by Kaplan and Norton (1992) and seen as a management system designed for the clarification and formalisation of company strategies. In Rabardel's work the author finds a grid for decoding this tool, particularly its evolution, the use for which it is intended and its use in the public organisations studied.

The observations carried out reaffirm the contingency principle of management tools; there are almost as many BSC models as departments that have adopted them. Nevertheless, the diversity in the results cannot be explained by the contingency principle alone because different adaptations of this tool have been noted in the same organisation. This diversity can be explained by the action of the people who intervene in the choice of the tool and in the appropriation process of the artefact, which Rabardel calls the 'instrumental genesis'.

Summary Sheet (Thesis 8)

The Axioms

Axiom of the transforming nature of the tool: through the learning that it brings about, the tool allows the subject to realise the object of his/her activity. At the same time the tool participates in shaping goals for those who use it because, implicitly or explicitly, it carries the aims fixed by its designers.

Axiom of tool–organisation interaction: management tools and organisations – in the sense of organising actions – are entangled. Collective learnings are forged through their interaction.

Axiom of the dual nature of the instrument: any instrument is made up, on the one hand, of an artefact (cognitive, psychological or semiotic) and, on the other, of schemes that can be defined as the organisers of the subjects' actions.

Key Concepts

Activity system: a socially organised set of individual or collective actors, objects of work to which they confront each other, and tools that mediate their relations by allowing actors to act upon objects.

Artefacts: term used by anthropologists to designate technical, material or symbolic objects; a table, a computer, or an accounting standard are all artefacts.

Instrument: the instrument contains an indissociable material or symbolic *artefact* (allowing it to act upon the object), and a *method of use* (in the form of diagrams for use). The instrument is what the artefact becomes when it is used in work situations by users: it can be activated by being used and in return it can modify users' work.

Rules of the Method

General principle of analysis: the interactions between the different components of the activity system must be analysed.

Posture: anthropocentric perspective in which humankind occupies a central place in the relation with techniques.

Procedure: describes, by analysis and/or intervention, the processes of instrumental genesis (transformation of artefacts into instruments).

Features of Speech

Mediation: the tool marks mediation between the human entity and the environment. It allows the transformation of the object (pragmatic mediation), but also its knowledge (epistemic mediation). What is more, it facilitates the achievement of common goals (collaborative mediation). 'There is no activity without instruments.'

A Few Authors and Key Texts

Engeström (1996, 2001), Lorino (2013), Rabardel (2001, 2002, 2003).

Thesis 9:

The Tool as a Language Being

This thesis is part of the narrative paradigm of the study of organisations, which postulates that if management claims to belong to the world of decision-making then it belongs mainly to the world of words (Boje, 1991; Brown, 1990; Czarniawska-Joerges and Joerges, 1988; Girin, 1990). The emphasis is on the fundamentally communicative dimension of organisations and especially on narrating events in daily life, or storytelling. Narration is an effective message (easily read, understood and remembered) that presents a certain ambiguity. According to Brown (1990) making a story of something reduces uncertainty and fosters commitment from the members of the organisation by giving a meaning to their experience, situating it in the framework of the organisation's culture. However, for Boje (1991), narration is not limited to the production of meaning; it also constitutes a means of intervention by which managers fabricate narratives that serve as supportive arguments when they undertake or justify an action.

At first, these ideas did not seem too disturbing to either practitioners or scientists (Giroux and Marroquin, 2005). However, when applied to management tools, they remind us once more of the teaching of the history of techniques, according to which the vocal production of words and the manual production of objects are humans' two great systems of expression. Indeed, in *Gesture and Speech*, Leroi-Gourhan (1993) points out that language and tools appeared simultaneously. The dematerialisation of the technical object has simply continued the progressive exteriorisation of tools, which are no longer linked to the body except by language. It is easy to note, even today, that there has been no technological transformation without accompanying modifications in language. This explains the attempts to establish reversibility between the tool as language and language as a tool, as they are both mobilised in communication activities.

In the functionalist approach, words and the written texts that carry them are seen as simple means in the service of the transmission of information. The research discussed here disrupts this perspective. A first strand shows that things written at work, above and beyond the basic functions of recording and transmitting information, constitute acts that produce effects on the organisation. A second strand locates management tools in interactional processes of the creation of meaning. For a third strand, the management tool presents itself as a text, shaping the representations of its users.

Compared to the positivist tradition, the publications scrutinised (see Table 5.3 below) consider management tools as informational artefacts, fully justifying an analysis that does not reduce the value of the tool to its operative role.[7]

WRITTEN TEXT AS A MANAGEMENT TOOL

Many written texts produced or used by an organisation have the character of tools. In this line of thinking the work carried out by the French Language and Labour Network (Borzeix and Fraenkel, 2001), which began in 1986 and included sociologists, linguists, psychologists and managers, has analysed the uses and functions of language in organisations in order to reassess the relations between communication, cognition and action.

One of the fields of study, considerably enriched by Béatrice Fraenkel, is specifically about writing at work. It is firmly rooted in the notion of performativity. Initially developed by J. L. Austin, the author of *How To Do Things with Words* (1975), the notion of performativity was met with great success in the social sciences (Denis, 2006). Performativity helps to show that managerial statements, far from being reflections of a reality or propositions that need to undergo a test of validity, are acts that orient behaviour. There are

---

[7] Lorino (2002) suggests a pragmatic and semiotic theory of management instruments.

Table 5.3 *A selection of publications of the discursive approaches*

Authors	Approach to the tool	Objects of study	Most significant contributions
Writing as a management tool			
Fraenkel (1995)	Traceability as a function of writing at work.	Writing at work as 'writing acts' the succession of which gives insights for organising action and following up on it.	Apart from their function for informing and recording, writing acts have a performative function (responsibility imposed by the writing and organisation of the action).
Delcambre (2009)	The activity of evaluation, in a case study of social and medico-social establishments.	Activity of dealing with the information system imposed by the evaluators.	Beyond the technical means imposed by law, evaluation appears as a succession of two language acts: collection of information and argumentation for evaluation.
Cochoy et al. (1998)	ISO 9000 insurance quality standards.	The systematic documentation of work practices seen as a tool that guides behaviours at work.	The quality assurance system puts each actor in a dilemma between obtaining a written

Table 5.3 (*cont.*)

Authors	Approach to the tool	Objects of study	Most significant contributions
			recognition of their responsibilities and the emergence of a possibility of increased control arising from written documentation of work practices.

The management tool as a support for sensemaking

Authors	Approach to the tool	Objects of study	Most significant contributions
Fincham (2002), Fisher and Howell (2004)	The process contributing to the success or failure of the introduction of new technologies.	The tool as an element of organisational change, a factor of uncertainty and confusion.	The meaning given to the introduction of new technologies is a social construction resulting from a process of interpretation.
Pereira (2002), Scott and Barrett (2005), Seligman (2006)	The problems posed by the adoption of a new tool.	The tool as an object in the appropriation process.	Identification of socio-cognitive factors influencing the adoption of a new tool.

The management tool as text

Authors	Approach to the tool	Objects of study	Most significant contributions
Davidson (1999)	The organisational and social	The tool as a support for mental images	The suggestive metaphors permeating the

Table 5.3 (*cont.*)

Authors	Approach to the tool	Objects of study	Most significant contributions
	implications of the metaphorical notion of data warehousing.	fashioning the interpretation of 'reality'.	conception of new information and communication technologies have implications for the meaning and application of the data used and for relations between the actors concerned.
Fauré and Gramaccia (2006)	The budgetary process in a large construction firm.	Management tools help to structure organisations via communication processes.	The language of numbers exercises a pragmatic influence in organisations through a work of enunciation around the authorised and legitimate definition of the calculation.
Lorino (2018)	The theoretical status of the tool.	Management tools as semiotic mediation.	Implementation is design: the tool is a text that writes itself in the use that is made of it.

circumstances where 'writing is doing' (Fraenkel, 2007). In law, a signature is obviously a performative act, not simply a straightforward graphic sign. But in management, many other pieces of writing, from a simple checklist to a note from the director, or a balanced scorecard can hold the same power and constitute acts that modify the course of events. This is the case with evaluation, which, according to Delcambre (2009), is a 'communicative act of writing' that blends analysis, argumentation and a comparison of points of view.

Likewise, Cochoy et al. (1998) study the application of ISO 9000 quality assurance standards in a company and show that these norms reorder the state of affairs in the firm. These standards require the company's management process to be described in detail. Thus, they help the client and the auditor – each point described is checked during an audit – pinpoint changes and almost always cause change in the way the firm functions. It is not the norm on its own that structures the action but the state of relations that it engenders by creating a 'writing dynamic'.

THE MANAGEMENT TOOL AS A SUPPORT FOR SENSEMAKING

In the English-speaking world the psychologist Karl E. Weick is recognised as having had considerable influence on the study of organisational communication, which he conceives as an action and a relation that create reality. The author of *The Social Psychology of Organizing* (Weick, 1979) might not have dealt directly with management tools but his work on sensemaking (Weick, 1995) has inspired considerable research in this field (David, 2006). For Weick, social practices take the form of structures because they feed the dominant discourses. Naming or describing some elements drawn from the environment (and thus creating them) are processes that Weick designates as sensemaking. In an environment that is often chaotic and ambiguous, sensemaking allows one to organise the chaos.

Language plays a central role in this process. It emerges as a medium for sensemaking during the course of collective action when a series of organisational situations and events is translated into words, when action is captured in written or spoken texts, or even through reading, writing, conversation and publishing. Situations where there is communication between individuals are crucial moments for the articulation of cognitive schemes and the production of collective meaning.

Weick's theoretical infrastructure has been used to broaden understanding of the success or failure of new information and communication technologies. There have been numerous failures in IT projects, so it is important to understand better what contributes to such negative results. Such research on information systems is generally concentrated on the use made of these technologies and on the reactions arising from users. Researchers who base their work on this theoretical framework are interested in the interpretative process that accompanies the introduction of new technologies (Fincham, 2002; Fisher and Howell, 2004; Scott and Barrett, 2005).

Other authors have tried to give an account of the methods of appropriating technological innovation (Pereira, 2002; Seligman, 2006). Turning their backs on the evolutionist models of classical authors, like Everett Rogers (1995), which were based on the idea of a linear dissemination of innovations, these authors see the adoption of new technologies as a process of giving meaning and analyse it starting from the sensemaking properties described by Weick (1995).

THE MANAGEMENT TOOL AS TEXT

It was particularly Roland Barthes (1972) who extended the idea of text to horizons beyond literary works. With Barthes, the concepts of the object and the relations with objects took a linguistic turn at the end of the 1950s. The theory of text states that a text works and makes us work. This Barthesian perspective can be applied to management tools, particularly to accounting documents, that can be analysed as a system of signs including a wide range of communication methods (figures, tables, graphs, commentaries) organised according to a language. There is no shortage of works showing

that semiotic analysis helps in the reconceptualisation of accounting communication.[8]

As a fixed text, the management tool maintains and disseminates a collective representation. Relations between management tools
can thus be considered as conversations between different types of
text, in a space of meaning (intertextuality) that constitutes the organisational discourse at the crossroads of different texts. From this point
of view, it is useful to understand how the conditions for the production (writing) and for the reception (reading) of these texts help the
construction of a coherent discourse (Detchessahar and Journé, 2007).

To deepen the understanding of management tools as texts also
implies analysing their rhetoric and the stylistic features that distinguish them, particularly metaphors. Whether they are superficial or
deeply rooted in the socially constructed reality, metaphors are present
in texts about the conception of information technologies and their use.
For example, the desktop metaphor has ever since inspired the conception and development of computer software and hardware. Metaphors
provide a useful device for promoting access to innovations but their
use can also raise false expectations about how real IT systems are
operated.

Recourse to metaphors can have undesirable effects as Davidson
(1999) shows in his study on the metaphor of 'data warehouses'. This
notion conjures up a physical place where neutral data might be
available after having been collected and stocked in an electronic
format. The total amount of data would constitute a unique version
of economic reality. For Davidson, this metaphor suggests unrealistic
expectations about the results of such warehousing. Data cannot be
handled as physical entities. They only have value at the moment
when they are interpreted by users. Moreover, there are different
versions of 'reality' and most often also different information systems
to represent them.

---

[8] Davison (2011) studies works of accounting research that claim to be in the
Barthesian tradition.

Skills-Management Tools as Discourse

(Detchessahar and Journé, 2007)

The authors studied the case of a factory within a large pharmaceutical company that introduced skills-management tools. In this organisation, which was undergoing a transformation, quality- and efficiency-related management tools (lean production, six sigma, ABC method, charter of values, etc.) fed into an organisational discourse centred on the company.

The management tool is seen as a script directing the actors' moves with a view to achieve better performance. Operators and first-level managers interpret the tool as consistent with other managerial instruments: this leads them to use the new skills-related management tool as a means of remuneration and motivation. But the tool was not relevant to just this one single logic. For example, the logic of polyvalence, also present in the tool, was ignored because it was in dissonance with other management tools.

The analysis of the case shows that the effectiveness of a management tool depends on the way in which the actors read and interpret the text that the tool conveys. Also, among the multiple dimensions of the skills-management tool users only retained those that echoed texts that were already existing and read within the organisation.

Summary Sheet (Thesis 9)

The Axioms

Communicative nature of the tool: a management tool cannot be understood outside its place in the flow of communication.

The tool as a narrative story-maker: the management tool carries narratives or accounts that contribute to sensemaking, manipulation of symbols and control of power. These accounts help to model representations and orient action.

Textuality of the management tool: management tools are texts that participate in the construction of organisational discourse.

Key Concepts

Organisational discourse: a dominant and normative system of statements defining the best ways to behave and to think in the organisation

(Phillips et al., 2004). When participating in organisational discourse, management tools relate to the creation of meaning and the control of power.

Sensemaking: the meaning given by individuals to situations is constructed in action, even retrospectively. Organisations also rebuild narratives after the event. Sensemaking constitutes a social process that aims at collectively reducing the ambiguity of a situation. The management tool supports the creation of meaning.

Intertextuality: a space of signification created by the collection of texts carried by the management tools.

Performativity: characteristic of management tools as they are not limited to representing the world but also help to produce it. For example, a performance indicator does not just describe a fact but also is a constitutive element of this fact.

Rules of the Method

General principle of analysis: management tools are bearers of narratives, which must be revealed, in competition with each other.

Posture: narrative approach, consisting of analysing management tools as narratives and cultural productions in their organisational and social dimensions.

Procedure: studying narrative structures, either as texts – a series of statements – or as acts of communication, in relation to the situations in which they are inscribed.

Features of Speech

Storytelling (constructing a narrative): narratives as the vectors of creation and dissemination of meaning.

Traceability: possibility of finding the origin and history of an article or an operation by means of recorded traces that are associated with them.

A Few Authors and Key Texts

Borzeix and Fraenkel (2001), Lorino (2002), Weick (1979, 1995).

Thesis 10:
The Effects of the Tool Are Conditioned by What Actors Do

The theory of the strategic actor that was developed by Crozier and Friedberg (Crozier, 1964; Crozier and Friedberg, 1980) constitutes the foundation of this thesis. It states that action is not the result of determinisms – whether economic, technical, cultural or others – but arises from the strategic intentions of social actors who aim to achieve certain goals. The origins of this thesis are found in American research on decision-making in organisational contexts. This work was led by Barnard (1938), Simon (1947) and especially March and Simon (1958). These authors renewed the theory of organisations from a perspective that brought together the study of human relations and a rationalist approach.[9] Crozier took up Barnard's idea that the acceptance of organisational life is the result of the calculation of the advantages and disadvantages linked to different organisational behaviours. He also borrows from Simon the concept of bounded rationality: the actor displays rational behaviour but this rationality is bounded by the array of choices that the actor's environment and ability to handle information allow. Therefore, the actor will decide for the first option that is perceived as satisfactory.

Many of the strategic actor theory analyses were carried out in the Centre for the Sociology of Organisations (CSO) which Crozier set up in Paris at the beginning of the 1960s. These researchers do not ignore technique but consider that it has very little direct influence on organisations' functioning, even when organisational changes they study are built around management tools. This research stream highlights management tools but does not put them at the heart of the analysis nor does it

---

[9] Crozier, in the preface to the French edition of March and Simon (1958).

question their content. From this perspective, management tools are relegated to being part of the formal system and its role is relativised. However, it is not impossible to extend Crozier's analytical framework to the properties of the tool itself, as several researchers have attempted to do.[10]

THE RELATIVISATION OF THE FORMAL SYSTEM

For the most part, proponents of strategic actor theory were reluctant to recognise the structuring nature of tools, particularly because, from the outset, they had had to break with the school of structural contingency and the technological neo-determinism that accompanied it.[11] Starting from the idea that no rationalisation can really bring order to an organisation, these authors rather tend to consider tools as toys manipulated by social actors.

This thesis offers an analysis of the instrumentation of management that seems to be subject to actors' strategies. At best the management tool is, through the rules it incorporates, a power resource – both at the level of its formulation and in its uses – in the service of the interests of a group of actors who manipulate their environment to impose themselves on it.

CSO researchers looked at the power games organised around tools, considered as elements of a formal system, and at the cultural, ideological and institutional factors that influence the behaviours of those involved in management practices. As an element of the formal system, the management tool, like formal rules, is only imperfectly applied. It is distorted and skewed. Opposition between actors always reorients the way it is used.

---

[10] Pavé (1989) shows that although information technology does not determine the way social systems are governed it gives rise to a particular way of thinking, hyperfunctionalism, which refers to a streamlined and rationalised reality. See also Justin (2004) for whom actors' strategies are crystallised in the tools of control.

[11] The critique of the structural contingency theory is the theme of chapter 4 in Crozier and Friedberg (1980).

For these researchers, the specialists of different management tools (computer scientists, management controllers, process engineers, etc.) have a tendency to conceive the future of organisations on the basis of hypotheses that serve their interests as actors. And however advanced it may be, the technology upon which these tools are based still remains dependent on the verdict of its users. The formal structure is opposed by the 'concrete system of action', where role-plays are acted out by actors who are caught up in power struggles to maintain the margins of uncertainty that give them power and to retain mastery over their work.

Cultural analysis, considered by Crozier and Friedberg (1980) as 'the other side of strategic analysis', was developed by Sainsaulieu (1977), who marked this discipline with his works on professional identity. Following on from Talcott Parsons (1951), who postulated that the cognitive evolution of individuals can be influenced by their social environment, Sainsaulieu insisted that organised work has a profound influence on mental structures and plays a role in the formation of professional identities. The direction of this research could have led Sainsaulieu to take an interest in management tools but there are very few traces of such an interest, except in his analysis of the relation between the interpersonal and the formal in offices.

CHANGE RATHER THAN FUNCTIONING

Researchers following strategic actor theory are probably more interested (especially in recent developments) in change than in functioning (Bernoux, 2004b; Dupuy, 2004). Thus it is through the analysis of change that these sociologists of organisations encounter management tools.

The introduction of a new tool can modify the balance of power via the transparency effects that it produces. It can also be associated with the production of new rules of play, which affect actors' ability to control, to maintain or seize power. However, actors can resist these rules, refuse and transform them. The rationalising effect of instruments is undermined by actors' strategies and the areas of uncertainty that they manage to preserve or reconstitute. The results that the tools produce are therefore distorted. Management tools can be used strategically, as much in the change strategies of the promoters of the tools as in the possible strategies of circumvention.

The Crozierian perspective on organisations, extended into a sociology of change, argues against the idea that actors' autonomy disappears progressively under the pressure of new management tools (such as ISO norms, enterprise resource planning, just-in-time, total quality management, etc.).[12] It underlines actors' autonomy in organisations, their ability to refuse these tools, resist, transform, change or adapt them. This perspective insists on the fact that change is only effective when actors find meaning in the actions they undertake.

TOOL AND/OR RULES?

At the end of the 1980s, the theory of social regulation advanced by Reynaud (1979, 1988, 1997) extended the sociological analysis of power relations by renewing the opposition between formal and informal organisation. What he calls 'social regulation', considered as the process of producing and transforming rules, combines two seemingly contradictory and complex phenomena that coexist in organisations: control and autonomy. The theory examines the dynamics of rule creation engendered by these phenomena. Social regulations aim at control, but actors never let themselves become totally imprisoned in control frameworks. Their response to these constraints is to make claims, negotiate and act. Actors exercise their autonomy by gradually gaining margins for manoeuvre or by negotiating.

This theory allows the management tool to be conceptualised not as a purely technical object with a material shape, but also as a social object, assembling rules that aim to coordinate and guide action. The theory also supplies a guide for analysing implementation in more detail, taking into account actors' reactions when confronted

---

[12] Bernoux (2004a) in particular defends this position.

with the rules that accompany management tools, as well as the negotiations that lead to the construction of new social orders.

Table 5.4 presents a list of representative works in strategic actor theory.

Table 5.4 *A selection of publications on strategic actor theory*

Authors	Approach to the tool	Objects of study	Most significant contributions
Balle and Peaucelle (1972)	The social dimensions of the activity of computerised design.	Technique as a regulatory element in organisational transformations.	Computer scientists tend to design organisations on the basis of presumptions that serve their interests as actors.
Pavé (1989, 1993), Pichault (1990)	Computerised management systems.	The management tool as a coercive arrangement of the world of work.	Technology submitted to the verdict of its users. The logic of negotiation wins over logical reason.
Christiansen and Skaerbaek (1997)	Setting up budgetary control at the Royal Danish Theatre.	Implementing a management tool to induce actors' strategies and conflicts.	The political perspective allows the understanding and anticipation of the behaviour of different groups implicated in or concerned by the setting up of a new accounting system.
Segrestin (1997, 2004)	Major projects in managerial innovation.	The management tool as an element of a project for organisational change.	In order to be disseminated, a managerial innovation needs a debate between actors and agreement on the resulting arrangements.

Table 5.4 (*cont.*)

Authors	Approach to the tool	Objects of study	Most significant contributions
Pichault and Nizet (2000)	HRM practices.	Tensions between desire for transparency and attempts to maintain control.	HRM devices are inscribed in the organisational arrangements that change through actors' conflict.
Reynaud (1979, 2001), Havard and Krohmer (2008)	Skills-based management	An analysis in terms of rules and regulation.	A proposition is acceptable if the addressee agrees to treat it as a rule of conduct.
Bernoux (2004a, 2004b)	Determinants of change.	Management tools leave actors freedom of interpretation. If they try to direct behaviour, they cannot impose it.	If the actors do not appropriate the tools proposed, change cannot take place.
Justin (2004)	Management control tools.	Management tools and economic agents are linked by a use relation.	Control tools are complex objects in which actors' strategies are encoded.
Bernard (2008)	The itinerary of an indicator into a management unit of public forests.	Indicators as emerging instruments in management situations.	Actors mobilise around an indicator, measure themselves, and find ways to cooperate without the indicator directly prescribing practices.

The Paradoxes of Quality Norms

(Segrestin, 1997)

At first sight, quality norms of the ISO 9000 kind seem to be devices for standardisation, which is achieved by reinforcing work directives and by limiting the autonomy of the personnel involved in the codification of the company's know-how in work procedures. However, the importance of employees' participation in setting up the quality assurance undertaking must not be forgotten.

These international norms, which are believed to standardise functioning, in fact, contribute towards the differentiation of firms among themselves since the question of their appropriation by the actors is posed. ISO standards reduce recipients' uncertainties relative to the acceptability of certain principles of operation. But, in parallel, they increase the uncertainties relating to the conditions of its implementation and, because of this, of its effects. Ultimately, quality norms only take shape in local configurations that give them a concrete existence.

Summary Sheet (Thesis 10)

The Axioms

Axiom of homo strategicus: the social actor is an opportunist and adapts to circumstances by adopting a strategic behaviour, determined by a desire to appear unpredictable to other actors. This is done to maintain or increase the actor's power. The actor is never deprived of all means, nor totally constrained by management tools.

Axiom of innovation and power: the introduction of a new tool causes a redistribution of power, which, even when this is only minimal, arouses resistance from those who see their power threatened.

Axiom of the tool as an opportunity for playing with the rules: the management tool is not interesting in itself, but only insofar as it constrains the actors' actions and becomes the object of games between actors. The strategies that arise around the tool rely on regulations that are also the object of play and negotiations.

Key Concepts

The social actor: whether an individual or a group, the actor is relatively free. The actor can play around with the role, allowing some latitude with regard to the rules that the organisation has laid down and the management devices that transmit them.

The stakes: what an actor thinks will be gained (positive stake) or lost (negative stake) in case of change.

Power: power basically lies in exchange relations and interactions. The resources of power are knowledge of the rules of functioning, skills, mastering relations with the environment and mastering communication. All these things are more or less inscribed in the uses of management tools and the tools themselves.

The zone of uncertainty: every organisation is subject to many uncertainties (economic, technical, social). Whoever has the faculty of mastering them has power over the actor for whom they are important. The general requirements that come with the uses of management tools generate zones of uncertainty in which the actors obtain a margin for manoeuvre.

The system of concrete action: between interdependent actors whose interests may be divergent or even contradictory, there is a set of relations, in the shape of informal but nevertheless structured games. This system is different from the formal system and explains better the actual functioning of the organisation.

Rules of the Method

Principle of general analysis: in order to understand how collective actions are constructed and the roles that management tool play in them, one must analyse the concrete situations as they are perceived by the actors.

Posture: sociology of organised action which postulates a rational and intentional subject who pursues her/his own goals and who primarily seeks to seize opportunities rather than to maximise personal gains.

Procedure: starting with actors' testimonies about the process under study in order to rebuild, via crosschecks and progressive approximations, the strategies pursued, the stakes they embody, and the system of relations (power structure) in which they are inscribed.

Features of Speech

Misappropriation or neutralisation of tools.

A Few Authors and Key Texts

Various titles by Bernoux (2004a, 2004b), Crozier (1964), Crozier and Friedberg (1980), Dupuy (2004), Pavé (1989, 1993), Pichault (1990), Pichault and Nizet (2000), Reynaud (1979, 1997), Segrestin (1997, 2004).

PART III Synthesis

The first part of the book laid the foundations of a general understanding of management tools: by tracing the evolution of thought about technique in general, and management techniques in particular. The second part presented different approaches and research currents that have focused on management tools and which, put together, reveal them as 'total social facts' (Mauss, 1966), i.e., facts that simultaneously reflect the expressions of all sorts of social institutions and have a number of moral, political, legal and economic implications.

This literature shows the sociological thickness of objects that guide decisions and organise action on a daily basis. But it leaves open the practical question of mobilising and articulating these works. Thus, in this third part, we would like to supplement the preceding theoretical developments with methodological contributions. We will begin by presenting an analytical framework for studying the functions of management tools and their effects on individuals and social relationships. In conclusion, we will explore some uses of this social science perspective on management instrumentation, and the avenues it opens for future research. Some methodological tips are provided in the appendices.

6 The Agency of Management Tools

The many pieces of research examined in the preceding chapters have revealed the social importance of management tools and recognised their role, place and influence in the coordination of organisational action, thereby justifying, in return, the efforts made in the research. As an extension of this work, we would like to propose an integrating analytical framework that would allow us to examine the different facets of what we call the 'agency' of management tools.[1] We chose this term because it accounts for the fact that tools have a capacity to act on and influence the world and human beings.

The moment in the life of a management tool that interests us most in this chapter is not the period of their genesis or institutionalisation. In fact, when explaining the arrival of tools in organisational contexts as well as the struggles and problems that accompany them, human actors are usually attributed the leading roles. In these stories, the tools themselves are described as malleable and either incorporate human intentions or are rejected or circumvented. If the social science approaches to management tools that we have discussed in this book need to make room for 'non-humans' in these situations, we are nevertheless still in that comfortable zone where action is specific to humans. It seems to us that we need to go one step further and wonder whether tools are likely to act without the intervention of people and whether they do possess what we call 'their own effects'. We should therefore pay careful attention to what happens when a tool is taken for granted, when it is characterised by a state of 'peace in fairness'

---

[1] An earlier version of this chapter appeared, in French, in a work on recent trends in organisation studies (Chiapello and Gilbert, 2016).

and not a 'dispute in justice' (Boltanski, 2012),[2] when the tool is finally taken for granted, is 'black boxed' and the controversies seem extinguished (Latour, 1987). The tool seems all the more effective when it is embedded in situations to the point where it becomes inseparable from the situational context, when it is institutionalised and has become an 'obligatory passage point' (Callon, 1984; Latour, 1987).[3] Once it is inscribed in the situations, humans must accommodate its existence. Of course human action was necessary to incorporate it in the first place and what has been constructed can be deconstructed, and of course the maintenance of management tools supposes that they are continually confirmed and reinstituted in social action. Yet nevertheless, talking about the agency of a tool remains relevant since the situation and the action are marked by its presence. Both would be different if the tool was not there. Its effect on social reality is just as concrete as the effects produced by mechanical tools on the physical word. Management tools do have agency. This affirmation, which the classic authors on organisations would have doubtlessly deemed incongruous or even scandalous, will not surprise the reader who has read this far. Yet besides this affirmation, we still lack an integrating framework that clarifies the role of management tools in action.

How do management tools act? What are their functions? Clarifying and organising these questions seemed necessary to us in order to validate the project for a sociology of management tools that develops its own perspective and its own method. The analytical framework that we propose borrows from the different theses mentioned in this book, whose complementarity is thus highlighted. We do not prefer one school of thought over any other; instead, we have sought to organise the various perspectives insofar as they make a significant contribution to our question regarding the agency of

---

[2] 'To a regime of disputes in justice, I shall thus oppose, first of all, a regime of peace in fairness' (Boltanski, 2012, p. 70).

[3] We must note that its materiality, in the sense of its physicality, is only one aspect, and not necessarily the most important, of this 'institutionalisation'.

management tools. The purpose is no longer to propose, as we did with the identification of the ten theses, a classification of theoretical approaches. Rather, we aim at considering what the different approaches have to say on the specific topic of agency. Such a constructive confrontation on a specific issue allows us to go beyond the seeming eclecticism of our theoretical resources.

We begin by presenting the analytical framework before looking at the different aspects of the agency of management tools in detail.

A FRAMEWORK FOR THE ANALYSIS OF MANAGEMENT TOOLS

Vocabulary Issues

In order to describe the different ways in which tools act, we use the notion of 'function'. Management tools have 'functions'. As the notion of function has different applications from one theoretical school of thought to another and spontaneously evokes teleological explanations, some preliminary clarification is necessary. Unlike some authors, such as Malinowski (1922) and Radcliffe-Brown (1952), we are not advancing any kind of functionalist hypothesis that would ascribe to management tools the satisfaction of some to-be-identified needs.

The term 'function' as we use it does not necessarily imply intentionality or a causal link. Although the function does relate to things that the tool allows people to do, the existence of the tool is not explained by the function. It is rather the other way round. According to the meaning postulated by Wright (1973), function appears as the consequence of the existence of the tool in a given situation. Being a 'consequence of' does not mean being 'guaranteed by the presence of' (Wright, 1973, p. 160). The 'official' functions of the tool, being basic mental operations (ranking, calculating, comparing, etc.) or the basis of greater ambitions (strategy deployment, organisational integration, monitoring of operational performance), do not exhaust all its possible functions and only allow an imperfect description of what the tool does. Thus, beyond the explicit functions vaunted by their promoters, management tools in fact carry out a range of 'implicit functions' (Gilbert, 1998b), which superimpose themselves on preceding 'explicit' and 'intended' functions and contribute their own dynamics.

While the identification of 'functions' allows us to identify some categories for the agency of tools, we also want to understand how this agency of management tools affects the world. This means looking at effects. Effects are indeed the consequences of the presence of tools in situations, just like 'functions', but they are understood not so much from the viewpoint of the tool's functioning but rather from the transformations it produces. If, for example, we say that one possible function of a hammer is to hit objects, one possible effect of that action is destruction, while another is displacement.

To conclude, we have made an effort to distinguish between 'specific effects' (first-order effects) and second-order effects. The former are the direct consequences of tools whose presence affects situations and the action that takes place. They are the direct effects of the inscription of the tool into social situations. Our main focus here will be to identify these immediate effects. Second-order effects are linked to people's reactivity[4] to first-order effects. For example, a ranking table has a first-order effect of evaluation and ranking, as well as a second-order effect in that the people classified react to their ranking and change their behaviour (Espeland and Sauder, 2007). Beyond the second-order effects linked to their reactivity, we could also mention systemic effects and chain reactions (such as constructing hierarchised markets) – but these effects suppose a more distant causality that is more difficult to establish, which is why we will not tackle these in this chapter.

Functions

There are three principal functions of management tools: *epistemic* (enable knowledge), *pragmatic* (enable actions and decisions) and *political* (enable influence, control, domination, and so on) ones.

---

[4] See thesis 5 ('Tools as investment in forms').

- The epistemic function largely relates to cognition and the treatment of information: tools order, classify, measure, evaluate, make visible, etc.
- The pragmatic function concerns the relationship between workers and their tasks and is linked to most of the explicit functions of management tools: they are supposed to equip organisational action. The pragmatic function produces effects because people act by relying on these tools, which are enabling and constraining at the same time (Giddens, 1984).[5] They allow action but the price to pay is that the action is then subject to norms, framed, and directed.
- The political function concerns the relations of influence between people. Here, action, even individual action, is thought of as social from the outset. To highlight this function necessitates a wide identification of the people involved, beyond just those who are the subjects or the objects of the managerial action.

This typology can be made clearer by placing management tools at the heart of the social psychology triad proposed by Moscovici (Moscovici and Markova, 2006), which has allowed us to conceive Figure 6.1 (Gilbert, 1998a, p. 60). In this process of interactions the four terms make up a system: *Ego* represents the subject (user, professional, manager); *Alter* represents all the people directly or indirectly concerned by the implementation of the tool in the situation; and *Object* represents whatever the action, with the help of the instrument, is directed towards (data, people, etc.).

In the case of the management tool, the instrument thus allows three types of mediation. The first two were conceptualised by Rabardel (2002, p. 40),[6] who works using only two of the three points of the triad (*Ego* and *Object*): *pragmatic* mediation in which the instrument enables a transformative action directed towards the object and *epistemic* mediation in which the instrument is a means of developing knowledge of the object. In accordance with the psychosocial view, we propose adding *social* mediation, in which the instrument is a means of regulating relations between social actors (for example

---

[5] See thesis 6 ('Technology is both constraining and enabling').
[6] See thesis 8 ('The tool is nothing outside the activity system')

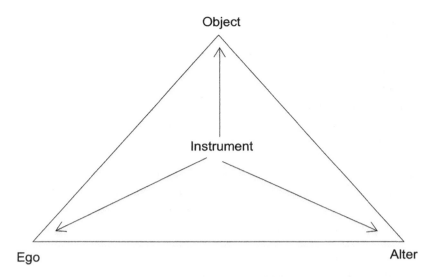

FIGURE 6.1 **Process of interaction involving the tool**

through the distribution of roles, or the standardisation of behaviours to adopt, etc.) (Gilbert, 1998a).

The typology of functions takes up this former conceptualisation, but while the notion of mediation makes the tool an instrument of the *Ego* that it serves, the notion of function suggests that the tool can impose its own knowledge, practices and politics on *Ego* as much as on *Alter*; it is in this sense that we understand the agency of tools, that is to say the way in which they impose themselves on people.

It must be emphasised that these three types of functions are not independent and are more analytical than empirical distinctions. The epistemic and pragmatic functions are strongly linked, just like cognition and action. The notion of learning, which is sometimes used to understand the roles of management tools, also mixes fairly broadly the epistemic and pragmatic functions.[7] As for the effects in terms of power implied by the political function, we know since

---

[7] For example, Lorino (2002) insists on the idea that management control tools are not 'faithful images' but are 'imperfect and temporary aids to learning'. See also Moisdon (1997) on the learning processes induced by tools.

Foucault[8] (1977, 1980) how much the production of knowledge (proper to the epistemic function) is linked to the exercise of power that requires, permits and uses it. Finally, it is clear that tools must serve action or knowledge and thus actualise their pragmatic and/or epistemic function to yield any political effects.

Nevertheless, these three functions allow us to give an account of the different 'specific effects' management tools have on people. We will concentrate on what tools do beyond explicit expectations and what they were intended for. For example, an accounting system has an explicit epistemic function, which is to reveal certain economic balances within a company. But this epistemic function also allows an accounting system to convey numerous calculation conventions,[9] which are likely to structure in depth the cognition of the decision-makers. The same is true for the pragmatic function. We will not list everything that tools enable or all the purposes for which they have been designed. Instead, we will try to identify the effects these tools have on action from the very fact that they are used to perform it. For example, we can see that tools that are not built for knowledge (and hence have no explicit epistemic function) nevertheless tend to impose their knowledge on users and therefore have an implicit epistemic function.

To sum up, the agency of management tools can be analysed through

- their epistemic function: the tools propose/impose their knowledge on people;
- their pragmatic function: the tools allow action and propose/impose their practices/forms of action/decisions;
- their political function: the tools produce or reproduce power relations even when they have not been designed for that purpose.

Effects

We have distinguished between first-order effects (specific effects), which are the immediate effects of the tools, and second-order effects

---

[8] See thesis 2 ('The tool as a technique for discipline and government')
[9] See thesis 5 ('Tools as investment in forms').

Table 6.1 *Management tools' agency analysed through unintended effects*

Functions	First-order (proper) effects	Second-order effects (human reactivity)
Epistemic: tools create and offer knowledge	Veridiction Valuation	Subjectification Performativity
Pragmatic: tools help and hinder action	Structuration Selection/ Distribution	Manipulation/ Circumvention/ Diversion Isomorphism
Political: tools act on power relations	Reification Legitimation	Domination/ Confrontation

(reactivity effects). To reveal second-order effects requires taking into account how people react to tools' agency, for example by resisting or letting things happen. In this chapter, only explicitly unintended effects interest us, insofar as we try to understand tools' agency: indeed intended effects can be imputed to human agency and not to tools' agency. Table 6.1 features a series of effects that we study in detail hereafter.

THE EPISTEMIC EFFECTS OF TOOLS

First-Order Effects Linked to Epistemic Function

We will address the epistemic function through two notions: veridiction and valuation. Veridiction deals with the role of management tools in 'telling the truth'; valuation relates to their role in constructing judgements and attributions of value.[10]

---

[10] For Berry (1983) these two types of effect were evoked through a function of reducing the complexity that was assumed by management tools, a reduction allegedly necessary in order to gain time. Management tools therefore offer two types of 'short cut': the abbreviation of 'what is true' and the abbreviation of 'what is good'.

Veridiction

The notion of veridiction is inseparable from the work of Foucault[11] that is infused with the question of 'regimes of truth': 'Each society has its regime of truth, its "general politics" of truth: that is, the types of discourse which it accepts and makes function as true; the mechanisms and instances which enable one to distinguish true and false statements, the means by which each is sanctioned; the techniques and procedures accorded value in the acquisition of truth; the status of those who are charged with saying what counts as true' (Foucault, 1980, p. 131). In philosophy, truth appears as the result of discourse. From this perspective, management tools make an essential contribution to the production of managerial 'truth telling' and therefore take part in the fabrication of truths about business affairs. They organise the selection, confection and distribution of legitimate information and can thus be read as taking part in an order of discourse (Foucault, 1971).

Management information systems that aim to give an account of what is happening in a firm are particularly concerned with the effects of veridiction. For example, the financial statements produced through accounting allow managers to follow the state of some variables that are crucial to them, such as turnover, cash-flow, or profit. The head of the profit centre registers these figures as being the truth about the activity of her department. Management indicators used to monitor an activity take part in establishing the truth about it. Other truth discourses would be possible, associated with other kinds of information but this would require competing sources of knowledge that are not always existing, because it is costly to produce indicators. Considerable technical and human means are needed for any accounting system. Companies generally adopt a single set of standards and stick to it, so that in the end there is only one economic image of the firm, even though it is deeply conventional. This representation, which is only one among possible others, becomes nevertheless the

---

[11] See thesis 2 ('The tool as a technique for discipline and government').

only available truth. To counter this situation one must sometimes construct other 'calculation centres' and produce other figures – otherwise, those that exist hold the monopoly of truth. In this way, management tools help to produce the truth about the world in which they operate. Here, the study of the systems of categories incorporated in tools is particularly enlightening. The sociology of quantification and classification[12] makes a valuable contribution to these topics.

Job Classification Systems as a Truth Technique

On a social and wage scale, the status of a 'worker' (blue-collar) is normally valued less than the status of an 'employee' (white-collar) even though, with the transformation of industrial work, differences have been attenuated. This has given rise to debates about the criteria used to classify people in management categories. Faced with criticism from labour unions regarding the 'empirical methods' used to define status (and therefore salaries), the Belgian steel firm Cockerill opted, in the late 1980s, for a so-called 'scientific' method. To distinguish between 'workers' and 'employees', it adopted a classification system with six subdivided criteria. Each subdivision contained a number of points that were added up using a weighting system. If the final rating of the worker reached a previously established threshold, then the worker was granted the status of 'employee'. As Lomba (2004, p. 50) points out: 'It was the argument of the mathematical measurement that was deployed to stabilise and neutralise the negotiations of status' (our translation). This example shows the instituting force of certain managerial devices that can decide who is a worker and who is an employee.

Source: Lomba (2004)

Beyond these effects, management tools themselves rely on theories, whose validity may be more or less scientifically established, that they convey and promote. A theory of the world that the tools

[12] See thesis 5 ('Tools as investment in forms')

help to manage is incorporated in them. The knowledge deposited in the tool contributes to the production of new knowledge that reinforces it. The tool participates in the production, implementation and dissemination of knowledge.

Graphs Showing Statistical Control of Production Quality as Conveyors of Knowledge

Industrial methods of quality control were transformed by the 'probabilistic revolution' at the beginning of the twentieth century, which introduced the idea of partly random variability of manufactured elements. Industrial products were then endowed with new properties and their quality was redefined. According to the new conceptualisation, quality became a synonym for containing variations between pre-established boundaries. Shewhart, an engineer at the Bell Laboratories, was one of those responsible for introducing statistics for quality control; he also perfected control charts that were graphical representations on which measures made at regular intervals could be plotted. These charts – real production management tools – made it possible to perceive theoretical notions as statistical spread while showing limits to dispersion within which production was considered as under control. The control chart has facilitated the transformation of a complex group of abstract reasoning processes into a work procedure that makes use of widely available capacities (vision and simple arithmetical calculations). Its simplicity and its ease of use were no doubt determining factors in the adoption of the statistical theory of quality. For those who use it in the workplace, the control chart looks like a patient's temperature curve: there is no need to understand the sophisticated underlying theories in order to use it.

Source: Bayart (1995)

Valuation

Here we define 'valuation' as the process of attributing value to objects, persons, actions and entities. The notion of 'valuation' that emerged from the pragmatist tradition (Dewey, 1939) allows us to shift the discussion about value in the economy. The notion of valuation draws attention to the fact that value is produced in the relation between the object and the person who estimates it (Lamont, 2012). It is the result of practical operations (Beckert and Aspers, 2011; Kornberger et al., 2015; Muniesa, 2011). Like truth in veridiction, value is the result of a process in which management tools play a crucial role. We differentiate the term valuation from that of evaluation, which is even more systematically employed by managers themselves who never cease evaluating. Valuation is about drawing attention to what is at stake in these managerial activities, namely that values are produced even when the explicit aim is evaluation.[13] Attributing value has different steps: the identification and selection of objects of attention (which also means that some are not selected); the qualification of the value or of the viewpoint according to which the value is attributed; and the estimation of the objects' worth[14] relative to the employed criteria. This last operation can itself bring into play a more or less elaborate technique and produce a quantification of value. Management tools play a role in each of these processes. For example, an evaluation interview sheet predefines the criteria according to which an employee's value is assessed. Internal competition in a sales department also produces a ranking and designates 'good' salespeople. The discounted cash-flow calculation of forecasts associated with an investment plays an active part in determining the interest of the project for the company (Chiapello, 2015; Doganova and Eyquem-Renault, 2009).

---

[13] Vatin (2013) has also proposed a distinction between evaluation and valorisation that does not immediately overlap with ours.

[14] Boltanski and Thévenot's (2006) model of economies of worth makes it possible to think simultaneously of the plurality of possible judgement principles and the operations that attribute worth (the states of 'big' and 'little'). They also highlight the importance of the 'tests' to which objects and people are submitted, allowing us to agree on their relative worth. (For a shift in this model towards devices for evaluating performance, see Bourguignon and Chiapello, 2005 and thesis 5, 'Tools as investment in forms'.)

In companies, just as in the public sector, the objectivity of figures is sought after (Porter, 1995). But whatever the quality of the measurement, it cannot completely hide its underpinning values, which a researcher may unravel by shedding light onto the conventions of quantification. The quantification of values tends to produce another effect: that of commensuration, which enables the comparison of different objects. Certain quantification practices – such as cost–benefit analyses, scoring or rating – organise the encounter of different values, according to different criteria, for the same object. Metrics establishing equivalences allow then the weighting of each view in an overall judgement. Commensuration is a process that entails the comparison of the qualities of different entities according to a common metric (Espeland and Stevens, 1998). Commensuration is a technique of inclusion, because disparate qualities are taken into account and compared; but it is equally and indissociably a technique of exclusion, because whatever is not 'commensurate' does not exist. Commensuration neglects some information and reorganises what is left into a new shape.

The work carried out by the 'economy of conventions'[15] has drawn attention to the importance of practices of qualifying products or persons for the functioning of markets – of course, management tools contribute to this. Tools incorporate criteria and procedures of judgement and help to coordinate the representations of those engaged in the situation, who need to agree on the relative value to be attributed to the 'things' that are discussed and that might be exchanged.

Management tools therefore impose truths and tend to order and classify things and people according to various value systems. Managers rely on these productions in order to make decisions. Although in general the 'truths' and 'values' displayed and produced by the tools themselves do not trigger actions automatically, this may nevertheless happen – for example, when a bank customer

---

[15] See thesis 5 ('Tools as investment in forms').

sees her/his payments automatically refused due to an overdraft. The weight of the tool in the course of action is therefore determining.

We now turn to reactivity effects. This won't be a question of recalling, as in the former example, the links between the epistemic and the pragmatic functions (cognition informs action) of management tools, but rather of showing the effects of reactivity on the epistemic function itself.

Effects of Reactivity Linked to the Epistemic Function

If management tools propose truths and distribute values, they produce recursive effects because by using tools, humans contribute to solidifying their engrained categories and qualities which make them more difficult to alter despite their arbitrary nature. Management tools create new realities, just like administrative practices create what they claim to describe (professional classes, types of beneficiaries of social services, etc.) (Hacking, 1999).

The effects of subjectification and the construction of the self via the tools are part of the effects of reactivity.

Subjectification

This perspective is supported by the works of Foucault.[16] When faced with evaluations and representations of the self, the individual is moulded by this process, either by auto-introjection of the evaluations and self-discipline or by falling into deviance. One part of the process does not derive from external powers but supposes the active engagement of the subjectified individual. In any case, before it became an instrument of productivity, discipline had always been a technique appreciated by ascetics.

---

[16] See thesis 2 ('The tool as a technique for discipline and government'). See also Lupton (2013, 2016).

Quantifying Self

What researchers call 'self-quantification' is in a way the prolongation of surveillance, normalisation and the necessity for performance through the distributed valorisation of the self. In February 2012, *Quantified Self*, a movement that groups together tools, principles and methods that allow the measurement, analysis and sharing of personal data, counted over 500 tools, most of which were supported by digital devices (smartphone or web apps, specific sensors, etc.). The fields of application are numerous, from sport to health and lifestyle (food, sleep, weight, etc.) or even the management of work and leisure time. Pharabod and colleagues describe three effects, or 'logics of use' – surveillance, regularity and performance – produced by these management tools of the self. They note that these tools can play as important a role as the practice monitored. For example in sports: '[The use of self-quantifying tools] is part of the identity-building process of the individual as a sportsperson' (Pharabod et al., 2013, p. 112, our translation).

Source: Pharabod et al. (2013)

The notion of performativity allows us to address other reactivity effects linked to the knowledge content of management tools.

Performativity

The notion of performativity, which was discussed in the interactional approaches,[17] is borrowed from the linguistic field of pragmatics and the work of J. L. Austin (1975). It was introduced into economic sociology by Callon (2006) with the affirmation that economic science was performative in the sense that instead of describing the world it tends to transform it such that it conforms to the theory.

---

[17] See Chapter 5 and especially thesis 7 ('The tool is a human/non-human arrangement') and thesis 9 ('The tool as a language being').

The works of MacKenzie in particular have illustrated this statement. MacKenzie and Millo (2003) have for example demonstrated how Black and Scholes's financial model has been used by people exchanging stock options on markets in order to estimate the price. In so doing, little by little, the observed prices began to match those predicted by the model. Thus, the model was not describing the market prices but had in fact created them. However, in order for ideas to be able to fashion the world according to their image, a great number of socio-technical mediations are necessary. In the case of option pricing, MacKenzie and Millo (2003) describe how market operators relied on systems to make their prices (such as price sheets and, after the emergence of computer technology, calculation software). Muniesa and Callon (2009, p. 300, our translation), insisting on the active role played by artefacts, developed the notion of 'distributed performation' to describe the process by which 'performative programmes meet and enter into relations of cooperation, free or forced, or into relations of competition and sometimes parasitism'.

An older figure of performativity is that of the self-fulfilling prophecy. according to which behaviours are modified in such a way that the prophecy is turned into reality, or in other words, validate *a posteriori* the *a priori* judgements.[18]

The epistemic function of tools (the fact that they help us to know the world) highlights a series of direct effects (veridiction and valuation effects) or second-order effects due to the reaction of actors to what tools propose as truth or value. Reactivity thus accentuates the efficacy of these judgements, which, in turn, acquire a greater materiality (through performative effects and effects of subjectivation).

We now look at the effects linked to the pragmatic function of tools. Their habilitating character is not sufficient to describe all that tools do, because it is contained in their explicit function as they exist to serve some purpose. Under the cover of allowing action, tools often impose themselves on an action and structure it in depth.

---

[18] See thesis 5 ('Tools as investment in forms').

THE PRAGMATIC EFFECTS OF MANAGEMENT TOOLS

The Specific Effects of Tools Linked to Their Pragmatic Function

Management tools tend to norm and frame action. We bring these effects together under the heading of structuration.

Structuration

Management tools do not only allow management acts to be performed – they also stimulate actors to make specific choices. Using a tool changes the structure of an activity and the result may well be a displacement of the goals to be met. For activity theory,[19] this property is inherent to all tools. The Danish psychologist Ellen Christiansen (1996) notes that a tool must serve the dual goal of enabling something to be done but also reminding that it should be done.

Segmentation of Clients and Offers in Banking Products

In a study of the evolution of the work organisation in a French public bank (Banque Postale) since the 1990s, Vézinat shows the impact of a software package handling knowledge of customers on the work of local bankers and their relation with their clients. This software organises a 'filing system' of customers who are put into different categories according to their age, their known needs, the length of time they had been customers, etc. The customer file is updated at every client meeting. Based on this information, the system sends bankers lists of things to do (such as contacting customers to propose a mortgage savings plan), identifies the bank's products associated with each targeted client category, and supplies ready-made lines of argument, thereby strongly guiding the work to be done. The software also structures the relationship with the customer. Some bank advisers

---

[19] See thesis 8 ('The tool is nothing outside the activity system').

> use the customer information to decide, for example, which customers to spend more time with, cancelling appointments with other clients deemed to be uninteresting. Vézinat highlights varying degrees of docility and autonomy among the bankers regarding the recommendations made by the system. However, whether they obeyed it or willingly moved away from it, they cannot ignore the importance of its role in carrying out their tasks.
>
> Source: Vézinat (2011)

In his theory of structuration, Giddens (1984) proposed the concept of 'the duality of structure' to signify that while the properties of a structure (the rules and resources that are engaged in the production and reproduction of social systems) are constraining (for the action and the actors), they are also facilitating.[20] They simultaneously constitute the medium and the result of practices that they organise in a recursive fashion.

Selection/Distribution

The selection/distribution effect is a direct result of the valuation effect. In fact, value judgements conveyed by management tools normally trigger, almost automatically, the distribution of social goods: reputation, monetary advantages, and advantages in terms of status or power. For example, systems for evaluating performance are strongly connected to reward and sanction systems (salary increases, bonuses, etc.) and career management. In the educational environment, the classification that follows entrance exams has significant distribution effects as the opportunities offered to the last successful candidate can diverge hugely from those offered to the first failed candidate – and yet there may be little or no differences between the candidates themselves. Similar effects can be observed in management consulting.

---

[20] See thesis 6 ('Technology is both constraining and enabling')

Performance Evaluation in a Management Consulting Firm

This multinational consultancy was founded in the 1960s in the USA. During the 1990s, researchers became interested in the effects produced by performance evaluation in its Swedish subsidiary (300 staff). Taking into account the dispersed nature of the work, carried out over many different missions, the evaluations were aimed at supplying information to ensure that resources (consultants) were being properly used and to take the most appropriate decisions according to the 'up or out' system ('make progress or you leave'), which was widely favoured in international consultancies. About 60 people left the firm every year, which was seen as normal in the sector.

The researchers showed that performance evaluations allowed the hierarchy to distribute sanctions or rewards, which in turn helped them to discipline behaviour to comply with the company's goals, inculcating and reproducing the associate values.

Source: Bergström et al. (2009)

The field of accounting also offers interesting examples where it is impossible to dissociate valuation from distribution. Thus, although the determination of profit is a largely conventional exercise, accounting figures, once disclosed, trigger all kinds of distribution: dividends, interest rate changes, bonuses, taxes, and so on.

In some cases actors may try to work around tools, particularly if they are aware of the influence of tools on their actions (structuration) and resource distributions. We discuss this phenomenon next.

The Effects of Reactivity Linked to the Pragmatic Function of Tools

Manipulation/Circumvention/Diversion

During the development of management tools, actors' reactivity to devices is often explicitly taken into account. Reward and sanction systems are configured in the hope that people will react to the incentives that are displayed. Thus managers constantly seek to manipulate the motivations of their subordinates, as well as the overall system of constraints, in order to make them do what they want them to do.

However, this project may fail for the exactly same reasons as those that may make it work: the actors themselves play with the system, circumventing or diverting it. They can produce what managers call 'perverse effects', and all sorts of 'unintended effects'.

This type of reactivity has been highlighted particularly by the theory of the strategic actor.[21] According to this approach, social actors are opportunists and adapt to circumstances. They adopt strategic behaviour and may especially try to make themselves unpredictable vis-à-vis others in order to maintain or increase their power. They are never totally deprived of means to act nor totally constrained by management tools. Actors never let themselves be imprisoned within frameworks of dependency – not even technical ones. They make claims, negotiate and act, thereby always responding strategically when faced with constraints. Actors exercise their autonomy by expanding their margins of manoeuvre, or by opposing and negotiating.

Manipulating Public Policy Evaluation Measures: The Case of Contemporary Music

When public policy evaluation measures were set up in France in the 1980s, they were strongly criticised by 'high culture' networks and unions. However, those involved with contemporary music have adopted a different position: they neither criticised the introduction of numbers, nor questioned the growing importance of economic concern. On the contrary, standardisation became an opportunity to gain legitimacy and they embarked on a 'partnership' with the French Ministry of Culture to create a 'shared method' that would allow them

---

[21] See thesis 10 ('The effects of the tool are conditioned by what actors do').

to show that their music is massively attractive and lucrative. Today's music federations went even further. Anticipating occasional enquiries from public administrations, they emancipated themselves by creating their own 'sustainable' and 'reproducible' information collection system over time. Their strategy was to progressively take over the entire production of data and to present these data in a favourable light, thereby limiting the intervention of public statistics. Thus, associations of classical music as well as popular music both had evaluation devices imposed on them. But faced with the same rules, two different strategies emerged: one that ran counter to the devices and one that absorbed them and reappropriated them to master their effects.

Source: Guibert (2011)

Isomorphism

The phenomenon identified as isomorphism (i.e., conformity of practices at the level of an organisational field)[22] can also be read as a kind of second-order effect linked to actors' reactivity. Some management tools become institutional references to such an extent that adopting them reinforces the legitimacy of the adopting firms or actors. Similarly, the way actors react to the directions given by tools can be analysed through the prism of institutional pressures.

Isomorphism as a Response to the Criticism of Elitism of the French Grandes Écoles

In the early 2000s, the French *Grandes Écoles* were criticised for their lack of openness and their role in reproducing social inequalities. *Sciences Po* in Paris was the first university to propose integration measures affecting its entry selection procedure, which led all *Grandes*

---

[22] See thesis 4 ('Management tools influenced by institutional strategies').

Écoles to develop similar concerns. An array of devices began to be developed (codes of conduct, 'best practices', partnerships with secondary schools located in poor neighbourhoods, student grants and statistical disclosure on their numbers), which other schools largely followed. Buisson-Fenet and Draelants (2013) showed how the question of social openness changed into a positioning strategy. The universities 'tried, collectively, to reaffirm and to relegitimise the specific nature of the French model of elite education while seeking, individually, to improve their position within the field of *Grandes Écoles*' (Buisson-Fenet and Draelants, 2013, p. 57, our translation). The authors enumerated different strategies adopted by the schools that showed different levels of decoupling between the adoption of devices and the effective transformation of selection processes.

Source: Buisson-Fenet and Draelants (2013)

The effects linked to the pragmatic function of tools can be largely linked to the issue of power. Tools convey prescriptions, some of which are chosen while others are deliberately not. Tools therefore exercise forms of power over actors who respond with varying degrees of docility. It is a question of power to make people do things, to have power over action. The political effects that we look at in the next section are of another kind, in the sense that they go well beyond the asymmetries of power that are linked to the realisation of tasks. We are rather dealing with asymmetries between social groups that can be captured by the notion of domination.

THE POLITICAL PRACTICES OF MANAGEMENT TOOLS

Because they are inscribed in a political space, that is, a space structured by power where interests diverge, the political function of management tools is omnipresent. For some actors, the two other functions of management tools are subordinate to the political one. Thus, some researchers criticise management tools as instruments of domination or exploitation[23] while more clinically oriented research-ers point to the role of tools in producing suffering at work.[24]

Political Effects That Are Proper to Management Tools

There seem to be two main ways in which management tools reinforce domination: reification and legitimation. In both cases, the 'technical' aspect of tools is decisive and acts as a veil covering the balance of power and thus tends to naturalise the asymmetries so as to make them look normal.

Reification

The Marxist philosopher Georg Lukács (1971) defined the concept of reification as giving the character of a thing to a relationship between people.[25] As most management tools rely on the standardisation of what is to be managed and on the formalisation of how to manage it, reification appears as a process that is baked into any management operation. The management of 'human resources' – the expression itself can be seen as reification – is a good example of this phenom-enon. As Gilbert et al. (2018) show, the reification of a management model contributes to its implementation by redefining relations of influence.

Legitimation

Since Max Weber (1922), the claim to legitimacy is linked to any kind of domination, that is, to any situation in which dominant groups hope to be obeyed routinely. Legitimation is the process whereby an act, organisation or practice finds itself legitimised and accepted. In terms of relations of domination, successful legitimation increases the chances that the domination remains unchallenged. Since they conceal the constructed character and arbitrary nature of the

---

[23] See thesis 1 ('Tools implicated in relationships of domination').

[24] See thesis 3 ('The tool alienates and dehumanises').

[25] See thesis 1 ('Tools implicated in relationships of domination').

conventions that they convey beneath a supposedly neutral technique, management tools help to legitimise social asymmetries.

The Legitimisation of Shareholders' Domination by the Discourse on Value Creation and Its Instruments

The wide diffusion of a discourse on shareholder value creation and the popularity of Economic Value Added (EVA) during the 1990s can be linked to evolutions of corporate governance that are inseparable from a new macroeconomic regime centred on financial markets. Close analysis of the EVA calculus reveals its incorporated political and economic assumptions. One of these is the right of any shareholder to receive a minimal payout (at the average market rate) for their capital contribution (a right which is, however, contrary to the status of shareholders, who are supposed to bear the risks of a company). A second assumption is that, once they have been compensated according to the level of risk taken, they are entitled to receive all additional profits generated by the firm. Finally, the EVA calculations assume a 'natural' risk–return link, not acknowledging that the relations between risk and return have shifted in recent years in favour of the shareholders. The level of the expected return rate is considered as dictated by the market, and not as a political construction produced by the balance of power in the economy. EVA calculation therefore tends to reinforce the apparently factual and non-controversial character of the expected rate and therefore reinforces the favourable position of shareholders in the distribution of added value.

Source: Lordon (2000)

Reactivity and the Political Effects of Management Tools

Reactivity is based on the principle that human beings have agency and that they react to the actions of tools, either reinforcing them, going along with them, or trying to escape them. In the case of political effects, second-order effects either mark the success of the political operation and thus a reinforcement of the domination, which gains legitimacy and is naturalised, or they mark opposition to domination or even its failure.

In the case of 'success', the second-order effects are directly related to the first-order effects of the political function (reification, legitimation). The cases of 'failure' are more complicated. They can be analysed using the same concepts as those that serve as second-order effects of the pragmatic function (manipulation, circumvention, diversion). In fact, it is not rare during the implementation of management tools that some of the subjected human actors develop what managers call 'a resistance to change' that prevents the institutionalisation of the tool, or organise circumventing or deviating from it.[26] Opposition is more probable during the implementation phase, rather than when the tools are firmly in place and have acquired legitimacy.

However, tools are not inevitably oriented towards domination. One might imagine the implementation of emancipatory management tools. In that case, instead of reinforcing the effects of domination, these tools would have liberating effects, which may trigger new types of second-order effect. As the tool favours emancipation, people could manage to free themselves from other management tools.

Other kinds of situation may trigger emancipation rather than domination, for example when people are immersed in situations permeated by tools with contradictory actions. This generates room for manoeuvre and unexpected effects.

CONCLUSION

Building on the literature discussed in the preceding chapters, our aim in this chapter was to propose a framework for the analysis of the different direct effects of management tools, and to distinguish these

---

[26] The dominant idea is that resistance to change is a problem concerning only humans. However, there are many cases where management tools are resisting (see Teglborg et al. (2015)).

first-order effects from those supposing a reaction from humans to the actions of tools (second-order effects).

The described effects are not inevitably produced by any tool in any context, but they always exist at least potentially. Therefore, each tool can be studied from the angle of its three – epistemic, pragmatic and political – functions. These functions describe the agency of management tools. Tools acts in the sense that they propose knowledge and values, they frame and format actions, they organise and justify social relations. The analytical distinctions proposed, distinguishing clearly between functions and various effects, aim at facilitating their identification and analysis. However, these phenomena are deeply intertwined in social situations. The effects are thus linked to each other: for example, distribution is a consequence of valuation and reification is enabled by veridiction. We furthermore have to take into account systemic interactions, where several effects can occur at the same time or successively.

General Conclusion

Our intention in writing this book was to introduce objects – management tools – into the analysis of social, organisational and economic phenomena. Their lack of visibility up until now and their apparent banality seemed to ignore any substantial problems tools might pose. Readers will have understood that we are not interested in management tools in the way technicians or managers would be; our idea is to view tools, which are omnipresent in our society, as an analyser of the specific situations that mark our time and so deserve to be studied.

On a wider scale, we want to contribute to a project of emancipation by setting our proposal in the tradition of socio-technical system theory whose field of application and methods we are trying to renew and enlarge. This perspective also allows us to review some older issues and to uncover what we might not see otherwise: the social, which is both hidden and revealed by socio-technical analysis.

STUDYING MANAGEMENT TOOLS: A PROJECT OF EMANCIPATION

The Analysis of Management Tools as Counter-Expertise

It has become indispensable to establish a new perspective on management tools because societies are increasingly regulated by mechanisms that arise from management and the place occupied by management tools is now quite considerable. They have left the confines of large companies and have invaded the third sector, the state, public organisations and society in general. They are as present in government systems as they are in individual interactions and have become indispensable mediators of social relations.

Our approach arises from a reasoning that could be described as anti-expertise, counter-expertise or second opinion. In fact, we have taken tools out of a closed field where discussions and arguments about technical authority were the concern of specialists and we have placed them in the field of social analysis. Recognising the importance of technique does not imply submitting to its dictatorship. By applying a different lens to the study of management tools, we want to give everybody the chance to introduce these objects into debates from which they had been excluded. It is not a question of setting specialists and amateurs against each other but of trying to attain a 'dialogic democracy', according to the expression used by Callon et al. (2009), which would put an end to the monopoly of experts and encourage exchanges.

In the pursuit of this aim, we have presented alternative reading grids to those of the experts of the investigated areas. This book is therefore the complete opposite of a management technique manual. It does not describe the procedures to be set up in different areas of management in order to make the tools work. It does not tell you how to draw up a profit and loss account, how to do a market survey, how to do effective payroll budgeting, draw up a Gantt chart, etc. Without neglecting the need to understand technique in order to be able to discuss it, we have attempted to 'de-professionalise' management tools and take them out of the reserved area to which they have been confined. We would like each and every one of us to be able to interpret and analyse management tools in a way that specialists, despite their familiarity with these objects – or maybe because of it – cannot necessarily do. Of course, this presupposes that newcomers get familiar with the language and logic of the management tool to be studied. They need to get an overview of its general anatomy and functioning without being confined by it.

Because they enable and constrain action, because they relay power relations and governmental regimes, and because they uphold social compromises, management tools belong to the world of politics. Some, who have understood this, developed a critique. However, the emancipatory project is not the monopoly of critical theses. It is important to root the project in dimensions other than only denunciation. We cannot be satisfied with just looking at these phenomena from above and at a distance without entering into the actual construction and functioning of the object. We need a global vision, but also a close analysis in order to deconstruct managerial instruments. The big picture requires proximity to the tool and long and attentive examination of it. It is important to combine an 'externalist' vision, which is concerned with actors, social groups, their power relations and their stakes and beliefs, with an 'internalist' approach to management tools that considers them as objects fabricated from a multitude of conventions and incorporating judgement models, political philosophies and forms of knowledge.

Towards a New Socio-Technical Approach

The perspective we have adopted aspires to be a prolongation and renewal of the socio-technical approach. The socio-technical system theory has its origins in Trist and Bamforth's (1951) study of English coal mines that used an extraction method known as 'longwall'. This method, characterised by a fixed series of simple and repetitive standardised operations, was adopted in substitution for manual cutting methods. But it caused many psychological and social problems (rivalry, individualistic reactions, compensatory absenteeism, etc.). After the researchers' analysis, some organisational innovations were introduced without changing the technical system, and they managed to increase productivity, interest in work and social cohesion. Trist and Bamforth showed that the introduction of new procedures and technical methods has repercussions for the social structure that influenced the technical system in return.

The original socio-technical approach was a diagnosis and restructuring approach to work environments; it was also a democratic project involving the recognition of workers' abilities to organise their work. It arose from a counter-movement to the mechanistic dynamics of Taylorism. After the first British experiments, the socio-technical system theory inspired the industrial democracy programme in Norway at the beginning of the 1960s (Emery et al., 1969). This programme, at the scale of a whole country, had its roots in the recognition of a gap between the social democratisation of the country and the hierarchical structure of organisations. It was about finding new ways of pursuing the country's industrial growth on bases other than the rationalisation of work, which was provoking increasing criticism. The socio-technical approach therefore accompanies a project of democracy at work, which implies power-sharing between all those engaged in industrial work – as opposed to a concentration of power in the hands of a minority.

The core lessons of this approach remain highly valuable and relevant, so we can make them ours:

- the affirmation of the indisputably socio-technical nature of all realities of work, especially organisations: they all have a dual social and technical reality;
- the hypothesis that technique limits and orients employees' behaviours just as these behaviours facilitate or limit the transformations that technique aims to achieve;
- the importance of simultaneously understanding operating systems and the economic, psychological, political and cultural aspects of the organisation's functioning;
- the will to pay attention to actual work practices and to take uncertainty into account.

Since these seminal works, the project of thinking together the technical system and the social system has been renewed by the acknowledgment that the 'great division' between the technical and the social does not actually exist in reality (Latour, 1991): despite its claims of autonomy and its capacity to produce objects, even after the process of hardening and concretisation, the technical sphere cannot be detached from what is political, social, moral or cultural. So, in accordance with the socio-technical school of thought, management tools analysts consider tools as parts of larger systems that include human and organisational elements. Expanding the first socio-technical approaches, Foucauldian authors focus on tools' participation in 'devices' or 'apparatuses', and sociologists of science and technology show that tools are also intrinsically social and political constructs.

The socio-technical school of the Tavistock Institute was primarily interested in the industrial world and its manufacturing techniques; in this book we propose to extend our view to other objects and techniques that are allegedly mainly immaterial. In this we follow Callon (1981) who advises us not to limit the study of technological controversies to 'carefully signposted territories' and 'to explore and make visible the territories where the techniques and the sciences are not yet constituted, where there is a fight to articulate socio-economic logics and economic logics' (Callon, 1981, p. 399, our translation).

No conceptual framework alone seems to be able to provide answers to the variety of issues raised by the management tools and serve our project. This is why, in this book, we have chosen to multiply the angles of analysis while trying to establish dialogues between the theoretical grids themselves.

AN APPROACH FOR A PROJECT

Multiply the Angles of Analysis

The understanding of a management tool cannot be considered exhaustive when using only one analytical grid. It is therefore necessary to multiply points of view and to take a pluralistic approach to management tools. This methodological choice arises from what others have qualified as multi-referential analysis (Ardoino, 1990). We had to make a choice from the multitude of theories and we tried to avoid any facile, inconsistent eclecticism or superficial syncretism. The authors whom we have grouped together in the same 'theses' have ideas in common. The comparison of different lines of thought then consists in noting possible links between them and pointing out specific contributions of each approach. Each analytical grid has its own language and distinct reference system, and is more or less appropriated to a type of description and a type of tool.

In order to illustrate what we mean, let us consider the distinctions between 'actor', 'agent', 'actant' and 'subject' as characters moving about on the social stage of managerial practices. From a determinist perspective, the 'agent' is the interchangeable bearer of the demands of a productive system; the 'actor' plays a role in the system because of the position and resources he or she possesses; the 'actant' is correlative to the concept of a 'system in action' in which the object acquires a status equivalent to that of the human actor; the 'subject' makes the action her/himself. Each of these terms suggests a particular type of analysis. Every one of these perspectives has its own zone of relevance within a general framework that we could qualify as anthropological, and helps to draw material for observation from the field and seek an overall understanding.

The object, the 'management tool', is first seen in relation to this or that theoretical analytical grid. It exists outside these grids, and it is at least in part constructed by them. To apprehend our object, a multitude of theories are applicable.

What should guide our choice is the expected contribution from using the different theories. Depending on the scales of analysis or the research questions, one should employ one grid or another. A multiplication of views will yield a detailed topography or the 'big picture', as long as the multiple perspectives do not lead to a simple superimposition of what they produce. This requires putting the chosen analytical grids into dialogue with each other.

Dialogue between the Grids Themselves

Although the different grids are based on different theoretical foundations – which could lead to opposing them – they should not be considered as alternatives, but on the contrary, as complementary. They can reinforce and/or complete one another even if their premises are different and have a specific descriptive language. Our purpose here is to go beyond what we proposed in the chapter that was dedicated to understanding how management tools act in social situations. Theoretical approaches are not only complementary to understand the multiple 'direct effects' tools can have. They can also be cross-mobilised to address other types of questions. This is why to ease the choice between the different theses presented in this book and to create a dialogue between them, we propose a few elements to bring these approaches together according to the research problem or question being asked (see Appendix 1). Meeting points between the theoretical grids we discuss are possible – in fact, this is frequently the case, as demonstrated by many authors who hybridise these theories.[1] As we will now examine, there are many links between the different theories.

The human and non-human are generally thought of as interacting rather than in opposition, whether in the sociology of translation[2] (Latour, Callon), the theory of activity[3] (Rabardel, Engeström) or the structurationist approach to management tools[4] (Orlikowski). Technique is seen as both produced by the social and producing the social. On the one hand, it is a social construct, whether the accent is on its conception (Giddens, Latour) or on its deployment (Rabardel's collective use schemes of the instrument, or negotiation logic in the Crozierian theory of the strategic actor[5]). On the other hand, it constructs social reality and the performative aspects of the tool are generally recognised (see narrative approaches to the tool,[6] Callon's calculative devices, or conventions theory[7]). There are no simple, linear causalities but rather process effects. Causality is attributable neither to human actors directly, nor to artefacts alone. The effects

---

[1] This hybridisation is totally normal insofar as the analysis is made to help the understanding of a phenomenon and not to serve a theory. This also explains why, whereas authors often have more complex thoughts, we had to make difficult choices as to which authors and texts to include in what thesis.

[2] Thesis 7 ('The tool is a human/non-human arrangement').

[3] Thesis 8 ('The tool is nothing outside the activity system').

[4] Thesis 6 ('Technology is both constraining and enabling').

[5] Thesis 10 ('The effects of the tool are conditioned by what actors do').

[6] Thesis 9 ('The tool as a language being').

[7] Thesis 5 ('Tools as investment in forms').

are often unexpected (particularly for Giddens, Weick, Foucault and Latour[8]); they emerge, borne by a processual rationality that cannot be reduced to the properties of the human and non-human elements that constitute it.

The ambivalence of the management tool is highlighted both by structuration theory (structure enables and constrains[9]) and activity theory (the instrument develops the power to act and at the same time exercises a pragmatic constraint on the way work is carried out[10]). Although for Foucault,[11] tools forge discipline and subjectification, this is not a totalitarian influence as there are failures and resistance. Individuals are neither completely free nor completely constrained. There is no absolute technological determinism, not even a managerial one.

The acceptance of a new tool by its users supposes a more or less profound modification, even a transgression. This can be done because tools are malleable: there is always uncertainty in their use. The sociology of organisations[12] has familiarised us with deviations made in the usage of management tools and deformations of the tools' action. There are structuration effects but nothing implies the resignation of agents submitting to technical imperatives. The tool does not generate action – it mediates it. But as explained in Chapter 6, this does not mean that the effects of management tools are null. With a given tool, not everything is possible; the game is not completely open. There may be malleability in the tool but it is no greater than that in humans. Orienting human action in certain directions, accompanying their gestures, tools may cause more problems than they provide solutions. They can also be fallible. Sometimes, like in the industrial world of Chaplin's *Modern Times*, tools are focused on things and forget people, who are only asked to serve the 'management machines' (Girin, 1983). At the same time,

---

[8] See also Chapter 6.   [9] Thesis 6 ('Technology is both constraining and enabling').
[10] Thesis 8 ('The tool is nothing outside the activity system').
[11] Thesis 2 ('The tool as a technique for discipline and government').
[12] Thesis 10 ('The effects of the tool are conditioned by what actors do').

the game is never completely over: breakdowns appear and the technique becomes obsolete. Management tools require constant maintenance.

Another feature characterises all the approaches studied and gives them unity: as the title of this book suggests, these approaches are 'social' and therefore distant from methodological individualism. According to these approaches, neither the property of individuals nor their singular actions are sufficient to account for the phenomena surrounding the use of management tools. The individual is never left to a solitary confrontation with objects considered external to her- or himself.

The approach we propose applies in principle to all types of management tool, the diversity of their uses and the situations in which they intervene. It allows a broadening of current issues and sheds fresh light on older questions.

REVISITING OLDER QUESTIONS

Going beyond the Macro–Micro Distinction

In the social science literature, it is common to distinguish between two levels of observation: the macro and the micro. This could even inspire a distinction between two types of tools. Basing our idea on Foucault we could, for example, separate 'disciplinary devices' that individualise, localise and create behavioural norms, from the government devices above them that totalise (as for statistics) and aim at overall results.[13] The former would be a micro approach and the latter a macro approach.

Nevertheless we should note that when we try to apprehend these categories using management tools we find that they are interlinked. Instead of being distinct tools, some at the 'macro' others at the 'micro' level, it is interesting to perceive them in several states or shapes. We can thus distinguish between states of 'being in

---

[13] Thesis 2 ('The tool as a technique for discipline and government').

circulation' and 'being inscribed'. In its circulating state, its 'macro' form, the tool intervenes in a wide area that can be national or even international. In their inscribed state, their 'micro' form, tools are contextualised and specific to an organisation and its internal context.

In its circulating state, the tool appears in the form of rules of law imposed by the legislator or the market regulator, or in professional prescriptions, international norms, labels, best practices, manuals and customisable software packages. These generally valid forms are designed to travel far and be adopted, 'implemented' in a large number of situations. For the groups that promote them it is a question of making practices conform on a vast scale with a regulatory aim, or to profit from selling the tool – a trade that is all the more lucrative the more adopters exist. The market for management tools and standardised 'best practices' thus broadly sustains the sector providing services to organisations. Here the tool is a messenger, the product of a culture and intentions, or a carrier of conventions and of rules of a social game. It exists independent of its uses and the context in which it is applied. Besides, this circulating form constitutes the dominant state of certain tools, like software packages, or even their exclusive nature (as for accounting standards).

The field of circulating forms is densely populated and the same tool can exist in different guises according to the group that gives it its shape. Thus, an international agreement finds itself transformed when it is taken up by an EU directive, which is itself modified by its transposition into national law. International standards invented in transnational spaces can be adapted to national professional or sectorial contexts. On the software and consultancy markets the 'solutions' sold compete with one another. Management tools, considered in their circulating form, can be studied from the point of view of the circulation of ideas (Czarniawska and Sevon, 2005) or the struggles between management standards. The actors we meet on these stages are entrepreneurs of causes, pressure groups, employers' associations, professional groups, public regulators, parliamentarians, senior civil servants, international organisations, think tanks, consultancy and audit agencies, or software producers.[14]

The tool also exists in each situation where it is implemented in an inscribed or situated form. It is rarely created out of nothing and finds itself imported, adapted, adjusted, 'translated' and 'edited' (Sahlin and Wedlin, 2008) in a specific situation that is important to examine in order to understand what the tool effects. In this contextualised form, the tool only really exists in its situated uses: as an ad hoc realisation or an adapted, heavily customised import, it is what it is used for – whether by individuals or groups. In extreme cases, one tool can be used instead of another to satisfy uses for which it was not designed. This is what ergonomists call a catachresis (Béguin and Rabardel, 1999) and it would be wrong to interpret this as a mere diversion. The actors we meet in these situations are different: executives, managers, workers, consultants or information technology service providers who participate in managerial situations (Segrestin, 2004); but also depending on what is to be managed, one can meet in these situations other actors such as clients, rivers, smoke, or even steel bars. It is a different world. Although the intersections between the actors of circulating forms and those of inscribed forms are limited and infrequent (except as distant references or ceremonial quotations), they are nevertheless often significant: they allow identifying the tool entrepreneurs in the field or first-time adopters who, in fact, often participate in the construction of the norm they 'adopt'.[15]

These two states of the tool call for analysis and data collection methods that are adapted to them (see Appendix 2). This is always a question of examining the tool and the particular form it takes in its context, and linking it to the actors who are pertinent in order to understand the tool as well as those who designed it. In its situated

---

[14] See, for example, research on transnational communities that produce standards (Brunsson and Jacobsson, 2000; Djelic and Sahlin-Andersson, 2006).

[15] See, for example, Berland et al. (2008) and Berland and Chiapello (2009) whose analysis gives some importance to actors who are at the intersection of the different worlds of prescription and operational implementation.

state, the tool carries features that have been forged during the production of its circulating form, but that are then the object of translation and inscription tasks necessary to make it effective. This translation may also be a betrayal, a deviation, or even a reduction to powerlessness. Following the tool in all its states can be a means of changing levels of analysis. It enables linking in the same description macro-level elements related to the stage of a tool's invention as a 'circulating form' and micro-level elements concerning what it does when it is applied in the daily life of organisations and work.

The logic of democratic counter-expertise, which, as opposed to technical expertise, inspired our approach, supposes not to limit one's gaze to the local scene in which the management tool manifests its existence. Instead, it requires varying the scales and spaces of analysis to be able to understand its origins and implications. Our method is neither 'globalist' nor 'localist' but tries to go beyond the macro–micro distinction, which we know can sometimes hinder the understanding of phenomena. It is therefore desirable to integrate both levels into the analysis of the situations encountered (Cicourel, 1981).

Management tool analysis does not require changing methods of description and analysis according to scale, as some practices in sociological research invite us to do – such as, for example, considering on the macro level societal problems, general theories, and statistical data, and on the micro level limited problems, local theories, and ethnographic studies. Taking up the invitation of ethnomethodology (Hilbert, 1990), we have studied macro constructions through the same lens that we apply to micro process. Either we start with a situated observation of a management tool that increases in scope, or we consider a technical device with very large scope and follow its tracks and seek to identify its effects on increasingly smaller scales.

The management tool is subject to numerous factors that collaborated in its emergence, as well as in local contexts. As such it can be seen as a courier or carrier. We should therefore conduct the social analysis of tools on different levels, without changing the method.

Detailed analysis makes the researcher travel through distinct social scenes that may have impacts and reach wider than the local area.

Renewing the Theory of Organisations

The works accumulated over the past 50 years have successively questioned the organisational unity of the firm (political coalitions, actors' strategies) and its enclosed character (the firm as an open system). More recently, under the effects of change in management practices (break-up of the work community and hierarchical firms, development of *in situ* subcontracting, business alliances, rapid evolution of legal perimeters of the firms and capitalistic reconfigurations) and a change in the theoretical view (with more attention paid to interactions with stakeholders), we have come to consider that the company no longer really has any border and that it has become dissolved in networks in permanent reconfiguration.

The controversy between Williamson (1991) and Powell (1990) about the existence of a network form alongside market and hierarchy is one sign among others of the difficulties in conceiving a network as an organisation. Powell considered the network as an entirely separate organisational form while Williamson saw it only as a hybridisation of the market and the hierarchy. Looking at management tools can help us to get away from this sterile opposition between an organisation conceived as a unit of action, endowed with policies and the means for action (classically, the idea of hierarchy enters into this) and an organisation that has become dissolved in networks. Tools supply us with clues about the company's functioning in a network. They may equip 'distant proximities': the boss is distant in terms of space but remains present thanks to technologies of coordination and control. Here we find an illustration of Beniger's thesis (1986), which states that information technologies allow evolution in forms of control. Hierarchical control is indeed less necessary when it is possible, thanks to information technology, to monitor at a distance multiple flows on a global scale. Networks still need to be coordinated and controlled to do business, but these actions become less visible. Because management tools remain necessary to ensure this coordination, studying them allows us to describe new forms of division of labour, control of production and allocation of resources with greater precision as well as new power relations that arise from these new organisational configurations.

Our socio-technical approach contributes to the renewal of organisation theory by introducing a different conception of the organisation. The organisation is no longer seen first and foremost as a socially autonomous economic unit, separated from its environment by clearly marked boundaries. It appears less as a defined space than as a system of flows – physical, financial and information – that are channelled, coordinated and controlled by specific technical means that structure and maintain social relations, allow economic activities to take place, or establish in particular entities monetary surpluses called 'profit'. The organisation is no longer limited to a specific place, but neither is it dissolved in a sea of multiple links. It exists through the regulation of economic meso-systems that traverse through clients, suppliers, subcontractors, competitors or allies. The global coherence of these systems can be reconstructed and brought to light via a study of these regulations starting from the management tools that organise them and so allow a certain traceability.

This echoes with Callon and Latour (1981) and their understanding of how certain actors become 'greater' and can be considered 'macro-actors'. Their approach can be taken up here in order to understand how certain 'organisations' or 'companies' keep consistency in such a way that we can still think that these collective entities 'act' and 'have strategies', as stated in everyday language. Callon and Latour (1981) review all the tools, rules, walls and objects that allow associations to stabilise and actors to 'grow' by association with other forces. In the case of organisations, it seems to us that, among these artefacts, management tools play a central role because of their particular functions of coordination, organisation and direction.

Thinking about the Transformations of Capitalism

The management tools perspective can offer a new intelligibility of the economic system because of the two characteristics that we have just explored. First of all, it allows a new conception of the organisation, to decipher the firm, to understand how economic flows are organised and structured and how this structuring evolves over time. The ability of management tools to circulate through a very large number of situations also opens the way to a systemic analysis. Transformations of capitalism can therefore be studied at two levels: the daily organisation of activities on the one hand and the collective rules that contribute to regulate capitalism on the other.

On the level of daily operations, it should be noted that the way in which companies handle certain questions – for example, their expert personnel, the supply of certain raw materials or even their relations with different service providers – evolves over time. These transformations are accompanied by changes in the management tools used, knowing that it is not always easy to distinguish what the evolution of practices owes to the invention of new management tools (think of work and remote control capacities enabled by information systems), to the transformation of business models, or to the dominant representations of the management best practices. But in any case, a management tools research perspective improves our understanding of these transformations.

Once the researcher has identified the relevant transformations, the reasons why former management practices and tools have lost their impact and the kind of crisis they have suffered need to be researched, as does the way in which this transformation was started, how it unfolded, and how new devices were built in the process. The history of management contains many periods of craze for certain tools and practices, some of which have been analysed as 'fashions' (Abrahamson, 1996; Abrahamson and Fairchild, 1999; Clark, 2004; Czarniawska and Sevon, 2005), but whose transformative effects on the organisation of firms can be considerable. It thus makes sense to study certain managerial innovations according to their diffusion[16] to shed light on the wider, morphological transformations of capitalism.

A management tools perspective also allows us to show what has changed as well as what persists but is concealed. Such an analysis may for example explain how the standardisation of work endures as it is outsourced to external service providers. According to this analysis, the notion of 'one best way' developed by Taylor has not disappeared: less perceptible, it is updated in the 'best practices' of outsourced Taylorism and ingrained into inter-organisational management information systems.

The circulating character of management tools, likely to become norms that impose themselves on a set of actors, also allows situated analyses to be systematically referred to more global phenomena concerning the interactions between organisations in the same field, or even throughout the whole of an economic system. It also allows a better understanding of what is at stake in design discussions that operate in circulating spheres, since what is produced there is conceived for widespread dissemination.

The study of management tools may be facilitated by starting researching in circulating spheres that are usually easier to access. A certain number of these spheres where norms are produced are indeed committed to provide some transparency. The undemocratic nature of the rules that are developed in these spheres (i.e., not subject to parliamentary debate) is partly compensated via online communication of numerous pieces of information or public calls for comment in the context of 'due process'. As soon as the norms begin to have a serious impact on the functioning of the economic sphere, 'transparency' aims at supporting the legitimacy of the normative production spaces (Chiapello and Medjad, 2009). The current and important development of 'soft law' (that is to say, non-obligatory norms that companies adopt as rules of conduct for their global activities) aims

---

[16] They are also normally relayed by many different consultancies and a substantial normative literature.

at compensating for the difficulties in developing international law. But at the same time, it pushes back the desire for control by some states by emphasising the business world's capacity for self-regulation. However, the problem with these norms is that they are produced by the very actors to whom they are supposed to apply. This creates a legitimacy deficit that must be compensated for by a form of transparency, or by welcoming other stakeholders into the process. These arenas are therefore more accessible to enquiry than the internal functioning of companies and it is then possible to follow what becomes of these standards in different national, professional or entrepreneurial settings.

We think that the study of the economic system is also facilitated by the existence of a continuity between instruments of government that are used by public administrations to regulate some sectors and management tools used by organisations to coordinate and control their activities. Besides the fact that all the analytical grids presented in this book can be used to study instruments of government as well as management tools, it is not unusual that the laws and rules imposed on economic actors include managerial prescriptions and require the use of some management tools. Examples are information disclosure obligations, compulsory audits, or administrative authorisation procedures. Audits can indeed help ensure that the organisations manage themselves according to the rules laid down by the legislator. Multi-level studies seem also appropriate to understand the way in which an economic system structures itself. Such studies would start with an analysis of the debates on regulation, instruments of government and public policies, and then move on to studying their impacts and their implementation through tools and management practices in the respective organisations.[17]

Finally, we propose to expand the approach of some economic sociologists who seek to identify the contribution of management and

---

[17] See Baud and Chiapello (2015) for an example of this approach.

its tools to the construction and functioning of markets.[18] Cochoy (2007) shows the importance of these tools in his work on marketing, which is considered a technique that allows the market economy to be disciplined. Although usually seen as a visible vector for the promotion of the market, marketing has proved to serve as a strategy for avoiding competition. Its very existence denies the self-regulatory virtues of the market. It offers devices (advertising, packaging, brand names, surveys) through which large companies attempt to control the market rather than submit to it. The meeting of supply and demand only happens through 'marketing's mediating role' (Cochoy, 2007, p. 115) that relies on decision-making support (packaging, visualisation of products, brand names, labels) in the form of devices that format choices (Dubuisson-Quellier, 1999). In the market, the visible hand of management organises, structures and coordinates by attributing roles and defining courses of action. The observation of what is happening through the management tools, which is of obvious interest in the empirical analysis of the functioning of the markets, must therefore be extended to management issues other than that of the meeting with customers.

Management Tools Perspective: A Research Strategy

Although a large variety of works have already recognised the role of management tools, and despite the many models and analytical perspectives we have tried to synthesise in this book, it seems to us that the management tools perspective is still underused as a general research strategy. We propose to consider management tools as analysers that allow access to larger questions of work, organisations, markets and capitalism, but also to public action and the regulation of economic systems. Such analysers are all the more useful in that they

---

[18] See the call of Steiner (2005, p. 32) 'to enrich the landscape of our discipline by making room for approaches based on the resources offered by management sciences, for they are very interesting when it comes to understanding the functioning of the market as a concrete meeting place of supply and demand' (our translation). See also Steiner(2001).

allow us to move on various scenes and help to build a systemic, global understanding of organisational and economic functionings. In a world made up of organisations, where our lives are largely structured by organised systems that are themselves coordinated by management tools and regulated by instruments of government, research into these objects is of crucial importance. The time has come to give management tools all the attention they deserve in the light of their discrete but essential role in our current world.

Appendix 1
Cross-Reading the Theses on Some Generic Questions

The analytical frameworks that we have brought together in this book are not mutually exclusive and we believe dialogue or exchanges between them are possible. Below we present some questions that, in our opinion, can be better understood by combining several points of view. Obviously, it does not purport to be exhaustive; the aim is to emphasise the possibilities provided by the social analysis of management tools, recalling the different theses that have been examined in this book.

In response to some basic questions that we have identified, only the most directly usable theses are re-examined through their major contributions. These are just simple pointers whose essential elements are taken from the summary sheets in Chapters 3–5 (Part II). For the rest, we refer to the presentation of the theories.

HOW DID WE GET TO THIS POINT?

This question concerns the origins of the tool, the problematisations that brought about its production and the conditions for its implementation in the context where it is used.

Thesis 1: Axiom of domination (the creation and implementation of the tool are inscribed in a project for domination and exploitation). Concepts: exploitation, ideology. Method: interpret the tool by repositioning it in the more general framework of power relations that structure society (the struggle to dominate the field).

Thesis 2: Axiom of the microphysics of power. Concept: governmentality. Method: reconstitute the conditions where the tool emerged by simultaneously paying attention to the voices that have been silenced and to the discontinuities that made it possible (genealogy). Reconstitute the strategic function of the power relation.

Thesis 3: Axiom of the perversity of the dominant. Concepts: manipulation, reification. Method: listen to the subject's complaint in order to identify the forms of violence at the root of suffering.

Thesis 4: Axiom of the search for legitimacy. Concepts: isomorphisms, especially mimetic (management fashions), opposition and hybridisation of institutional logics, institutional entrepreneur. Method: analyse how legitimacy is built in a given field and understand the institutional games that preside over the adoption of the tool.

Thesis 7: Axiom of controversies. Concepts: translation process (problematisation, interessement, enrolment, mobilisation), spokesperson. Method: reconstitute the controversies, the irreversibilities and the not realised possibilities.

WHAT IS THE TOOL MADE OF?

This question paves the way towards a technical, internal analysis that goes beyond the most obvious descriptive aspects easily accessible. The research aims at identifying what is deposited in the tool, encapsulated and reified.

Thesis 1: Axiom of domination. Concept: ideology (the dominant conceal their intentions; hiding behind technique, they promote their ideology). Method: critical unveiling.

Thesis 2: Axiom of the microphysics of power. Feature of speech: power/knowledge (individuals are placed under surveillance). Method: study the coherent configuration of knowledge and power contained in managerial devices.

Thesis 5: Axiom of the conventional nature of social life. Concepts: convention, categorisation, classification. Method: find the representations, values and conventions incorporated in the tool.

Thesis 6: Axiom of the mediating role of technology in the structuration of social systems (technology conveys interpretative plans, resources and norms that are encoded in it). Concept: structural properties. Method: study the dimensions of the structural (signification, domination, legitimation).

Thesis 9: Axiom of the textuality of the management tool. Concepts: the tool as text, inter-textuality (the tool as an element of the organisational discourse). Method: reveal the narrations that the tool conveys and the way in which these contribute to organisational discourse.

HOW DOES IT WORK?

Going beyond the instructions for use drawn up during the technical description of the tool, here we reveal what holds the tool together and allows its use.

Thesis 4: Axiom of the search for legitimacy. Concept: isomorphism (legitimation of tools). Method: identify the institutions that support the management tool.

Thesis 7: Axiom of symmetry. Concepts: network, arrangement. Method: reconstitute the power relations and translation process that have allowed controversies to die away.

Thesis 8: Axiom of the dual nature of the instrument (artefact + plans for use). Method: analyse the interactions between the management tool and other components of an activity system; study the instrumental genesis (the tool's transformation into an instrument).

Thesis 10: Axiom of homo strategicus. Concepts: stakes, system of concrete action. Method: analyse the stakes and the system of relations in order to understand the cooperation between actors around the tool.

HOW DOES IT EVOLVE?

This question relates to the modification of the field in which the tool intervenes, to its being potentially thrown into crisis, to critiques and the de-legitimisation that accompany them, but also to new possibilities that might arise.

Thesis 1: Axiom of social conflict. Concept: the struggle for domination. Method: study the asymmetries of power and power relations.

Thesis 5: Axiom of the plurality of conventions. Concept: dynamic of tests. Method: study the moments of conventional uncertainty and critique.

Thesis 7: Axiom of controversies. Concepts: process of translation (problematisation, interessement, enrolment, mobilisation of allies), spokesperson. Method: think of the tool and actors as the temporary result of a network. The irreversible is created through the accumulation of connections.

Thesis 10: Axiom of innovation and power. The tool is an opportunity to manipulate the rules. Concept: social actor (can play around with management tools). Method: reconstitute the system of concrete action by analysing actors' games.

WHAT IS THE EFFECT?

This final question concerns the identification of what is produced or reproduced by the tool and its uses. We are particularly interested in changes in behaviour, identity, power relations, the nature of work carried out and skills sought, and the quality of life at work.

Thesis 1: Axiom of domination. Concepts: exploitation, domination. Method: identify the balance and relations of power that are present in the economic field and are reproduced or displaced by the tool.

Thesis 2: Axiom of subjectification. Concepts: disciplinary power, construction of the self, disciplined subject. Method: study the process of subjectification implemented in a knowledge-power device.

Thesis 3: Axiom of managerial reductionism (evacuation of subjectivity). Concepts: submission, manipulation, reification. Method: clinical (listen to the subject's complaint), reveal the forms of oppression.

Thesis 5: Axiom of the productive and interactive nature of conventions. Concepts: categorisation, classification, commensuration, test. Method: discover the conventions incorporated in the tool in order to understand how it coordinates actions and judgements, imparts ways of doing and thinking and constructs differences.

Thesis 6: Axiom of the mediating role of technology in the structuration of social systems. Axiom of the duality of technology. Concept: enabling/constraining. Method: study separately the effects of the management tool on the social (technology can create structure) and the effects of the social on the management tool.

Thesis 7: Axiom of society being made. Concepts: action at a distance, performation (the tool does not just represent the world but helps to produce the world). Method: study the way in which the tool acts on humans and non-humans.

Thesis 8: Axiom of the dual nature of the instrument. Feature of style: mediation. Method: analyse the interactions between the management tool and other components of an activity system to identify learning processes, changes in work relations.

Thesis 9: Axiom of the tool as a narrative story-maker. Concept: sense-making, performativity (the tool produces the social world, modelling its representations). Method: analyse acts of communication in relation to the use of management tools.

Thesis 10: Axiom of innovation and power (the introduction of a new tool causes a redistribution of power). Method: analyse actors' play, justifications for resistance and the stakes that motivate them.

Appendix 2
Studying the Tool in All Its Various States

It must be remembered that for the analyst's scrutiny, the management tool presents itself in two forms and in two different states: a circulating state and an inscribed state where actors and scenes are very different (see General Conclusion). In its circulating state, the tool acts within a vast national or even international perimeter. It might be the case, for example, of a legal norm, an integrated management software package, a management method package (Six Sigma, lean manufacturing, balanced scorecard, etc.). The inscribed state, which is the 'micro' form, corresponds to contextualised tools that are specific to an organisation and its local context. According to the perspective applied, some tools may relate to both: an integrated management software package can be largely adapted to a local situation; a balanced scorecard can take on different aspects, etc.

According to the cases and the theoretical frameworks mobilised, research has concentrated on either one form or another. Without being exclusive, critical and institutionalist approaches are more interested in circulating forms and interactional approaches more interested in inscribed forms. Our perspective is that it is difficult to study situated forms without taking at least a brief look at the origins of the tool; and that the pure analysis of circulating forms cannot be disconnected from an examination of the real influence of the tool in question. In the case of extensive dissemination and deep impact, the research work can contribute to analysis of broad social transformations; in the case of limited dissemination, research contributes more to the study of the failure of certain social forms.

Listed below are the data to be collected according to whether the form of a tool is circulating or inscribed. This simple, non-exhaustive tracking aims to provide clarity for the apprentice researcher thinking about beginning the social study of a management tool.

(1) THE CIRCULATING FORM (THE TOOL OUTSIDE A SPECIFIC SITUATION)

Describing the Management Tool as a Technical Object

Describe its physical aspect, instructions for its use, the infrastructure in which it is found.

Describe the recommended instructions for use (what it is supposed to do, how it is supposed to work).

Collect:

- for a tool of the 'standards' type: the texts that introduce it, encode it, regulate it and its instructions for use;
- for a tool of the 'software' type: the procedures, manuals, training support that accompany it. Make screen copies; follow the sequences present in the software.

Identify the terms and the key concepts used by the tool and in the discourse that accompanies it (technical vocabulary proper to the tool and to its use, managerial concepts, etc.).

Identify the Conventions, Representations, Models of Judgement and Action, Premises That Are Present in the Tool or That Support Its Purpose

Vision of the organisation, of what it means to work well, of the 'context' of the organisation and what is at stake: categories of analysis, categories of actors, what is managed and what is not. Conceptions of performance.

Behaviour required of the user, hypothesis about what drives the user and about what the working context should be.

Establish the History of the Tool

Understand the period, the cultural, economic and social environment surrounding the invention of the tool.

Who are the actors involved in the shaping of the tool (age, gender, social and professional story, nationality)? What are their intentions? What are their interests and ambitions? Where do their ideas and their references come from?

Who are the 'pioneers' (first adopters)? What relations do they have with the designers (epistemic community, political interests, ideological convergence)?

Collect the texts that have accompanied the construction of the tool (minutes of meetings, calls for feedback, contributions from different actors, denunciations and critiques).

Question the actors of the process. Observe the different places where the tool is discussed.

Reconstitute the debates and the chronology, and the different arenas of formalisation.

Study the Modes of Circulation

> Who are the actors who make the tool circulate? According to what modalities (media, teachings, rules of law, consultants' advice, etc.)? With what effects (appropriation, oppositions, debates, etc.)?

(2) THE INSCRIBED FORM (THE TOOL IN A SPECIFIC SITUATION)

Like for the circulating forms, the study of the inscribed form cannot overlook the analysis of the conventions deposited in the tool; however, here the analysis focuses on the organisational context where the tool comes into action.

Describe the Organisational Context

> The organisation in which the management tool has its place (size, sector of activity; general structure, culture).
>
> The part of the organisation (function, department) that is most directly concerned.
>
> The history of the tool in this place: When was it produced? With what aim? Who promoted it?
>
> The official discourse around the tool or its introduction: What was said? By whom? In what circumstances?
>
> Link these elements:
> - to other management tools used in the situation;
> - to other management practices in the same company that rely on the same representations and premises (similarities, incoherencies);
> - to the normative discourses external to the tool (management literature) that are taken up in the situation via training programmes, the work of consultants, discourses of justification, and which refer to the tool in its circulating form or to the tool in other given situations as an example.

Identify the Actors in Their Relation to the Tool

> List the actors (individuals or groups concerned and capable of intervening). Describe them in terms of age, gender, skill, training, social status and professional career path. Specify their function in the organisation, the nature of their activity and how this concerns the tool. Specify for each one the relation to use of the tool: design, dissemination, use.
>
> Give an idea of the intensity of this use (frequency, duration).
>
> Characterise their 'affective' relation to the tool (positive, neutral, negative).

Describe the interactions between these actors around the tool.

What are the stakes, risks, potential gains and losses of these actors (in terms of taking an interest in work, social status, income, quality of life)?

What resources are available to them?

Is it possible to identify in promoters and opponents the cultural and identity factors that are likely to explain their positions?

Reconstitute the History of the Tool in the Organisation

How can the adoption of the tool coming from elsewhere be explained? Mimicry? Coercion? Rational myth? Who are the prescribers?

What debates have occurred? Describe the processes of enrolment and commitment, the problems encountered, the configurations and modifications carried out during the project.

Chronology of the implementation (first steps, periodisation, key events).

Interactions between the actors and the characteristics of the technical device.

Evolution in use over time. Perception of successes and failures.

Identify the Different Effects of the Tool and/or the Transformations That Accompany It

Atmosphere at work, motivation at work, structure of jobs, content and division of labour, workers' profiles, employment conditions, effective uses of the tool, ways of appropriation, quality of the work carried out using the tool.

Transformation of frameworks of thinking, and of ways of representing work and routines.

Strategy of the organisation, the department.

Redistribution of powers within the organisation, modification of relations between professions, departments, people; transformation of areas of uncertainty.

Bibliography

Abrahamson, E. (1996). Management fashion. *Academy of Management Review*, 21(1), 254–85.

Abrahamson, E. and Fairchild, G. (1999). Management fashion: Lifecycles, triggers, and collective processes. *Administrative Science Quarterly*, 44(4), 708–40.

Aggeri, F. (2005). Les régimes de gouvernementalité dans le domaine de l'environnement. In A. Hatchuel, E. Pezet, K. Starkey and O. Lenay, eds., *Gouvernement, organisation et gestion. L'héritage de Michel Foucault*. Québec: Les Presses de l'Université de Laval, 431–67.

Aggeri, F. and Labatut, J. (2010). La gestion au prisme de ses instruments: Une analyse généalogique des approches théoriques fondées sur les instruments de gestion. *Finance, Contrôle, Stratégie*, 13(3), 5–37.

Ahnre, G., Brunsson, N. and Garsten, C. (2000). Standardizing through organization. In N. Brunsson and B. Jacobsson, eds., *A World of Standards*. Oxford University Press, 50–70.

Ahrens, T. and Chapman, C. (2002). The structuration of legitimate performance measures and management: Day-to-day contests of accountability in a U.K. restaurant chain. *Management Accounting Research*, 13(2), 151–71.

Akrich, M., Callon, M. and Latour, B. (2006). *Sociologie de la traduction. Textes fondateurs*. Paris: Presse École des Mines de Paris.

Alford, R. R. and Friedland, R. (1985). *Powers of Theory: Capitalism, the State, and Democracy*. Cambridge University Press.

Amado, G. and Enriquez, E. (2006). Editorial. *Nouvelle Revue de Psychosociologie*, 1.

Amblard, M. (2003a). Vers une théorie de la dynamique des conventions. In M. Amblard, ed., *Conventions et management*. Bruxelles: Éditions De Boeck Université, 139–58.

Amblard, M., ed. (2003b). *Conventions et management*. Bruxelles: Éditions De Boeck Université.

Amblard, M. (2004). Conventions et comptabilité: Vers une approche sociologique du modèle. *Comptabilité, Contrôle, Audit*, 10(3), 47–67.

Ardichvili, A. (2003). Constructing socially situated learning experiences in human resource development: An activity theory perspective. *Human Resource Development International*, 6(1), 5–20.

Ardoino, J. (1990). L'analyse multiréférentielle des situations sociales. *Psychologie clinique*, 3, 33–49.

Arnold, P. and Hammond, T. (1994). The role of accounting in ideological conflict: Lessons from the South African Divestment Movement. *Accounting, Organizations and Society*, 19(2), 111–26.

Aubert, N. and Gaulejac, V. de (1991). *Le coût de l'excellence*. Paris: Seuil.

Austin, J. L. (1975). *How To Do Things with Words*. Oxford University Press.

Balfet, H. (1991). *Observer l'action technique. Des chaînes opératoires pour quoi faire?* Paris: CNRS.

Balle, C. and Peaucelle, J. L. (1972). *Le pouvoir informatique dans l'entreprise*. Paris: Les Éditions d'organisation.

Barad, K. (2007). *Meeting the University Halfway: Quantum Physics and the Entanglement of Matter and Meaning*. Durham, NC: Duke University Press.

Barley, S. (1986). Technology as an occasion for structuring: Evidence from observations of CT scanners and the social order of radiology departments. *Administrative Science Quarterly*, 31(1), 78–108.

Barley, S. and Kunda, G. (1992). Design and devotion: Surges of rational and normative ideologies of control in managerial discourse. *Administrative Science Quarterly*, 37(3), 363–99.

Barnard, C. (1938). *The Functions of the Executive*. Cambridge, MA: Harvard Business Press.

Barraud de Lagerie, P. (2009). Objectiver la qualité sociale. In F. Vatin, ed., *Évaluer et valoriser*. Toulouse: Presses Universitaires du Mirail, 229–45.

Barrett, M., Grant, D., and Wailes, N. (2006). ICT and organizational change: Introduction to the special issue. *Journal of Applied Behavioral Science*, 42(1): 6–22.

Barrett, M., Oborn, E. and Orlikowski, W. (2016). Creating value in online communities: The sociomaterial configuring of strategy, platform, and stakeholder engagement. *Information Systems Research*, 27(4), 704–23.

Barrett, M. and Walsham, G. (1999). Electronic trading and work transformation in the London insurance market. *Information Systems Research*, 10(1), 1–21.

Barrey, S. (2007). Struggling to be displayed at the point of purchase: The emergence of merchandising in French supermarkets. In M. Callon, Y. Millo and F. Muniesa, eds., *Market Devices*. Oxford: Blackwell Publishing, 92–108.

Barthes, R. (1972). *Mythologies*. New York: Hill & Wang.

Barus-Michel, J., Enriquez, E. and Lévy, A., eds. (2003). *Vocabulaire de la psychosociologie. Références et positions*. Ramonville: Erès.

Baud, C. and Chiapello, E. (2015). How the financialization of firms occurs: The role of regulation and management tools – the case of bank credit. *Revue française de sociologie*, 56(3), 439–68. [English translation of the French article online] www.cairn-int.info/article-E_RFS_563_0439–how-the-financialization-of-firms-occurs.htm

Baudrillard, J. (1996). *The System of Objects*. London and New York: Verso [Original work published in 1968].

Baumard, P. (1997). Une école française de l'intervention, commentaire de l'ouvrage. In J. C. Moisdon, ed., *Du mode d'existence des outils de gestion*. Paris: Seli Arslan [*Revue française de gestion*, 114], 136–8.

Bayart, D. (1995). Des objets qui solidifient une théorie: L'histoire du contrôle statistique de fabrication. In F. Charue-Duboc, ed., *Des savoirs en action. Contributions de la recherche en gestion*. Paris: L'Harmattan, 139–73.

Beauvois, J. L. (1994). *Traité de la servitude libérale*. Paris: Dunod.

Beauvois, J. L. (1997). Cognitive dissonance theory: A radical view. *European Review of Social Psychology*, 8(1), 1–32.

Beauvois, J. L. (2005). *Les illusions libérales, individualisme et pouvoir social. Petit traité des grandes illusions*. Grenoble: Presses Universitaires de Grenoble.

Becker, H. S. (1963). *The Outsiders*. New York: Free Press.

Beckert, J. and Aspers, P., eds. (2011). *The Worth of Goods: Valuation and Pricing in the Economy*. Oxford University Press.

Béguin, P. and Rabardel, P. (1999). Concevoir pour les activités instrumentées. *Revue d'Intelligence Artificielle*, 14, 35–54.

Béguin, P. and Rabardel, P. (2000). Designing for instrument-mediated activity. *Scandinavian Journal of Information Systems*, 12, 173–90.

Benedetto-Meyer, M., Maugeri, S., and Metzger, J. L. (2011). *L'emprise de la gestion. La société au risque des violences gestionnaires*, Paris: L'Harmattan.

Beniger, J. (1986). *The Control Revolution: Technological and Economic Origins of the Information Society*. Cambridge, MA: Harvard University Press.

Benzerafa, M. (2007). L'introduction de la *Balanced Scorecard* dans les administrations de l'État en France: Premières conclusions d'une recherche empirique. *Politiques et management public*, 25(4), 81–97.

Bergström, O., Hasselbladh, H. and Karreman, D. (2009). Organizing disciplinary power in a knowledge organization. *Scandinavian Journal of Management*, 25(2), 178–90.

Berland, N., Alcouffe, S. and Levant, Y. (2008). The role of actor-networks in the diffusion of management accounting innovations: A comparative study of budgetary control, GP method and activity-based costing in France. *Management Accounting Research*, 19(1), 1–17.

Berland, N. and Chiapello, E. (2009). Criticisms of capitalism, budgeting and the double enrolment: Budgetary control rhetoric and social reform in France in the 1930s and 1950s. *Accounting, Organizations and Society*, 34(1), 28–57.

Bernard, B. (2008). Itinéraire d'un indicateur forestier: De l'émergence et de l'enrôlement. *Revue française de gestion*, 181, 97–110.

Bernoux, P. (2004a). Le changement dans les organisations: Entre structures et interactions. *Relations industrielles/Industrial Relations*, 57(1), 77–99.

Bernoux, P. (2004b). *Sociologie du changement dans les entreprises et les organisations*. Paris: Seuil.

Berry, M., ed. (1983). *Une technologie invisible? L'impact des instruments de gestion sur l'évolution des systèmes humains*. CRG-École polytechnique, Rapport pour le Ministère de la Recherche et de la Technologie.

Bessire, D. and Onnée, S. (2010). Assessing corporate social performance: Strategies of legitimation and conflicting ideologies. *Critical Perspectives on Accounting*, 21, 445–67.

Beunza, D. and Garud, R. (2007). Calculators, lemmings or frame-makers? The intermediary role of securities analysts. *Sociological Review*, 55(2), 13–39.

Bezes, P. (2004). Rationalisation salariale dans l'administration française: Un instrument discret. In P. Lascoumes and P. Le Galès, eds., *Gouverner par les instruments*. Paris: Presses de Sciences Po, 108–9.

Bidet, A. (2005). Quatre mesures du téléphone: L'invention d'une gestion téléphonique. *Économie et Sociétés*, série Socio-Économie du travail, 25(4), 601–23.

Bidet, A. (2010). Dessiner le marché, démultiplier le calcul: Les rationalisations matérielle et formelle dans la téléphonie au tournant des années 1980. *Revue française de socio-économie*, 1, 165–85.

Biencourt, O., Chasserant, C. and Rébérioux, A. (2001). L'économie des conventions: L'affirmation d'un programme de recherche. In P. Batifoulier, ed., *Théorie des conventions*. Paris: Economica, 193–218.

Bijan, A. (2017) Exploring materialization of institutional logics: A case of changing tax regimes and procedures. *Academy of Management Annual Meeting Proceedings*, 1, 11765.

Bijker, W. and Law, J. (1992). *Shaping Technology, Building Society: Studies in Sociotechnical Change*. Cambridge, MA: MIT Press.

Blandin, B. (2002). *La construction du social par les objets*. Paris: PUF.

Blau, P. M. (1955). *Dynamics of Bureaucracy: A Study of Interpersonal Relations in Two Government Agencies*. University of Chicago Press.

Boje, D. M. (1991). The storytelling organization: A study of story performance in an office-supply firm. *Administrative Science Quarterly*, 36(1), 106–26.

Boje, D. M. and Winsor, R. D. (1993). The resurrection of Taylorism: Total quality management's hidden agenda. *Journal of Management Studies*, 6(4), 57–70.

Boltanski, L. (1970). Taxinomies populaires, taxinomies savantes: Les objets de consommation et leur classement. *Revue française de sociologie*. 11(1), 34–44.

Boltanski, L. (1987). *The Making of a Class: Cadres in French Society*. Cambridge University Press.

Boltanski, L. (2012). *Love and Justice as Competences*. Cambridge: Polity Press.

Boltanski, L. and Chiapello, E. (2005). *The New Spirit of Capitalism*. London and New York: Verso.

Boltanski, L. and Thévenot, L. (2006). *On Justification: Economies of Worth*. Princeton University Press.

Borzeix, A. and Fraenkel, B., eds. (2001). *Langage et travail*. Paris: Presses du CNRS.

Bouilloud, J. P. and Lécuyer, B. P. (1994). *L'Invention de la gestion. Histoire et pratiques*. Paris: L'Harmattan.

Bourguignon, A. (2005). Management accounting and value creation: The profit and loss of reification. *Critical Perspectives on Accounting*, 16(4), 353–89.

Bourguignon, A. and Chiapello, E. (2005). The role of criticism in the dynamics of performance evaluation systems. *Critical Perspectives on Accounting*, 16(6), 665–700.

Boussard, V. (2001). Quand les règles s'incarnent: L'exemple des indicateurs prégnants. *Sociologie du travail*, 43(4), 533–51.

Boussard, V. (2008). *Sociologie de la gestion*. Paris: Belin.

Boussard, V. and Maugeri, S., eds. (2003). *Du politique dans les organisations. Sociologie des dispositifs de gestion*. Paris: L'Harmattan.

Bowker, G. C. and Star, S. L. (2000). *Sorting Things Out: Classification and Its Consequences*. Cambridge, MA: MIT Press.

Bowker, G. C. and Star, S. L. (2007). Enacting silence: Residual categories as a challenge for ethics, information systems, and communication. *Ethics and Information Technology*, 9(4), 273–80.

Brabet, J. (1999). Peut-on enseigner autre chose que le modèle instrumental en gestion des ressources humaines ? *Gérer et comprendre*, 58, 72–85.

Braverman, H. (1974). *Labour and Monopoly Capital: The Degradation of Work in the Twentieth Century*. New York: Monthly Review Press.

Breton, P. (1987). *Histoire de l'informatique*. Paris: La Découverte.

Briers, M. and Chua, W. F. (2001). The role of actor-networks and boundary objects in management accounting change: A field study of an implementation of activity-based costing. *Accounting, Organizations and Society*, 26(3), 237–69.

Brivot, M. (2008). *Une auto-rationalisation douce du travail par le knowledge management dans les firmes de services professionnels: Le cas d'un cabinet d'avocats français*. Ph.D. thesis, HEC Paris.

Brown, M. H. (1990). Defining stories in organizations: Characteristics and functions. *Annals of the International Communication Association*, 13(1), 162–90.

Brunel, V. (2004). *Les managers de l'âme*. Paris: La Découverte.

Bruno, I. (2008). *A vos marques, prêts ... cherchez ! La stratégie européenne de Lisbonne, vers un marché de la recherche.* Bellecombes en Bauges: Éditions du croquant.

Brunsson, N. (2002). *The Organization of Hypocrisy: Talk, Decisions and Action in Organizations.* New York: Wiley.

Brunsson, N. and Jacobsson, B., eds. (2000). *A World of Standards.* Oxford University Press.

Buchli, V., ed. (2002). *The Material Culture Reader.* Oxford and New York: Berg.

Buisson-Fenet, H. and Draelants, H. (2013). School-linking processes: Describing and explaining their role in the social closure of French elite education. *Higher Education,* 66(1), 39–57.

Burawoy, M. (1983). Between the labor process and the state: The changing face of factory regimes under advanced capitalism. *American Sociological Review,* 48(5), 587–605.

Burns, J., Englund, H. and Gerdin, J. (2010). Twenty-five years of Giddens' structuration theory in management accounting research: Achievements, limitations and the future. Working paper. HEC Paris.

Burns, T. and Stalker, G. M. (1961). *Management of Innovation.* London: Tavistock Publications.

Caglio, A. (2003). Enterprise resource planning systems and accountants: Towards hybridization? *European Accounting Review,* 12(1), 123–53.

Callon, M. (1981). Pour une sociologie des controverses technologiques. *Fundamenta Scientae,* 2(3–4), 381–99.

Callon, M. (1984). Some elements of a sociology of translation: Domestication of the scallops and the fishermen of St Brieuc Bay. *Sociological Review,* 32(1 suppl.), 196–233.

Callon, M. (2006). What does it mean to say that economics is performative? In D. MacKenzie, F. Muniesa and L. Siu, eds., *Do Economists Make Markets? On the Performativity of Economics.* Princeton University Press.

Callon, M., Lascoumes, P. and Barthe, Y. (2009). *Acting in an Uncertain World: An Essay on Technical Democracy.* Cambridge, MA: MIT Press.

Callon, M. and Latour, B. (1981). Unscrewing the big Leviathan; or how actors macrostructure reality, and how sociologists help them to do so. In K. D. Knorr and A. Cicourel, eds., *Advances in Social Theory and Methodology: Toward an Integration of Micro and Macro Sociologies.* London: Routledge & Kegan Paul, 277–303.

Callon, M., Millo, Y. and Muniesa, F., eds. (2007). *Market Devices.* Oxford: Blackwell Publishing.

Capron, M., ed. (2005). *Les normes comptables internationales, instruments du capitalisme financier*. Paris: La Découverte.

Carmona, S., Ezzamel, M. and Gutierrez, F. (2002). The relationship between accounting and spatial practices in the factory. *Accounting, Organizations and Society*, 27(3), 239–74.

Carpenter, V. L. and Feroz, E. H. (2001). Institutional theory and accounting rule choice: An analysis of four US state governments' decisions to adopt generally accepted accounting principles. *Accounting, Organization and Society*, 26(7), 565–96.

Carruthers, B. G. (1995). Accounting, ambiguity, and the new institutionalism. *Accounting, Organization and Society*, 20(4), 313–28.

Chiapello, E. (2005). Les normes comptables comme institution du capitalisme. Une analyse du passage aux IFRS en Europe à partir de 2005. *Sociologie du travail*, 47(3), 362–82.

Chiapello, E. (2007). Accounting and the birth of the notion of capitalism. *Critical Perspectives on Accounting*, 13(3), 263–96.

Chiapello, E. (2015). Financialisation of valuation. *Human Studies*, 38(1), 13–35.

Chiapello, E. (2017). Critical accounting research and neoliberalism. *Critical Perspectives on Accounting*, Special Anniversary Issue, 43, 47–64.

Chiapello, E. (2018). The work of financialisation. In I. Chambost, M. Lenglet and Y. Tadjeddine, eds., *The Making of Finance*. London: Routledge, 192–200.

Chiapello, E. and Baker, C. R. (2011). The introduction of French theory into English language accounting research. *Accounting, Auditing & Accountability Journal*, 24(2), 140–60.

Chiapello, E. and Desrosières, A. (2006). La quantification de l'économie et la recherche en sciences sociales: Paradoxes, contradictions et omissions. Le cas exemplaire de la *Positive accounting theory*. In F. Eymard-Duvernay, ed., *L'économie des conventions. Méthodes et résultats, Tome 1: Débats*. Paris: La Découverte, 297–310.

Chiapello, E. and Gilbert, P. (2009). La gestion comme technologie économique. In P. Steiner and F. Vatin, eds., *Traité de sociologie économique*. Paris: PUF, 325–65.

Chiapello, E. and Gilbert, P. (2012). Les outils de gestion, producteurs ou régulateurs de la violence au travail? *Le travail humain*, 75(1), 1–18.

Chiapello, E. and Gilbert, P. (2013). *Sociologie des outils de gestion. Introduction à l'analyse sociale de l'instrumentation de gestion*. Paris: La Découverte.

Chiapello, E. and Gilbert, P. (2016). L'agence des outils de gestion. In F. X. De Vaujany, A. Hussenot and J. F. Chanlat, eds., *Théories des organisations. Nouveaux tournants*. Paris: Economica, 177–226.

Chiapello, E. and Godefroy, G. (2017). The dual function of judgment devices: Why does the plurality of market classifications matter? In K. Krenn, ed., *Historical Social Research/Historische Sozialforschung, Special Issue of* Market Classification, 42(1), 152–88.

Chiapello, E. and Godelier, E. (2015a). *Management multiculturel. Tome 1: Pratiques de management comparées.* Paris: Presses de l'école polytechnique.

Chiapello, E. and Godelier, E. (2015b). *Management multiculturel. Tome 2: Explorations indiennes.* Paris: Presses de l'école polytechnique.

Chiapello, E. and Medjad, K. (2009). An unprecedented privatization of mandatory standard-setting: The case of European accounting policy. *Critical Perspectives on Accounting*, 20(4), 448–68.

Chiapello, E. and Ramirez, C. (2004). La sociologie de la comptabilité: Une introduction. *Comptabilité-Contrôle-Audit*, 10(3), 3–5.

Cho, S., Mathiassen, L. and Nilsson, A. (2008). Contextual dynamics during health information systems implementation: An event-based actor-network approach. *European Journal of Information Systems*, 17(6), 614–30.

Christiansen, E. (1996). Tamed by a rose: Computers as tools in human activity. In B. A. Nardi, ed., *Context and Consciousness: Activity Theory and Human–Computer Interaction.* Cambridge, MA: MIT Press, 174–98.

Christiansen, J. K. and Skaerbaek, P. (1997). Implementing budgetary control in the performing arts: Games in the organizational theatre. *Management Accounting Research*, 8(4), 405–38.

Cicourel, A. (1981). Notes on the integration of micro- and macro-levels of analysis. In A. Cicourel and K. Knorr-Cetina, eds., *Advances in Social Theory and Methodology: Toward an Integration of Micro- and Macro-Sociologies.* London: Routledge & Kegan Paul, 51–80.

Clark, T. (2004). The fashion of management fashion: A surge too far? *Organization*, 11(2), 297–306.

Clot, Y. (1995). *Le travail sans l'homme. Pour une psychologie des milieux de travail et de vie.* Paris: La Découverte.

Cochoy, F. (1999). *Une histoire du marketing. Discipliner l'économie de marché.* Paris: La Découverte.

Cochoy, F. (2007). A sociology of market-things: On tending the garden of choices in mass retailing. *Sociological Review*, 55(Suppl. 2), 109–29.

Cochoy, F., Garel, J. P. and Terssac, G. de (1998). Comment l'écrit travaille l'organisation: Le cas des normes ISO 9000. *Revue française de sociologie*, 39(4), 673–99.

Colette, C. and Richard, J. (2000). *Comptabilité générale. Les systèmes français et anglo-saxons.* Paris: Dunod.

Conein, B., Dodier, N. and Thevenot, L., eds. (1993). *Les objets dans l'action. De la maison au laboratoire* (Raisons Pratiques 4). Paris: EHESS.

Covaleski, M. A. and Dirsmith, M. W. (1988). An institutional perspective on the rise, social transformation, and fall of a university budget category. *Administrative Science Quarterly*, 33(4), 562–87.

Covaleski, M. A., Dirsmith, M. W., Heian, J. B. and Samuel, S. (1998). The calculated and the avowed: Techniques of discipline and struggles over identity in big six public accounting firms. *Administrative Science Quarterly*, 43(2), 293–327.

Cresswell, R. (1983). Transfert de techniques et chaînes opératoires. *Techniques et culture*, 2, 143–63.

Crozier, M. (1964). *The Bureaucratic Phenomenon.* University of Chicago Press.

Crozier, M. and Friedberg, E. (1980). *Actors and Systems: The Politics of Collective Action.* University of Chicago Press [Original work published in 1977].

Currie, G. and Spyridonidis, D. (2016). Interpretation of multiple institutional logics on the ground: Actors' position, their agency and situational constraints in professionalized contexts. *Organization Studies*, 37(1), 77–97.

Cyert, R. and March, J. (1963). *A Behavioral Theory of the Firm.* Englewood Cliffs, NJ: Prentice Hall.

Czarniawska, B. (2002). *A Tale of Three Cities, or the Glocalization of City Management.* Oxford University Press.

Czarniawska-Joerges, B. and Joerges, B. (1988). How to control things with words: Organizational talk and control. *Management Communication Quarterly*, 2(2), 170–93.

Czarniawska, B. and Sevon, G. (1996). *Translating Organizational Change.* Berlin: Walter de Gruyter.

Czarniawska, B. and Sevon, G., eds. (2005). *Global Ideas: How Ideas, Objects and Practices Travel in the Global Economy.* Malmö: Liber & Copenhagen Business School Press.

Dagognet, F. (1989). *Eloge de l'objet. Pour une philosophie de la marchandise.* París: Vrin.

Dagognet, F. (1996). *Les dieux sont dans la cuisine. Philosophie des objets et objets de la philosophie.* Paris: Synthélabo Groupe.

Dambrin, C. and Lambert, C. (2017). Beauty or not beauty: Making up the producer of popular culture. *Management Accounting Research*, 35, 35–46.

Daumas, M. (1963). Le mythe de la révolution technique. *Revue d'histoire des sciences et de leurs applications*, 16(4), 291–302.

David, A. (1996). L'aide à la décision entre outils et organisation. *Entreprises et Histoire*, 13, 9–26.

David, A. (1998). Outils de gestion et dynamique du changement. *Revue française de gestion*, 120, 44–59.

David, A. (2006). *Sensemaking, outils de gestion et activités de conception: Quatre rapprochements*. In D. Autissier and F. Bensebaa, eds., *Les défis du sensemaking en entreprise. Karl Weick et les sciences de gestion*. Paris: Economica, 249–72.

Davidson, E. J. (1999). What's in a name? Exploring the metaphorical implications of data warehousing in concept and practice. *Journal of End User Computing*, 11(4), 22–32.

Davie, S. S. K. (2000). Accounting for imperialism: A case of British-imposed indigenous collaboration. *Accounting, Auditing & Accountability Journal*, 13(3), 330–59.

Davison, J. (2011). Barthesian perspectives on accounting communication and visual images of professional accountancy. *Accounting, Auditing & Accountability Journal*, 24(2), 250–83.

Deal, T. E. and Kennedy, A. A. (1982). *Corporate Cultures: The Rites and Rituals of Corporate Life*. Reading, MA: Addison-Wesley.

Dechow, N. and Mouritsen, J. (2005). Enterprise resource planning systems, management control and the quest for integration. *Accounting, Organizations and Society*, 30(7–8), 691–733.

Dejours, C. (1990). Nouveau regard sur la souffrance humaine dans les organisations. In A. Chanlat, ed., *L'individu dans l'organisation. Les dimensions oubliées*. Québec: Les Presses de l'Université Laval & les Éditions Eska, 687–708.

Dejours, C. (1995). *Le facteur humain*. Paris: PUF.

Dejours, C. (2003). *L'évaluation du travail à l'épreuve du réel. Critique des fondements de l'évaluation*. Versailles: INRA Éditions.

Dejours, C. (2006). Subjectivity, work and action. *Critical Horizons*, 7(1), 45–62.

Dejours, C. (2007). *Conjurer la violence. Travail, violence, santé*. Paris: Payot.

Dejours, C. and Deranty, J. P. (2010). The centrality of work. *Critical Horizons*, 11(2), 167–80.

Delcambre, P. (2009). L'activité d'évaluation et les systèmes d'information. L'évaluation est aussi un travail: langagier, assisté, organisé. *Études de communication*, 33, 79–100.

Deleuze, G. (1992). Postscript on the societies of control. *October*, 59, 3–7.

Denis, J. (2006). Les nouveaux visages de la performativité. *Études de communication*, 29, 8–24.

DeSanctis, G. and Poole, M. (1994). Capturing the complexity in advanced technology use: Adaptive structuration theory. *Organization Science*, 15(2), 121–47.

Desrosières, A. (1977). Éléments pour l'histoire des nomenclatures socio-professionnelle. *Pour une Histoire de la Statistique, Economica*, 1, 155–231.

Desrosières, A. (2004). Pour une politique des outils du savoir: le cas de la statistique. Presented at the conference 'Politics and knowledge: Democratizing knowledge in times of the expert'. University of Bergen, 21–22 June.

Desrosières, A. (2008). *Pour une sociologie historique de la quantification. L'argument statistique I*. Paris: Presses des Mines.

Desrosières, A. and Thévenot, L. (1988). *Les catégories socioprofessionnelles*. Paris: La Découverte.

Detchessahar, M. and Journé, B. (2007). Une approche narrative des outils de gestion. *Revue française de gestion*, 177, 77–92.

Dewey J. (1939). *Theory of Valuation*. University of Chicago Press.

Diaz-Bone, R. and Didier, E., eds. (2016). Special Issue: *Conventions and Quantification – Transdisciplinary Perspectives on Statistics and Classifications*. *Historical Social Research*, 41(2).

Diaz-Bone, R. and Salais, R., eds. (2011). Special Issue: *Conventions and Institutions from a Historical Perspective*. *Historical Social Research*, 36(4).

Didier, E. (2009). *En quoi consiste l'Amérique? Le statistiques, le new deal et la démocratie*. Paris: La Découverte.

DiMaggio, P. and Powell, W. (1983). The iron-cage revisited: Institutional isomorphism and collective rationality in organizational field. *American Sociological Review*, 48, 147–60.

Dirsmith, M. W., Heian, J. B. and Covaleski, M. A. (1997). Structure and agency in an institutionalized setting: The application and social transformation of controls in the big six. *Accounting, Organizations and Society*, 22(1), 1–27.

Djelic, M. L. and Quack, S. (2008). Institutions and transnationalization. In R. Greenwood, C. Oliver, K. Sahlin and R. Suddaby., eds., *The SAGE Handbook of Organizational Institutionalism*. London: Sage, 299–324.

Djelic, M. L. and Sahlin-Andersson, K., eds. (2006). *Transnational Governance: Institutional Dynamics of Regulation*. Cambridge University Press.

Doganova, L. and Eyquem-Renault, M. (2009). What do business models do? Innovation devices in technology entrepreneurship. *Research Policy*, 38(10), 1559–70.

Douglas, M. (1986). *How Institutions Think*. Syracuse University Press.

Drori, G. S., Meyer, J. W. and Hwang, H. (2006). *Globalization and Organization: World Society and Organizational Change*. Oxford University Press.

Dubuisson-Quellier, S. (1999). Le prestataire, le client et le consommateur: Sociologie d'une relation marchande. *Revue française de sociologie*, 40(4), 671–88.

Dupuy, F. (2004). *Sociologie du changement*. Paris: Dunod.

Durkheim, É. and Mauss, M. (1963). *Primitive Classification*. University of Chicago Press [Original work published in 1903].

Ellul, J. (1964). *The Technological Society*. New York: Knopf.

Ellul, J. (1980). *The Technological System*. New York: Continuum.

Ellul, J. (1990). *The Technological Bluff*. Grand Rapids, MI: Eerdmans.

Emery, F. E., Thorsrud, E. and Trist, E. L. (1969). *Form and Content in Industrial Democracy: Some Experiences from Norway and Other European Countries*. London: Tavistock Institute.

Emery, F. E. and Trist, E. L. (1960). Socio-technical systems. In C. W. Churchman and M. Verhulst, eds., *Management Sciences: Models and Techniques*, vol. 2. Oxford: Pergamon Press, 83–97.

Engeström, Y. (1987). *Learning by Expanding*. Helsinki: Orienta-Konsultit Oy.

Engeström, Y. (1996). Development as breaking away and opening up: A challenge to Vygotsky and Piaget. *Swiss Journal of Psychology*, 55, 126–32.

Engeström, Y. (2001). Expansive learning at work: Toward an activity theoretical reconceptualization. *Journal of Education and Work*, 14(1), 133–56.

Engeström, Y. and Middleton, D. (1998). *Cognition and Communication at Work*. Cambridge University Press.

Englund, H., Gerdin, J. and Burns, J. (2011). 25 years of Giddens in accounting research: Achievements, limitations and the future. *Accounting, Organizations and Society*, 36(8), 494–513.

Enriquez, E. (1982). Structures d'organisation et contrôle social. *Connexions*, 41, 97–124.

Enriquez, E. (1989). L'individu pris au piège de la structure stratégique. *Connexions*, 54, 145–65.

Enriquez, E. (1997a). *Les jeux du pouvoir et du désir dans l'entreprise*. Paris: Desclée de Brouwer.

Enriquez, E. (1997b). The clinical approach: Genesis and development in Western Europe. *International Sociology*, 12(2), 151–64.

Erlingsdottir, G. (1999). *Förförande idéer – kvalitetssäkring i hälso – och sjurkvarden*. Lund: KFS AB.

Erlingsdottir, G. and Lindberg, K. (2005). Isomorphism, isopraxism, and isonymism: Complementary or competing processes? In B. Czarniawska and G. Sevon, eds., *Global Ideas: How Ideas, Objects and Practices Travel in the Global Economy*. Malmö: Liber & Copenhagen Business School Press, 47–70.

Espeland, W. and Sauder, M. (2007). Rankings and reactivity: How public measure recreates social worlds. *American Journal of Sociology*, 113(1), 1–40.

Espeland, W. and Stevens, M. (1998). Commensuration as a social process. *Annual Review of Sociology*, 24, 313–43.

Espeland, W. and Stevens, M. (2008). A sociology of quantification. *Archives Européennes de Sociologie/European Journal of Sociology*, 49(3), 401–36.

Eymard-Duvernay, F. (1989). Conventions de qualité et formes de coordination. *Revue Economique*, 40 (2), 329–59.

Eymard-Duvernay, F., ed. (2006a). *L'économie des conventions. Méthodes et résultats, Tome 1: Débats*. Paris: La Découverte.

Eymard-Duvernay, F., ed. (2006b). *L'économie des conventions. Méthodes et résultats. Tome 2: Développements*. Paris: La Découverte.

Eymard-Duvernay, F. and Marchal, E. (1997). *Façons de recruter. Le jugement des compétences sur le marché du travail*. Paris: Métailié.

Eyraud, C. (2004). Comptabilité (publique et d'entreprise) et sociologie, ou l'analyse sociologique des catégorisations sociales. *Comptabilité, Contrôle, Audit*, 10(3), 29–45.

Eyraud, C. (2011). Une comptabilité d'entreprise pour les Etats? Un dispositif de quantification économique soumis à l'analyse sociologique. *Le cas français. Sociologie et Sociétés*, 43(2), 91–116.

Ezzamel, M., Xio, J. Z. and Pan, A. (2007). Political ideology and accounting regulation in China. *Accounting, Organizations and Society*, 32(7/8), 669–700.

Fauré, B. and Gramaccia, G. (2006). La pragmatique des chiffres dans les organisations: De l'acte de langage à l'acte de calcul. *Études de communication*, 29, 25–37.

Favereau, O. (1989). Marché interne/marché externe. *Revue économique*, 2, 273–328.

Fayol, H. (1949). *General and Industrial Management*. London: Pitman [Original work published in 1916].

Fincham, R. (2002). Narratives or success and failure in systems development. *British Journal of Management*, 13(1), 1–14.

Fisher, S. L. and Howell, A. W. (2004). Beyond user acceptance: An examination of employee reactions to information technology systems. *Resource Management*, 43(2–3), 243–58.

Foucault, M. (1970). *The Order of Things: The Archaeology of Human Sciences*. London: Tavistock Publications [Original work published in 1966].

Foucault, M. (1971). The order of discourse: Inaugural lecture delivered at the Collège de France. *Social Science Information*, 10(2), 7–30.

Foucault, M. (1972). *The Archeology of Knowledge & the Discourse on Language*. New York: Pantheon Books [*The Archaeology of Knowledge* originally published in 1969].

Foucault, M. (1977). *Discipline and Punish: The Birth of the Prison*. New York: Vintage Books.

Foucault, M. (1978). *The History of Sexuality*. New York: Pantheon Books.

Foucault, M. (1980). *Power/Knowledge: Selected Interviews and Other Writings, 1972–1977*, ed. C. Gordon, L. Marshall, J. Meplam and K. Soper. Brighton: Harvester Press.

Foucault, M. (1988). *Madness and Civilization: A History of Insanity in the Age of Reason*. New York: Vintage Books [Original work published in 1961].

Foucault M. (2001 [1976]). Les mailles du pouvoir. In *Dits et écrits II, 1976–1988*. Paris: Gallimard, 1001–20 [Originally presented at a conference at Bahia University of Philosophy, 1976; first published in 1981].

Foucault, M. (2001 [1977]). Le jeu de Michel Foucault. In *Dits et écrits II, 1976–1988*. Paris: Gallimard, 298–329 [Original interview published in *Ornica, Bulletin Périodique du champ freudien*, 10, July 1977].

Foucault, M. (2008a). *Security, Territory, Population: Lectures at the Collège de France*, trans. G. Burchell. Basingstoke: Palgrave Macmillan.

Foucault, M. (2008b). *The Birth of Biopolitics: Lectures at the Collège de France*. Basingstoke: Palgrave Macmillan.

Fourcade, M. (2011). Cents and sensibility: Economic valuation and the nature of nature. *American Journal of Sociology*, 116(6), 1721–77.

Fraenkel, B. (1995). La traçabilité: Une fonction caractéristique des écrits de travail. *Connexions*, 65, 63–75.

Fraenkel, B. (2007). Actes d'écriture: Quand écrire c'est faire. *Langage et société*, 121–22, 101–12.

Friedland, R. (2009). Institution, practice and ontology: Towards a religious sociology. In R. E. Meyer, K. Sahlin and M. J. Ventresca, eds., *Research in the Sociology of Organizations*, vol. 27. Bingley: Emerald Group Publishing, 45–83.

Friedland, R. (2011). The institutional logic of religious nationalism: Sex, violence and the ends of history. *Politics, Religion and Ideology*, 12, 1–24.

Friedland, R. (2013). God, love, and other good reasons for practice: Thinking through institutional logics. In M. Lounsbury and E. Boxenbaum, eds., *Institutional Logics in Action, Part A*. Bingley: Emerald Group Publishing, 25–50.

Friedland, R. and Alford, R. R. (1991). Bringing society back in: Symbols, practices, and institutional contradictions. In W. W. Powell and P. J. Di Maggio, eds., *The New Institutionalism in New Organizational Analysis*. University of Chicago Press, 232–66.

Friedmann, G. (1964). *The Anatomy of Work: Labor, Leisure and the Implications of Automation*. New York: Macmillan.

Fritz, J. M., ed. (2007). *International Clinical Sociology*. New York: Springer.

Furusten, S. (2000). The knowledge base of standards. In N. Brunsson and B. Jacobsson, eds., *A World of Standards*. Oxford University Press, 71–84.

Gadrey, J. (2006). Les conventions de richesse au cœur de la comptabilité nationale: Anciennes et nouvelles controverses. In F. Eymard-Duvernay, ed., *L'économie des conventions, méthodes et résultats. Tome 1: Débats*. Paris: La Découverte, 311–24.

Gallhofer, S. and Haslam J. (2003). *Accounting and Emancipation: Some Critical Interventions*. New York: Routledge.

Gates, W. H. (1999). *Business @ the Speed of Thought*. New York: Warner Books.

Gaulejac, V. de (2005). *La société malade de la gestion. Idéologie gestionnaire, pouvoir managérial et harcèlement social*. Paris: Seuil.

Gaulejac, V. de (2008). On the origins of clinical sociology in France: Some milestones. In J. M. Fritz, ed., *International Clinical Sociology*. New York: Springer, 54–71.

Gendron, Y. and Baker, C. R. (2005). On interdisciplinary movements: The development of a network of support around Foucaultian perspectives in accounting research. *European Accounting Review*, 14(3), 525–69.

Giddens, A. (1984). *The Constitution of Society*. Cambridge: Polity Press.

Giddens, A. (1990). *The Consequences of Modernity*. Cambridge: Polity Press.

Giddens, A. and Pierson C. (1998). *Conversations with Anthony Giddens: Making Sense of Modernity*. Cambridge: Polity Press.

Gilbert, P. (1998a). *L'instrumentation de gestion*. Paris: Economica.

Gilbert, P. (1998b). Fonctions implicites et explicites des instruments de gestion des ressources humaine. *Psychologie du Travail et des Organisations*, 1, 118–30.

Gilbert, P. and Gonzalez, D. (2000). Les progiciels intégrés et la GRH: Quand l'ambiguïté des enjeux est fonctionnelle. *Gérer et Comprendre, Annales des Mines*, 59, 26–33.

Gilbert, P. and Leclair, P. (2004). Les systèmes de gestion intégrés: Une modernité en trompe-l'œil? *Sciences de la société*, 61, 17–30.

Gilbert, P., Raulet-Croset, N., and Teglborg, A. C. (2018). How the materialization of a managerial model contributes to its take up: The case of 'liberating management' in France. In N. Mitev, A. Morgan-Thomas, P. Lorino, F.-X. de Vaujany and Y. Nama, eds., *Materiality and Managerial Techniques*. Cham: Palgrave Macmillan, 281–305.

Gille, B., ed. (1986). *The History of Techniques*, Vol. 1. New York: Gordon and Breach Science Publishers.

Girin, J. (1983). Les machines de gestion. In M. Berry, ed., *Le rôle des outils de gestion dans l'évolution des systèmes sociaux complexes*, CRG-École polytechnique, Report for the ministry of Research and Technology.

Girin, J. (1990). Problèmes du langage dans les organisations. In F. Chanlat, ed., *L'individu dans l'organisation. Les dimensions oubliées*. Québec: Presses de l'Université Laval/Éditions Eska, 37–78.

Giroux, N. and Marroquin, L. (2005). L'approche narrative des organisations. *Revue française de gestion*, 159, 15–42.

Glendinning, C. (1990). Notes toward a neo-Luddite manifesto. *Utne Reader*, 38(1), 50–3.

Goffi, J. Y. (1988). *La philosophie de la technique*. Paris: PUF.

Gomez, P. Y. (1994). *Qualité et théorie des conventions*. Paris: Economica.

Gomez, P. Y. (1997). Information et convention: Le cadre du modèle général. *Revue française de gestion*, 112, 64–77.

Gordon, C., ed. (1980). *Foucault. Power/Knowledge: Selected Interviews and Other Writings, 1972–1977*. New York: Pantheon.

Gouldner, A. W. (1954). *Patterns of Industrial Bureaucracy*, New York: Free Press.

Greenwood, R. and Hinings, C. R. (1996). Understanding radical organizational change: Bringing together the old and the new institutionalism. *Academy of Management Review*, 21(4), 1022–54.

Greenwood, R., Oliver, C., Sahlin, K. and Suddaby, R. (2008). Introduction. In R. Greenwood, C. Oliver, K. Sahlin and R. Suddaby, eds., *The SAGE Handbook of Organizational Institutionalism*. London: Sage, 1–46.

Greenwood, R., Raynard, M., Kodeih, F., Micelotta, E. R. and Lounsbury, M. (2011). Institutional complexity and organizational responses. *Academy of Management Annals*, 5(1), 317–71.

Guibert, B., Laganier, J. and Volle, M. (1971). Essai sur les nomenclatures industrielles. *Économie et Statistiques*, 20(1), 23–36.

Guibert, G. (2011). Détourner le contrôle? Le cas de la Fédération des lieux de musiques actuelles. *Sociologies Pratiques*, 22, 79–92.

Hacking, I. (1999). *The Social Construction of What?* Cambridge, MA: Harvard University Press.

Halpern, C., Lascoumes, P. and Le Galès, P., eds. (2014). *L'instrumentation de l'action publique. Controverse, résistances, effets*. Paris: Presses de Sciences Po.

Halpern, C. and Le Galès, P. (2011). Pas d'action publique sans instruments propres. *Revue française de sciences politiques*, 61(1), 51–78.

Halström, K. T. (2000). Organizing the process of standardization. In N. Brunsson and B. Jacobsson, eds., *A World of Standards*. Oxford University Press, 85–99.

Hatchuel, A. (2000). Quels horizons pour les sciences de gestion? Vers une théorie de l'action collective. In A. David, A. Hatchuel and R. Laufer, eds., *Les nouvelles fondations des sciences de gestion. Eléments d'épistémologie de la recherche en management*. Paris: Vuibert, 7–44.

Haudricourt, A. G. (1955). Biogéographie des araires et des charrues. *Compte rendu sommaire des séances de la Société de biogéographie*, 280, 77–83.

Haudricourt, A. G. (1964). La technologie, science humaine. *La Pensée*, 115, 28–35.

Havard, C. and Krohmer, C. (2008). Création et articulation des règles dans le cadre d'un management des compétences. *Revue de Gestion des Ressources Humaines*, 70, 1–14.

Henning, R. (2000). Selling standards. In N. Brunsson and B. Jacobsson, eds., *A World of Standards*. Oxford University Press, 114–24.

Henry, O. (1992). Entre savoir et pouvoir: Les professionnels de l'expertise et du conseil. *Actes de la recherche en sciences sociales*, 95, 37–54.

Herzberg, F. (1966). *Work and the Nature of Man*. New York: World Publishing.

Hilbert, R. A. (1990). Ethnomethodology and the micro-macro order. *American Sociological Review*, 55, 794–808.

Hoffman, A. (1999). Institutional evolution and change: Environmentalism and the US chemical industry. *Academy of Management Journal*, 42, 351–71.

Hofstadter, D. (1979). *Gödel, Escher, Bach: An Eternal Golden Braid*. New York: Basic Books.

Hopper, T. and Armstrong, P. (1991). Cost accounting, controlling labour and the rise of conglomerates. *Accounting, Organizations and Society*, 7(5/6), 405–38.

Hopper, T. and Macintosh, N. (1993). Management accounting as disciplinary practice: The case of ITT under Harold Geneen. *Management Accounting Research*, 4(3), 181–216.

Hoskin, K. W. and Macve, R. (1988). The genesis of accountability: The West Point connections. *Accounting, Organizations and Society*, 13(1), 37–73.

Isaac, H. (1998). Les normes de qualité dans les services professionnels: Une lecture des pratiques à travers la théorie des conventions. *Finance Contrôle Stratégie*, 1 (2), 89–112.

Jack, L. (2005). Stocks of knowledge, simplification and unintended consequences: The persistence of post-war accounting practices in UK agriculture. *Management Accounting Research*, 16(1), 59–79.

Jones, T. C. and Dugdale, D. (2002). The ABC bandwagon and the juggernaut of modernity. *Accounting, Organizations and Society*, 27(1–2), 121–63.

Joule, R. V. and Beauvois, J. L. (2002). *Petit traité de manipulation à l'usage des honnêtes gens*. Presses Universitaires de Grenoble.

Justin, J. (2004). Proposition d'un cadre conceptuel d'analyse des jeux d'acteurs cristallisés dans et par les outils de contrôle. *Comptabilité-Contrôle-Audit*, 10(3), 213–36.

Kaplan, R. S. and Norton, D. P. (1992). The balanced scorecard: Measures that drive performance. *Harvard Business Review*, 1, 71–9.

Karpik, L. (2010). *Valuing the Unique: The Economics of Singularities*. Princeton University Press.

Kennedy, M. T. and Fiss, P. C. (2009). Institutionalization, framing, and diffusion: The logic of TQM adoption and implementation decisions among US hospitals. *Academy of Management Review*, 52(5), 897–918.

Kiesler, C. A. (1971). *The Psychology of Commitment*. New York: Academic Press.

Kipping, M., Furusten, S. and Gammelsaeter, H. (2003). Converging towards American dominance? Developments and structures of consultancy fields in Europe. *Entreprises et Histoire*, 33, 25–40.

Kletz, F., Moisdon, J. C. and Pallez, F. (1997). Zoom sur l'organisation. Les grilles de classification: Un dispositif photographique problématique. In J. C. Moisdon, ed., *Du mode d'existence des outils de gestion. Les instruments de gestion à l'épreuve de l'organisation*. Paris: Seli Arslan, 91–112.

Kornberger, M., Justesen, L., Madsen, A. K. and Mouritsen, J., eds. (2015). *Making Things Valuable*. Oxford University Press.

Kurzweil, R. (2005). *The Singularity Is Near: When Humans Transcend Biology*. New York: Viking Books.

La Boétie, E. (1975). *The Politics of Obedience: The Discourse of Voluntary Servitude*. Montréal: Black Rose Books.

Lambert, C. and Pezet, E. (2011). The making of the management accountant: Becoming the producer of truthful knowledge. *Accounting, Organizations and Society*, 36(1), 10–30.

Lamont, M. (2012). Toward a comparative sociology of valuation and evaluation. *Annual Review of Sociology*, 38(21), 201–21.

Lascoumes, P. (2004). La gouvernementalité: De la critique de l'État aux technologies du pouvoir. *Le portique [en ligne]*, *Revue de philosophie et de sciences humaines* (http://le portique.revues.org).

Lascoumes, P. and Le Galès, P., eds. (2004a). *Gouverner par les instruments*, Paris: Presses de Sciences Po.

Lascoumes, P. and Le Galès, P. (2004b). Introduction: L'action publique saisie par ses instruments. In P. Lascoumes and P. Le Galès, eds., *Gouverner par les instruments*. Paris: Presses de Sciences Po, 11–44.

Lascoumes, P. and Le Galès, P. (2007). Introduction: Understanding public policy through its instruments – from the nature of instruments to the sociology of public policy instrumentation. *Governance*, 20(1), 1–21.

Latour, B. (1987). *Science in Action: How to Follow Scientists and Engineers through Society*. Cambridge, MA: Harvard University Press.

Latour, B. (1991). Technology is society made durable. In J. Law, ed., *A Sociology of Monsters: Essays on Power, Technology and Domination*. London: Routledge, 103–31.

Latour, B. (2000). The Berlin key or how to do words with things. In P. M. Graves-Brown, ed., *Matter, Materiality and Modern Culture*. London: Routledge, 10–21.

Latour, B. (2005). *Reassembling the Social: An Introduction to Actor-Network-Theory*. Oxford University Press.

Law, J. (2003). Notes on the theory of the actor network: Ordering, strategy and heterogeneity. http://comp.lancs.ac.uk/sociology/papers/law-Notes-on-ANT.pdf

Law, J. (2009). Actor network theory and material semiotics. In B. S. Turner, ed., *The New Blackwell Companion to Social Theory*. Oxford: Blackwell, 141–58.

Lawrence, P. and Lorsch, J. (1967). Differentiation and integration in complex organizations. *Administrative Science Quarterly*, 12(1), 1–30.

Lejeune, A. and Harvey, P. L. (2007). L'analyse des systèmes d'activité, l'apprentissage extensif et le codesign en communauté: Une approche alternative à la réingénierie du système de santé au Québec. *Gestion 2000*, 24(5), 143–59.

Lemieux, C. (2007). À quoi sert l'analyse des controverses? Mil neuf cent. *Revue d'Histoire Intellectuelle*, 25, 191–212.

Lemonnier, P. (1976). La description des chaînes opératoires: Contribution à l'analyse des systèmes techniques. *Techniques et culture*, 1, 100–51.

Lemonnier, P. (1986). The study of material culture today: Toward an anthropology of technical systems. *Journal of Anthropological Archaeology*, 5(2), 147–86.

Lemonnier, P. (1991). Technique (système). In P. Bonte and M. Izard, eds., *Dictionnaire de l'ethnologie et de l'anthropologie*. Paris: PUF, 697–8.

Lemonnier, P. (2012). *Mundane Objects: Materiality and Non-Verbal Communication*. Walnut Creek, CA: Left Coast Press.

Lenay, O. (2005). L'ergonomie de la gouvernementalité: Le cas du système hospitalier français. In A. Hatchuel, E. Pezet, K. Starkey and O. Lenay, eds., *Gouvernement, organisation et gestion. L'héritage de Michel Foucault*. Les Presses de l'Université de Laval, 395–428.

Leonardi, P. (2011). When flexible routines meet flexible technologies: Affordance, constraint, and the imbrication of human and material agencies. *MIS Quarterly*, 35(1), 147–67.

Leontiev, A. N. (1978). *Activity, Consciousness and Personality*. Englewood Cliffs, NJ: Prentice Hall.

Leroi-Gourhan, A. (1943). *Évolution et techniques. L'homme et la matière*. Paris: Albin Michel.

Leroi-Gourhan, A. (1945). *Milieu et techniques*. Paris: Albin Michel.

Leroi-Gourhan, A. (1993). *Gesture and Speech*. Cambridge, MA: MIT Press [Original work published in 1964].

Lévy, A. (1997). *Sciences humaines cliniques et organisations sociales*. Paris: PUF.

Lévy, P. (1994). *L'intelligence collective. Pour une anthropologie du cyberespace.* Paris: La Découverte.

Lewin, K., Lippitt, R. and White, R. K. (1939). Patterns of aggressive behavior in experimentally created social climates. *Journal of Social Psychology*, 10(2), 271–99.

Lewis, D. (1969). *Convention: A Philosophical Study.* Cambridge, MA: Harvard University Press.

Liang, H., Saraf, N., Hu, Q. and Xue, Y. (2007). Assimilation of enterprise systems: The effect of institutional pressures and the mediating role of top management. *Management of Information Systems Quarterly*, 31(1), 59–87.

Likert, R. (1967). *The Human Organization: Its Management and Value.* New York: McGraw-Hill.

Linhardt, R. (1983). Le taylorisme entre les deux guerres: Quelques problèmes. *Travail et Emploi*, 18, 9–15.

Loft, A. (1986). Towards a critical understanding of accounting: The case of cost accounting in the UK, 1914–1925. *Accounting, Organizations and Society*. 11(2), 137–69.

Lomba, C. (2004). Distinguer un ouvrier d'un employé dans l'industrie: Naturalisation et négociations des classifications. *Sociétés Contemporaines*, 2(54), 35–53.

Lordon, F. (2000). La création de valeur comme rhétorique et comme pratique. *Généalogie et sociologie de la valeur actionnariale. L'année de la régulation*, 4, 117–65.

Lorino, P. (2002). Vers une théorie pragmatique et sémiotique des outils appliquée aux instruments de gestion. Working paper. ESSEC, DR-02015.

Lorino, P. (2013). Management systems as organizational 'architextures'. In F.-X. de Vaujany and N. Mitev, eds., *Materiality and Space: Technology, Work and Globalization.* London: Palgrave Macmillan, 62–95.

Lorino, P. (2018). *Pragmatism and Organization Studies.* Oxford University Press.

Lounsbury, M. (2007). A tale of two cities: Competing logics and practice variation on the professionalizing of mutual funds. *Academy of Management Journal*, 50(2), 289–307.

Lukács, G. (1971). *History and Class Consciousness: Studies in Marxist Dialectics.* Cambridge, MA: MIT Press [Original work published in 1923].

Lupton, D. (2013). Quantifying the body: Monitoring and measuring health in the age of mHealth technologies. *Critical Public Health*, 23(4), 393–403.

Lupton, D. (2016). *The Quantified Self.* New York: John Wiley.

MacKenzie, D. and Millo, Y. (2003). Constructing a market, performing theory: The historical sociology of a financial derivatives exchange. *American Journal of Sociology*, 109(1), 107–45.

Maister, D. H. (1993). *Managing the Professional Service Firm*. New York: Free Press.

Malinowski, B. (1922). *Argonauts of the Western Pacific*. New York: Routledge.

March, J., Schulz, M. and Zhou, X. (2000). *The Dynamics of Rules: Change in Written Organizational Codes*. Stanford University Press.

March, J. and Simon, H. (1958). *Organizations*. New York: John Wiley.

Martin, L., Gutman, H. and Hutton, P., eds. (1988). *Technologies of the Self: A Seminar with Michel Foucault*. London: Tavistock Publications.

Maslow, A. (1943). A theory of human motivation. *Psychological Review*, 50(4), 370–96.

Maugeri, S., ed. (2001). *Délit de gestion*. Paris: La Dispute.

Mauss, M. (1923). *Essai sur le don*. Paris: PUF.

Mauss, M. (1948). Les techniques et la technologie. *Journal de psychologie*, 41, 71–8.

Mauss, M. (1966). *The Gift: Forms and Functions of Exchange in Archaic Societies*. London: Cohen & West.

Mauss, M. (1973). Techniques of the body. *Economy and Society*, 2(1), 70–88.

Mauss, M. (2007). *The Manual of Ethnography*. New York: Berghahn Books [Original work published in 1926].

Mayo, E. (1933). *The Social Problems of an Industrial Civilization*. London: Routledge.

McGrath, K. (2002). The golden circle: A way of arguing and acting about technology in the London Ambulance Service. *European Journal of Information Systems*, 11(4), 251–66.

McGregor, D. (1960). *The Human Side of Enterprise*. New York: McGraw-Hill.

McKenna, C. (1995). The origins of modern management consulting. *Business and Economic History*, 24(1), 51–8.

McKinlay, A. and Starkey, K., eds. (1998). *Foucault, Management and Organization Theory: From Panopticon to Technologies of the Self*. London: Sage.

McLuhan, M. and Fiore, Q. (1967). *The Medium is the Message: An Inventory of Effects*. New York: Bantam Books.

Mercier, E. (2003). Pour une lecture conventionnaliste du changement organisationnel: Le cas d'une entreprise publique de service. In M. Amblard, ed., *Conventions et management*. Bruxelles: Éditions De Boeck Université, 179–202.

Merton, R. K. (1949). *Social Theory et Social Structure*. New York: Simon & Schuster.

Meyer, J. and Rowan, B. (1977). Institutionalized organizations: Formal structure as myth and ceremony. *American Journal of Sociology*, 83(2), 340–63.

Miller, P. (1991). Accounting innovation beyond the enterprise: Problematizing investment decisions and programming economic growth in the U.K. in the 1960s. *Accounting, Organizations and Society*, 16(8), 733–62.

Miller, P. and O'Leary, T. (1987). Accounting and the construction of the governable person. *Accounting, Organizations and Society*, 12(3), 235–66.

Miller, P. and O'Leary, T. (1994). Accounting economic citizenship and the spatial reordering of manufacture. *Accounting, Organizations and Society*, 19(1), 15–43.

Miller, P. and Rose, N. (1990). Governing economic life. *Economy and Society*, 19(1), 1–31.

Minsky, M. (1985). *The Society of Mind*. New York: Simon & Schuster.

Mintzberg, H. (1979). *The Structuring of Organizations*. Englewood Cliffs, NJ: Prentice Hall.

Mitev, N. and Vaujany, F. X. de, eds. (2013). *Materiality and Space: Organizations, Artefacts and Practices*. London: Springer.

Modell, S. (2003). Goals versus institutions: The development of performance measurement in the Swedish university sector. *Management Accounting Research*, 14, 333–59.

Moisdon, J. C., ed. (1997). *Du mode d'existence des outils de gestion*. Paris: Seli Arsan.

Montmollin, M. de (1995). *Préface, Vocabulaire de l'ergonomie*. Toulouse: Octares.

Moscovici, S. and Markova, I. (2006). *The Making of Modern Social Psychology*. Cambridge: Polity Press.

Muniesa, F. (2005). Contenir le marché: La transition de la criée à la cotation électronique à la Bourse de Paris. *Sociologie du Travail*, 47(4), 485–501.

Muniesa, F. (2007). Market technologies and the pragmatics of prices. *Economy and Society*, 36(3), 377–95.

Muniesa, F. (2011). A flank movement in the understanding of valuation. *Sociological Review*, 59(s2): 24–38.

Muniesa, F. (2014). *The Provoked Economy: Economic Reality and the Performative Turn*. London: Routledge.

Muniesa, F. and Callon, M. (2009). La performativité des sciences économiques. In P. Steiner and F. Vatin, eds., *Traité de sociologie économique*. Paris: PUF, 281–316.

Murray, F. (2010). The oncomouse that roared: Hybrid exchange strategies as a source of distinction at the boundary of overlapping institutions. *American Journal of Sociology*, 116, 341–88.

Oakes, L. S., Townley, B. and Cooper, D. J. (1998). Business planning as pedagogy: Language and control in a changing institutional field. *Administrative Science Quarterly*, 43(2), 257–92.

Oldroyd, D., Fleischman, R. K. and Tyson, T. N. (2008). The culpability of accounting practice in promoting slavery in the British Empire and antebellum United States. *Critical Perspectives on Accounting*, 19(5), 764–84.

Oliver, C. (1991). Strategic responses to institutional processes, *Academy of Management Review*, 16(1), 145–79.

Orlikowski, W. (1992). The duality of technology: Rethinking the concept of technology in organizations. *Organization Science*, 3(3), 398–427.

Orlikowski, W. (2000). Using technology and constituting structures: A practice lens for studying technology in organizations. *Organization Science*, 11(4), 404–28.

Orlikowski, W. (2005). Material works: Exploring the situated entanglement of technological performativity and human agency. *Scandinavian Journal of Information Systems*, 17(1), 183–6.

Orlikowski, W. and Barley, S. (2001). Technology and institutions: What can research on information technology and research on organizations learn from each other? *MIS Quarterly*, 25(2), 145–65.

Orlikowski, W. and Robey, D. (1991). Information technology and the structuring of organizations. *Information Systems Research*, 2(2), 143–69.

Ouchi, W. (1981). *Theory Z: How American Business Can Meet the Japanese Challenge*. New York: Avon Books.

Pache, A. C. and Santos, F. (2010). When worlds collide: The internal dynamics of organizational responses to conflicting institutional demands. *Academy of Management Review*, 35(3), 455–76.

Pagès, M., Bonetti, M., Gaulejac, V. de and Descendre, D. (1998). *L'emprise de l'organisation*. Paris: Desclée de Brouwer.

Palpacuer, F., Seignour, A. and Vercher, C. (2007). *Sorties de cadre(s). Le licenciement pour motif personnel, instrument de gestion de la firme mondialisée*. Paris: La Découverte.

Parsons, T. (1951). *The Social System*. New York: Free Press.

Pavé, F. (1989). *L'illusion informaticienne*. Paris: L'Harmattan.

Pavé, F. (1993). Les nouvelles technologies de l'information et de la communication et l'organisation du travail. In C. Freeman and H. Mendras, eds., *Le paradigme informatique. Technologie et informatique sociales*. Paris: Descartes, 77–121.

Peaucelle, J. L. (2003). L'outillage administratif de Fayol. In J. L. Peaucelle, ed., *Henri Fayol, inventeur des outils de gestion*. Paris: Economica, 207–35.

Pereira, R. E. (2002). An adopter-centered approach to understanding adoption of innovations, *European Journal of Innovation Management*, 5(1), 40–9.

Perrin, J. (1988). *Comment naissent les techniques. La production sociale des techniques*. Paris: Publisud.

Perrow, C. (1985). Review essay: Overboard with myth and symbols. *American Journal of Sociology*, 91, 151–5.

Peters, T. and Waterman, R. (1982). *In Search of Excellence*. New York: Harper & Row.

Pharabod, A. S., Nicolski, V. and Granjon, F. (2013). La mise en chiffres de soi: Une approche compréhensive des mesures personnelles. *Réseau*, 1(177), 97–129.

Phillips, N., Lawrence, T. and Hardy, C. (2004). Discourse and institutions. *Academy of Management Review*, 29(4), 635–52.

Piaget, J. (1952). *The Origins of Intelligence in Children*. New York: International Universities Press.

Pichault, F. (1990). *Le conflit informatique. Gérer les ressources humaines dans le changement technologique*. Bruxelles: De Boeck Université.

Pichault, F. and Nizet, J. (2000). *Les pratiques de gestion des ressources humaines. Approches contingente et politique*. Paris: Seuil.

Poole, M. and DeSanctis, G. (1992). Microlevel structuration in computer-supported group decision making. *Human Communication Research*, 19(1), 5–49.

Poole, M. and DeSanctis, G. (2004). Structuration theory in information systems research: Methods and controversies. In M. Whitman and A. Woszczynski, eds., *The Handbook of Information Systems Research*. Hershey, PA: Idea Publishing, 206–49.

Porter, T. (1995). *Trust in Numbers: The Pursuit of Objectivity in Science and Public Life*. Princeton University Press.

Powell, W. W. (1985). The institutionalization of rational organization. *Contemporary Sociology*, 14(5), 564–6.

Powell, W. W. (1990). Neither market, nor hierarchy: Network form of organizations. *Research in Organizational Behavior*, 12, 295–336.

Powell, W. W. and DiMaggio, P. J. (1991). *The New Institutionalism in Organizational Analysis*. University of Chicago Press.

Pozzebon, M. and Pinsonneault, A. (2005). Challenges in conducting empirical work using structuration theory: Learning from IT research. *Organization Studies*, 26(9), 1353–76.

Preston, A. M. (2006). Enabling, enacting and maintaining action at a distance: An historical case study of the role of accounts in the reduction of the Navajo herds. *Accounting, Organizations and Society*, 31(6), 559–78.

Preston, A. M., Cooper, D. J. and Coombs, R. W. (1992). Fabricating budgets: A study of the production of management budgeting in the National Health Service. *Accounting, Organizations and Society*, 17(6), 561–93.

Rabardel, P. (2001). Instrument mediated activity in situations. In A. Blandford, J. Vanderdonckt and P. Gray, eds., *People and Computers XV: Interaction without Frontiers.* London: Springer, 17–30.

Rabardel, P. (2002). *People and Technology: A Cognitive Approach to Contemporary Instruments.* Saint Denis: Université Paris 8. https://hal.archives-ouvertes .fr/hal-01020705

Rabardel, P. (2003). From artifact to instrument. *Interacting with Computers,* 15, 641–5.

Rabardel, P. and Bourmaud, G. (2003). From computer to instrument system: A developmental perspective. *Interacting with Computers,* 15, 665–91.

Radcliffe-Brown, A. R. (1952). *Structure and Function.* London: Cohen and West.

Revel, J. (2002). *Le vocabulaire de Foucault.* Paris: Ellipses.

Reynaud, J. D. (1979). Conflict and social regulation: A sketch of theory of joint regulation. *British Journal of Industrial Relations,* 17(3), 314–21.

Reynaud J. D. (1988). Les régulations dans les organisations: Régulation de contrôle et régulation autonome. *Revue française de sociologie,* 29(1), 5–18.

Reynaud, J. D. (1997). *Les règles du jeu. L'action collective et la régulation sociale.* Paris: Armand Colin.

Reynaud, J. D. (2001). Le management par les compétences: Un essai d'analyse. *Sociologie du travail,* 43(1), 7–31.

Rivaud-Danset, D. and Salais, R. (1992). Les conventions de financement des entreprises: Premières approches théorique et empirique. *Revue française d'économie,* 7(4), 81–120.

Roberts, J., Sanderson, P., Barker, R. and Hendry, J. (2006). In the mirror of the market: The disciplinary effects of company/fund manager meetings. *Accounting, Organizations and Society,* 31(3), 277–94.

Robson, K. (1991). On the arenas of accounting change: The process of translation. *Accounting, Organizations and Society,* 16(5–6), 547–70.

Robson, K. (1992). Accounting numbers as inscription: Action at a distance and the development of accounting. *Accounting, Organizations and Society,* 17(7), 685–708.

Roethlisberger, F. J. and Dickson, W. J. (1939). *Management and the Worker.* Boston, MA: Harvard Business School Press.

Rogers, E. M. (1995). *Diffusion of Innovations,* 4th edition. New York: Free Press.

Rose, N. and Miller, P. (1992). Political power beyond the state: Problematics of government. *British Journal of Sociology,* 43(2), 173–205.

Sahlin, K. and Wedlin, L. (2008). Circulating ideas: Imitation, translation and editing. In R. Greenwood, C. Oliver, K. Sahlin and R. Suddaby, eds., *The SAGE Handbook of Organizational Institutionalism.* London: Sage, 218–42.

Sainsaulieu, R. (1977). *L'identité au travail*. Paris: Presses de la FNSP.

Salais, R. (1989). L'analyse économique des conventions du travail. *Revue économique*, 40(2), 199–240.

Sale, K. (1996). *Rebels against the Future: The Luddites and Their War on the Industrial Revolution – Lessons for the Computer Age*. New York: Perseus Press.

Sarker, S., Sarker, S. and Sidorova, A. (2006). Understanding business process change failure: An actor-network perspective. *Journal of Management Information Systems*, 23(1), 51–86.

Schein, E. H. (1985). *Organizational Culture and Leadership: A Dynamic View*. San Francisco, CA: Jossey-Bass.

Schmitz, K., Teng, J. and Webb, K. (2016). Capturing the complexity of malleable IT use: Adaptive structuration theory for individuals. *MIS Quarterly*, 40(3), 663–86.

Scott, R. W. (1981). *Organizations: Rational, Natural and Open Systems*. Englewood Cliffs, NJ: Prentice Hall.

Scott, S. V. and Barrett, M. L. (2005). Strategic risk positioning as sensemaking in crisis: The adoption of electronic trading at the London International Financial Futures and Options Exchange. *Journal of Strategic Information Systems*, 14(1), 45–68.

Scott, S. V. and Orlikowski, W. (2014). Entanglements in practice: Performing anonymity through social media. *MIS Quarterly*, 38(3), 873–95.

Segrestin, D. (1997). L'entreprise à l'épreuve des normes de marché: Les paradoxes des nouveaux standards de gestion dans l'industrie. *Revue de sociologie française*, 38(3), 553–85.

Segrestin, D. (2004). *Les chantiers du manager*. Paris: Armand Colin.

Seligman, L. (2006). Sensemaking throughout adoption and innovation decision process. *European Journal of Innovation Management*, 9(1), 108–20.

Selznick, P. (1949). *TVA and the Grass Roots: A Study in the Sociology of Formal Organization*. Berkeley, CA: University of California Press.

Selznick, P. (1957). *Leadership in Administration: A Sociological Interpretation*. New York: Harper & Row.

Sewell, G. (1998). The discipline of teams: The control of team-based industrial work through electronic and peer surveillance. *Administrative Science Quarterly*, 43(2), 397–428.

Simon, H. (1947). *Administrative Behavior*. New York: Macmillan.

Simon, H. (1960). *The New Science of Management Decision*. Englewood Cliffs, NJ: Prentice Hall.

Simondon, G. (1980). *On the Mode of Existence of Technical Objects*. London, ON: University of Western Ontario.

Siti-Nabiha, A. K. and Scapens, R. (2005). Stability and change: An institutionalist study of management accounting change. *Auditing and Accountability Journal*, 18(1), 44–73.

Sorokin, P. (1956). *Fads and Foibles in Modern Sociology and Related Sciences*. Chicago, IL: H. Regnery Co.

Star, S. L. and Griesemer, J. (1989). Institutional ecology, translations and boundary objects: Amateurs and professionals on Berkeley's Museum of Vertebrate Zoology. *Social Studies of Science*, 19(3), 387–420.

Starr, P. (1992). Social categories and claims in the liberal state. *Social Research*, 59 (2), 263–95.

Steiner, P. (2001). The sociology of economic knowledge. *European Journal of Social Theory*, 4(4), 443–58.

Steiner, P. (2005). Le marché selon la sociologie économique. *Revue Européenne des Sciences Sociales*, 43(2), 31–64.

Storper, M. and Salais, R. (1997). *Worlds of Production: The Action Frameworks of the Economy*. Cambridge, MA: Harvard University Press.

Supiot, A. (2002). Travail, droit et technique. *Droit social*, 1, 13–25.

Suzuki, T. (2007). Accountics: Impacts of internationally standardized accounting on the Japanese socio-economy. *Accounting, Organizations and Society*, 32, 263–301.

Swan, J., Bresnen, M., Newell, S. M., Robertson, M. and Dopson, S. (2010). When policy meets practice: Colliding logics and the challenges of Mode 2 initiatives in the translation of academic knowledge. *Organization Studies*, 31(9–10), 1311–40.

Tarde, G. (1969). *On Communication and Social Influence: Selected Papers*. University of Chicago Press.

Taylor, F. W. (1911). *The Principles of Scientific Management*. New York: Harper & Brothers.

Teglborg, A. C., Gilbert, P. and Raulet-Croset, N. (2015). The management device in the blind spot to resistance to change. *Revue de gestion des ressources humaines*, 98(4), 18–29.

Teulier, R. and Lorino, P., eds. (2005). *Entre connaissance et organisation: L'activité collective*. Paris: La Découverte.

Thévenot, L. (1979). Une jeunesse difficile: Les fonctions sociales du flou et de la rigueur dans les classements. *Actes de la recherche en sciences sociales*, 26–27, 3–18.

Thévenot, L. (1984). Rules and implement: Investment in forms. *Social Science Information*, 23(1), 1–45.

Thompson, E. P. (1963). *The Making of the English Working Class*. London: Victor Gollancz.

Thornton, P. and Ocasio, W. (1999). Institutional logics and the historical contingency of power in organizations: Executive succession in the higher education publishing industry, 1958–1990. *American Journal of Sociology*, 105(3), 801–43.

Thornton, P. and Ocasio, W. (2008). Institutional logics. In R. Greenwood, C. Oliver, K. Sahlin and R. Suddaby, eds., *The SAGE Handbook of Organizational Institutionalism*. London: Sage, 99–129.

Thornton, P., Ocasio, W. and Lounsbury, M. (2012). *The Institutional Logics Perspective: A New Approach to Culture, Structure, and Process*. Oxford University Press.

Tolbert, P. and Zucker, L. (1983). Institutional sources of change in the formal structure of organizations: The diffusion of civil service reform, 1880–1935. *Administrative Science Quarterly*, 28(1), 22–39.

Townley, B. (1993). Performance appraisal and the emergence of management. *Journal of Management Studies*, 30(2), 221–39.

Townley, B. (1995). Know thyself: Self-awareness, self-formation and managing. *Organization*, 2, 271–89.

Townley, B. (1997). The institutional logic of performance appraisal. *Organization Studies*, 18(2), 261–85.

Townley, B. (2002). The role of competing rationalities in institutional change. *Academy of Management Journal*, 45(1), 163–79.

Trist, E. L. and Bamforth, K. W. (1951). Some social and psychological consequences of the Longwall Method of coal-getting: An examination of the psychological situation and defences of a work group in relation to the social structure and technological content of the work system. *Human Relations*, 46(1), 3–39.

Trompette, P. and Vinck, D. (2009). Retour sur la notion d'objet-frontière. *Revue d'anthropologie des connaissances*, 3(1), 5–27.

Vatin, F. (2004). Mauss et la technologie. *Revue du MAUSS*, 23(1), 418–33.

Vatin, F. (2013). Valuation as Evaluating And Valorizing. *Valuation Studies*, 1, 31–50.

Vaujany, F.-X. de (2003). Les figures de la gestion du changement sociotechnique. *Sociologie du travail*, 45, 515–36.

Vaujany, F.-X. de (2006). Pour une théorie de l'appropriation des outils de gestion: Vers un dépassement de l'opposition conception-usage. *Management & Avenir*, 9, 103–26.

Vercher, C., Palpacuer, F. and Charreire-Petit, S. (2011). Codes de conduite et systèmes d'alerte éthique: La RSE au sein des chaînes globales de valeur. *Revue de la régulation*, 9.

Vezinat, N. (2011). Surveiller les professionnels, ficher les clients: Étude des contrôles de la Banque Postale. *Sociologies Pratiques*, 22, 35–47.

Villette, M. (2003). *Sociologie du conseil en management*. Paris: La Découverte.

Vygotski, L. (2012). *Thought and Language*. Cambridge, MA: MIT Press [Original work published in 1934].

Wagner, P. (1994). Dispute, uncertainty and institution in recent French debates. *Journal of Political Philosophy*, 2(3), 270–89.

Walsh, E. J. and Steward, R. E. (1993). Accounting and the construction of institutions: The case of a factory. *Accounting, Organizations and Society*, 18(7/8), 783–800.

Weber, M. (1922). *Wirtschaft und Gesellschaft. Grundriss der verstehenden Soziologie*. Tübingen: Mohr. Published as *Economy and Society: An Outline of Interpretive Sociology*. Berkeley, CA: University of California Press, 1978.

Wedlin, L. (2007). The role of rankings in codifying a business school template: Classifications, diffusion and mediated isomorphism in organizational fields. *European Management Review*, 4, 24–39.

Weick, K. E. (1979). *The Social Psychology of Organizing*. New York: McGraw-Hill.

Weick, K. E. (1995). *Sensemaking in Organizations*. London: Sage.

Weil, T. (2000). *Invitation à la lecture de James March*. Paris: Les presses de l'École des mines.

Westphal, J. D., Gulati, R. and Sortell, S. M. (1997). Customization or conformity? An institutional and network perspective on the content and consequences of TQM adoption. *Administrative Science Quarterly*, 42(2), 366–94.

Whittington, R. (1992). Putting Giddens into action: Social systems and managerial agency. *Journal of Management Studies*, 29(6), 693–712.

Williamson, O. E. (1991). Comparative economic organization: The analysis of discrete structural alternatives. *Administrative Science Quarterly*, 36(2), 269–95.

Woodward, J. (1958). Management and technology. In T. Burns, ed., *Industrial Man*. Harmondsworth: Penguin, 4–40.

Wren, D. A. (2003). The influence of Henri Fayol on management theory and education in North America. *Entreprises et histoire*, 34, 98–107.

Wright, L. (1973), Functions. *Philosophical Review*, 82(2), 139–68.

Xu, Y. and Xu, X. (2008). Social actors, cultural capital, and the state: The standardization of bank accounting classification and terminology in early twentieth century China. *Accounting, Organizations and Society*, 33(1), 73–102.

Zanarelli, C. (2003). *Caractérisation des stratégies instrumentales de gestion d'environnements dynamiques: Analyse de l'activité de régulation du métro*. Ph.D. Thesis, Université Paris 8.

Index